DOING BUSINESS
IN THE NEW INDONESIA

DOING BUSINESS IN THE NEW INDONESIA

TABLE OF CONTENTS

PREPARED AND PUBLISHED BY

Business International

757 THIRD AVENUE, NEW YORK, N. Y. 10017

Introduction

Indonesia—the fifth largest country in the world in terms of population—has only recently rejoined world markets that are open to your company. A dramatic and bloody series of events in 1965 paved the way for Indonesia to sever its ties with the communist world and to set about building a flow of investment, credits, and business from the west. Almost overnight, every major world company was obliged to take a reckoning of the new Indonesia and determine where it fitted into the company's pattern of world business and future growth.

The country's potential in terms of human and natural resources is astounding—as is the determination of Indonesia's new government to turn this potential into actual wealth. And the potential of this country is further increased by the interest of the noncommunist countries in realizing political stability and economic progress in the strategic area occupied by Indonesia.

The problems that confront Indonesia's new leaders are immense. Decades of mismanagement have nearly broken the back of the economy. Inflation is rampant, production of many key products has declined from the levels of the past, communications and infrastructure are largely nonexistent, and skills and capital are in deplorably short supply. All in all, Indonesia provides possibly the most difficult environment in the world today in which to do business.

Yet in the two years that the opportunity has been open to them, dozens of US, UK, European, Japanese, Australian, and other companies have accepted this most difficult of challenges and have started operations in Indonesia. Many have gone into ventures based on the country's rich resources of minerals, forests, fisheries, and agricultural produce. These are ventures that are essentially export-oriented—to them the present thinness, in per capita income terms, of the Indonesian market is not relevant. Other companies have seized opportunities deriving from Indonesia's desperate need for modern communications and infrastructure. Still others have set up manufacturing ventures postulated on the slow—but almost certain—growth of the Indonesian domestic market.

Every foreign firm that has set up in Indonesia, and all who propose to do so in the immediate future, will find that the first frustrating difficulty is the sheer lack of information about the country. The demoralization of the civil service, the collapse of infrastructure, and the chaos of recent years has meant, for one thing, that few reliable official statistics have been published. Vast areas of law, administration, and government policy were surrounded by confusion, and many of the most elementary facts on which to base business planning simply were not available.

This report covers all of these areas. It is based on more than 18 months of field work in Indonesia by BI's staff. A high proportion of the report is first hand information, never before collected and published. All of it has been checked for accuracy with official Indonesian sources, with foreign economic experts posted in Djakarta, and with top business executives based there.

This report covers every aspect of doing business in Indonesia—taxation, banking, finance, labor and land costs, government regulations, segments of the economy where growth will be fastest, incentives for foreign investors, problems arising from corruption and ethnic differences, the foreign exchange system, and the basic "how-to's" of setting up and registering a firm.

This report pulls no punches in its depiction of present-day Indonesian conditions. Nor is it too timid to make predictions about the country's future and how firms should organize in order to reap their share of the profits that this future will create.

This is the twelfth report that BI has produced on major countries of the world in its Research Report series. All are recognized for their thoroughness and practicality, but none we believe has opened up so much virgin territory in terms of practical business information than "Doing Business in the New Indonesia."

I—The Country and the People

THE REPUBLIC OF INDONESIA is the largest archipelago in the world. It lies in an arc, with the Indian Ocean to the west and south, and the Pacific Ocean to the east. To the north are the South China Sea, the Philippines, and the Asian mainland. Only a few miles separate Sumatra—one of the islands in the archipelago—from the Malay peninsula. Australia lies to the southeast.

Indonesia straddles the equator between 6 degrees North and 11 degrees South, stretching for some 3,200 miles from northwestern Sumatra to and including West Irian (Irian Barat). There it has one of its three land frontiers, a border with Papua and New Guinea, both of which are under Australian administration. Indonesia's other two frontiers are on Kalimantan (Borneo), where it borders Sabah and Sarawak, and on Timor, part of which is Portuguese.

Indonesia consists of more than 13,600 islands, of which about 1,000 are inhabited. They range in size from a few acres to the 539,460 square kilometers of Kalimantan, almost as large as France. The next largest are Sumatra (473,606 square kilometers), West Irian (421,951 square kilometers), Sulawesi (Celebes—189,035 square kilometers), and Java (132,174 square kilometers). The total land area is 735,381 square miles—about one fourth the size of the US—making Indonesia the third largest country in Asia, after Mainland China and India.

The most important of the islands is Java, which for centuries has dominated the archipelago. It is there that Hinduism, Buddhism, and later, Islam were assimilated and integrated into the already complex culture of traditional village life. And it is from Java that some of Indonesia's most important traditions come—for example, *gotong royong*, or mutual assistance for the common welfare; and *musjawarah* (deliberations) and *musfakat* (consensus).

The Land

The terrain of Indonesia shows sharp contrasts. Much of the country is mountainous or covered with heavily forested rolling hills (forests cover nearly two-thirds of the land). The rest is mainly marshland and tropical jungle. Only in Java and parts of Sumatra are there extensive dry flatlands. In Sumatra the hills and mountains follow the west coast and level out to broad expanses of lowland marshes to the east. In Java, the mountains lie close to the shoreline of the Indian Ocean, but they are less continuous than those of Sumatra, and allow frequent access between north and south. East Java is more mountainous and drier than the rest of the island, but even so, over 60% of the land is cultivated.

Central and East Java have fertile hills and plains between the volcanic mountains on the south and limestone plateaus on the north. These are the most highly cultivated areas in Indonesia. With the denseness of its population, and its miles of terraced rice paddies, Java is almost one continuous village surrounded by a man-made landscape.

The mountains of Kalimantan run mainly along the border with Sabah; south Kalimantan consists of vast lowlands and swamps. Sulawesi has high mountain peaks and narrow coastal plains. Nearly half the population earns its living from the sea. The mountains continue through many of the smaller eastern islands — the Lesser Sundas and the Moluccas (Spice Islands); on Bali, Lombok, and Ceram there are volcanic peaks of over 10,000 feet. West Irian is covered with dense forest and vast swamps, and its mountains are the highest in Indonesia.

Because of its position astride the equator, Indonesia has no seasons as they are understood in the temperate zones. The days and nights are each 12 hours long; there is less than 5 degrees Fahrenheit variation in average temperature between the warmest and coolest months, and humidity averages 80% throughout the year. Two main seasons are recognizable: one wet (November to March) and one dry (June to October). In most areas, rainfall is at least 40 inches a year, and in the equatorial rain belt that covers most of Sumatra, Kalimantan, and Sulawesi, rainfall often reaches 90 to 100 inches annually.

Population

Indonesia ranks fifth in population among the countries of the world, exceeded only by Mainland China, India, the USSR, and the US. The last official census, in 1961, placed the population at 97 million; today it is between 112 and 120 million. At its present growth rate — between 2.3% and 2.8% per year — Indonesia's population will reach 125 million in 1970 and about 250 million in 2000.

The population is unevenly distributed. Some areas, such as West Irian (four persons per square mile) and Kalimantan are sparsely populated, while others, such as Java (1,300 per square mile) are among the most densely populated in the world. About two-thirds of Indonesia's total population lives in Java and Madura, which together account for only about 6.5% of the total land area of the archipelago. Sumatra, about four times larger than Java, has only 16% of the population. Java's serious overpopulation problem and the underpopulation of the Outer Islands stem partly from history and tradition, but geographic and climatic factors have been important.

Indonesia is the most volcanic region in the world. It has some 400 volcanic peaks, of which roughly 100 are active (or were until recently). The volcanic ash enriches the soil, and since people settled where the soil was most fertile, Java, with the most volcanoes, became by far the most densely populated of the islands.

Only 15% of the population lives in urban communities. The largest of these cities is the capital, Djakarta, which had three million people in 1961, and has nearly five million now. Then come (according to the 1961 census) Surabaja (1.18 million), Bandung (1 million), Semarang (503,200), Jogjakarta (367,600), and Malang (341,700), all on Java. In Sumatra the main cities are

	Area in sq. m.	% of total area	Population in '000	% of total population	Density per sq. m.
TABLE 1.					
Indonesia's Population in the 1961 Census					
Java/Madura	48,842	6.5	63,059	64.9	1,291
Sumatra	183,000	24.6	15,739	16.2	86
Sulawesi	71,695	9.6	7,079	7.2	98
Kalimantan	189,106	25.4	4,102	4.2	21
Moluccas	32,300	4.3	790	0.8	24
West Irian	162,965	21.9	758	0.7	4
Other islands	55,976	7.7	5,558	6.0	98

(Statistical Pocket Book of Indonesia, 1961, Djakarta)

Medan (480,000), Palembang (475,000), and Padang (143,700). In Sulawesi are Makasar (394,200), and Menado (130,000); and in Kalimantan are Bandjermasin (214,000), Pontianak (151,200), and Balikpapan (91,700). (The population in the cities has grown rapidly since the end of the Japanese occupation in 1945. The struggle for independence against the Dutch in the 1940's and later internal rebellions brought chaos and insecurity to rural areas, and speeded the move to the cities. The trend is continuing, but most new city dwellers now are people seeking a better livelihood. (Out of a labor force of 40 million, there are some three million urban unemployed, but about 15 million people in the countryside are underemployed.)

The Population Explosion

Indonesia is clearly in need of active programs to reduce the birth rate and to influence in some degree the future location of the population. In both respects some first steps have already been taken, but neither is likely to have much effect in the near future. The Indonesian Planned Parenthood Association was established in 1957 and has continued its work since. (The Soekarno regime was not in favor of family planning, but the present government recognizes the need for it. At the first family planning conference, which met in Djakarta in 1967, all religious groups declared themselves in favor of family planning. So far there has been no budget appropriation for family planning, however; and the Government, though it does offer facilities and assistance to private groups promoting family planning, has not made family planning an official program.

The overpopulation of Java led the Government to encourage transmigration from Java to other, less densely populated islands as early as 1950. The civilian transmigration scheme is now administered by the newly created Ministry of Transmigration and Cooperatives. But the results so far have been far from encouraging. From 1951 to 1966, only 96,600 families (480,000 persons) were resettled. Farm families that resettle in the Outer Islands (mostly in Sumatra, Kalimantan, and Sulawesi) receive five acres of land and are provided with seed and fertilizer. But these advantages have not been able to overcome the traditional methods of subsistence farming. In addition, many of those who do go to the Outer Islands stay only a few years, and their migration outward is countered by natural migration from the Outer Islands to Java. The Soeharto Government is emphasizing the need for transmigration linked to the development of agricultural, forestry, and mineral resources outside Java, and is putting priority on improving interisland transportation to facilitate the transmigration. A faster tempo in resettlement is likely as investors begin to tap the resources in the Outer Islands, but even this will be far too little for the magnitude of the problem. A potentially more effective — but probably less workable — proposal is that the armed forces be demobilized and given a two or three year transitional period to be spent in the Outer Islands, where hopefully some would stay.

The People

At the most rudimentary level are the mountain tribes of Kalimantan and West Irian. Although these tribes have now largely turned to farming, some are still wandering hunters and food gatherers. Many Indonesians live by subsistence farming in traditional villages that serve as the unit of production.

Altogether, some 70% of the Indonesian labor force of 40 million are employed in agriculture; 5-10% are in trade, and another 5-10% in manufacturing. Most Indonesians are independent workers, whether as smallholder farmers or traders in the cities; less than a third are wage earners. There are some two million in the armed forces and the civil service, and 1-1.5 million are in the professions.

The elite of the society is made up of senior government officials, professional people, businessmen, intellectuals, leaders of political or quasi-political parties and organizations, and officers of the armed forces. Many of the elite have in common the university diploma. Academic titles proliferate: Dr., Drs. (Doctorandus — candidate for the Doctor of Philosophy degree), Mr. (Master of Law), Ir. (Master of Engineering). Education has increasingly become the route to social mobility. Over 50% of the population is literate, and the figure is much higher for the younger age group.

Indonesia's population is composed of 16 major and innumerable minor ethnic groups, ranging from Malays in the West to Oceanic Negroids in West Irian. The vast majority of Indonesians are of Malay stock, and the Javanese are the largest single ethnic group. There are distinctions between ethnic groups by language, culture, and stereotypes of temperament. Racial differences, however, have not been important in Indonesia, except that the colonial experience left some resentment against Westerners. The dominance of the Chinese minority in the modern sectors of the economy (and the Chinese reluctance to assimilate into Indonesian society) has caused discrimination against the Chinese. There are now three and a quarter million Chinese, of which about 1.5 million are Indonesian citizens; some 250,000 alien Chinese are citizens of Communist China. The Chinese control some 70% of the money economy. There are smaller groups of Indians (some in commerce, but most as agricultural laborers in Sumatra) and Arabs (mainly in commerce in the cities), and several thousand Europeans.

There are also wide religious differences. About 90% of the population is Moslem, but there is a fairly wide gap between the traditional Moslems and the "modernist" ones. A good number of the 90% are only "statistical Moslems." The Balinese are Hindu, and Hinduism, once widespread in the islands, has influenced other religions. There are several million Christians, and small numbers of Buddhists, Taoists, and Confucianists.

Underlying most religious beliefs in Indonesia are the mystical and ancestor cults, whose influence, especially in rural areas, is still important today. While there is normally religious harmony in Indonesia, religion does carry over into the political sphere. There are Moslem, Christian, and secular political parties; and there is a widespread fear among non-Moslems of a Moslem desire to make Indonesia a theocratic state.

Unity in Diversity

Despite all the ethnic, social, and religious diversity found in Indonesia, the nation has certain underlying characteristics that make for unity. One of these is a rich, sophisticated cultural heritage. The motto of the present Indonesian Republic, "Unity in Diversity," was first used in the 15th century when the Hindu empire of Madjopahit extended across the islands. The emergence of Islam as the dominant faith also served as a unifying force among culturally and ethnically varied groups. More recently, western influences have been the most dynamic unifying forces, both in the form of ideas and technology introduced during three centuries of Dutch rule, and in the Indonesian reaction to that domination. In the 1920's Bahasa Indonesia (basically Malay) was declared the national language. Although many local dialects are in use, the spread of Bahasa Indonesia has done much to draw together the diverse groups in the country. Most significant, however, have been the experience of a successful revolution against colonial rule, and with independence, the force of emerging economic, political, and social forms that are national rather than local in scope.

II—Politics and Administration

INDONESIA'S EARLY HISTORY was marked by the rise and decline, over several centuries, of various Hindu and Buddhist kingdoms, and the introduction of Islam in the 12th and 13th centuries. Beginning in the early 1600's, the entire archipelago was brought progressively under Dutch control; in the 300 years of Dutch rule that followed, Indonesia developed into one of the world's richest colonial possessions.

By the end of the 19th century, the Dutch had built up an efficient plantation economy with modern agricultural practices, factories with trained foreign managers who supervised the processing of plantation products, and an efficient commercial network to collect and market raw materials and products. Water and rail transport systems had been developed to serve the export trade. In the two decades before World War II, a growing consumer demand led a few foreign investors, usually non-Dutch, to establish factories. Prior to the Japanese occupation of Indonesia in 1942, the Indonesians had obtained some industrial experience in cottage and small-scale industry, but had little opportunity to get technical training or managerial experience in the Dutch plantations. Generally, only lower clerical positions in the Government were open to them.

During their three-year occupation of Indonesia, the Japanese, to further their war aims, sought the support of the nationalist movement that had been developing since the 1920's. Many Indo-nesians were appointed to positions in civil administration that had been almost closed to them under the Dutch. The Japanese also abolished the Dutch education system, replaced it with a new unified system, and encouraged the use of Bahasa Indonesia throughout the islands. The occupation made Indonesians more politically conscious, gave nationalist leaders experience in political leadership, and provided the nationalists with an army through the formation of a Japanese-trained Indonesian home guard. When the Japanese began to lose the war, they gave more power to the Indonesians, and in early 1945 set up a committee to prepare for independence.

The Struggle for Independence

On August 17, 1945, three days after the Japanese surrender, a small group of Indonesians led by two strong nationalists — Ir. Soekarno and Dr. Moh. Hatta — proclaimed the Republic of Indonesia. The leaders announced the famous five guiding principles of Indonesia, the Pantja Sila, which still form the philosophic basis of the country: Belief in One Supreme God, Humanitarianism, Nationalism, Democracy, and Social Justice. This was the beginning of the Soekarno era, and the forging of a nation from hundreds of diverse peoples and islands.

There followed four years of war as the Dutch tried to reestablish control. Some areas of the country were held by nationalists and others by the Dutch. The areas of control shifted, particularly with the two Dutch "police actions" of July 1947 and December 1948. Finally, in 1949, in response to pressures against the Netherlands in the United Nations, an agreement was reached at a conference at the Hague. The settlement provided that the Netherlands would transfer sovereignty to a federally constituted Republic of Indonesia; sovereignty over West Irian, however, was to be the subject of further discussions, and it remained an area of dispute between the two countries for some years. Indonesia agreed to assume over $550 million in financial obligations to the Netherlands, to keep its exchange rate tied to the Dutch guilder, and to guarantee Dutch investments in Indonesia. A few months later, a unitary Republic of Indonesia was established. The country was internationally recognized, and became the 60th member of the United Nations.

The economy of Indonesia suffered severely in the decade of occupation and revolution. First came heavy destruction when the Japanese advanced in 1942. This was followed by an allied blockade, and Japanese efforts to gear the economy to a war machine. After 1945, the economy was affected not only by the disruptions of war and guerilla activity, but also by a Dutch naval blockade that nearly cut off trade with the outside world, and by counterblockades by the nationalists to "starve" the Dutch-held cities. The guerilla army used scorched-earth tactics whenever the Dutch gained territory. It is estimated that overall, the loss in industrial output between 1938 and 1948 amounted to about 2% per year, due to war, occupation, and the struggle for independence.

The Soekarno Era

From 1945 to 1950 the independent portion of the country was governed under the Constitution adopted when independence was proclaimed in 1945. Power was concentrated in the hands of the revolutionary leadership, headed by Soekarno and Hatta. When the unitary Republic of Indonesia was established in 1950, with Soekarno as President and Hatta as Vice President, a new provisional Constitution was adopted. It made the President little more than a figurehead, and provided for parliamentary government; the cabinet

was made responsible to Parliament. Although until 1955 Parliament was appointed rather than elected, political parties played an important role. But party differences prevented any degree of government stability. Often these differences reflected the rivalry between Moslem and secular groups, and the deep division between Java and the Outer Islands, where fear of strong Javanese political control was strong. Fifteen coalition cabinets held office between 1950 and 1955. President Soekarno, through the strength of his personality and his prestige as a nationalist leader, was a strong political force despite the constitutional limits on his power. And it was clear that the Army and the regions outside Java were both potential political forces in themselves.

In 1955, two elections were held — one for members of a Constituent Assembly to draft a permanent constitution, and one for the People's Representative Council or Assembly, which was to serve as a parliament until the new constitution was ready. Since then no general elections have been held.

Four major parties — the nationalists (PNI), which had been founded by the revolutionaries in the 1930's; the Masjumi, a modernist Moslem party with substantial support outside Java; the Nahdatul Ulama (NU), representing the traditional Moslems; and the Communist Party (PKI) — were supported by the electorate in that order, and between them received 80% of the popular vote in the 1955 elections. The Socialist Party (PSI), which was important for its intellectual makeup but had little mass support, was virtually eliminated in the elections. The protestant Parkindo, the Catholic Party, and two smaller Moslem parties (PSII and Perti) won some seats; altogether some 30 political parties and organizations were represented in Parliament.

In 1956 and 1957, when the cabinet refused to accept communist members, Soekarno denounced political parties and the parliamentary system, and advanced his concept of "guided democracy." He proposed, in addition to a cabinet including the communists, the establishment of a National Council under his chairmanship to represent the major interests in the country and advise the cabinet. The cabinet was to be responsible to the Council, not Parliament; and Parliament, in effect, was to be reduced to a powerless debating society. The reaction was strong: Hatta resigned as Vice President; army commanders in Sumatra, Sulawesi, and Kalimantan took over administration of their regions and announced they no longer recognized the Government; and the Masjumi withdrew from the cabinet. But by mid-1957, Soekarno had established his National Council, directly or indirectly selecting the members himself. There were representatives of regional and functional groups — labor, farmers, religious groups, and armed forces — but most were Javanese, and there was no real opposition.

In theory at least, Soekarno's idea of guided democracy — by emphasizing the principles of deliberation and consensus — was more suited to Indonesian tradition than was the parliamentary system. But in practice it did not provide true representation, and the National Council was only a rubber stamp.

In the meantime, Indonesia had stepped up a campaign in the United Nations to force the Dutch to negotiate over the sovereignty of West Irian. When the campaign failed, Dutch property in Indonesia was seized, and put under government (military) control.

The most serious division the nation had experienced came in 1958, when a revolt broke out in Central Sumatra. The leaders of the province, joined by several important Indonesian leaders, formed a Revolutionary Council and demanded a new cabinet and an end to ''guided democracy.'' Underlying the political reasons for revolt were long-standing resentments in the other regions that they were supporting Java with their foreign exchange earnings. The rebellion in Sumatra was supported by a revolt in Sulawesi, but within a few months both were suppressed by the Army.

These events led Soekarno to conclude that the country was not ready for representative democracy. He dissolved the Constituent Assembly (which was on the point of agreeing on a constitution), restated the principles of guided democracy, and propounded the ideology of NASAKOM — the combination of nationalism, religion, and communism. The provisional Constitution of 1950 was abandoned and the more authoritarian one of 1945 was decreed to be the country's permanent charter. The elected parliament was dissolved and replaced by a ''mutual help'' parliament of 283 members, all appointed by the President. The new parliament, in turn, became a part of the larger Provisional People's Consultative Assembly (MPRS).

Although the Constitution of 1945 gives this body responsibility for determining the main lines of state policy, it was completely under the control of Soekarno, who, under the provisions of the Constitution, became Head of Government as well as Head of State. In 1960 he received the title ''President for Life.''

Tighter control over the economy, censorship of the press, and control of political parties were part of ''Guided Democracy.'' The Masjumi was outlawed for alleged participation in the 1958 rebellion, and other parties were limited to 10 in number. The effectiveness of the remaining political parties was greatly impaired. Measures were taken to discourage political dissent, and acceptance of the state ideology was required for appointment to important offices.

The Nationalizations

The takeover of the Dutch enterprises in 1958-1959 inevitably resulted in a substantial degree of de facto socialism. The West Irian dispute was the ostensible motivation for the seizure of the Dutch assets, estimated to be worth $1 billion. In the 1950's, after independence, with political control in the hands of the Indonesians, the Dutch were still responsible for over half of the total trade of the country. They still controlled inter-island shipping, and through their commercial and industrial activities retained an influential financial and economic position in Indonesia.

In order to assure essential supplies under the rather chaotic conditions following the nationalization of Dutch enterprises, a monopoly of the import of nine so-called essential items (including food, fuel, and clothing) was placed in the hands of government trading companies. Almost the entire modern section of the Indonesian economy came under state control. Through the combination of ideology and sheer necessity, the Government found itself involved in more and more diversified economic activities, from running estates and heavy industries to foreign trade and local retailing.

The measures that were taken to ''Indonesianize'' the main economic activities and to establish the basis for a ''guided economy'' greatly retarded the smooth operation of the economy. Measures in 1959 to limit the Chinese role in trade disrupted the economy even more. Shortages and strains developed, particularly in distribution. The Dutch management personnel were withdrawn from interisland merchant shipping, but the Government was unable to build a fleet to fill the vacuum their departure created. Part of the shipping capacity was also diverted to military operations in connection with the West Irian dispute and the Malaysian confrontation.

By 1963 it was clear that the economy was in a serious state of decline, and runaway inflation had set in. The President's Economic Declaration (DEKON) and subsequent economic regulations might have signaled a more rigorous approach to problems, but Indonesia's adventurist foreign policy eliminated any chance of this.

The dispute with the Netherlands concerning West Irian was finally resolved under the United Nations authority, and on May 1, 1963, Indonesia assumed full responsibility for that territory, with provision for a plebiscite in 1969 to determine whether the local population wants to remain permanently a part of the Republic of Indonesia.

The formation later in 1963 of Malaysia — by linking Malaya, the autonomous State of Singapore, and the former UK territories of Sabah and Sarawak — was denounced by Soekarno. Disregarding a United Nations survey of the results of a referendum in Sabah and Sarawak, Soekarno alleged that the new nation was a "puppet" of British imperialism. Subsequently, in September 1963, a military "crush Malaysia" campaign was launched by Indonesia. Within the framework of this "confrontation" policy pursued by Soekarno, Malaysian and UK interests in Indonesia were taken over and placed under the direct control of the Indonesian Government. The Singapore-owned soft drink manufacturing company, Fraser & Neave Co Ltd, was one such plant seized. Twenty-four Malaysian-owned remilling plants, processing annually in Sumatra and Kalimantan about 75,000 tons of rubber (i.e., almost all of the country's then existing remilling capacity), were also put under the supervision of either the Department of Agriculture or the regional military authorities.

Seventy-nine estates, administered by 10 UK companies and covering more than 160,000 acres, were placed under the supervision of the Department of Plantations. Four subsidiaries of UK manufacturing companies — Unilever (soap, edible oil), British-American Tobacco Co Ltd (cigarettes), Nebritex (textiles), and Dunlop (tires) — were put under the direct control of the Department of People's Industries and the Department of Basic Industry and Mining. Two other British firms — United Molasses Co Ltd (storage and export of molasses), and Maclaine Watson & Company (export-import) — were taken over by the Department of Trade. Ocean Insurance Co Ltd was taken over by the Department of Revenue, Expenditure, and Control. Later, the Chartered Bank was put under the control of the Minister for Central Bank Affairs. The other UK bank with a branch in Indonesia, the Hongkong & Shanghai Banking Corporation, quit when the trouble started. Similarly, two UK-owned insurance companies — the Union of Canton Insurance Co and the Semarang Sea & Fire Insurance Co — liquidated themselves before being taken over. The total British assets in Indonesia in 1963 were estimated at $200 million (including investments of the Shell Oil Company).

The two other foreign oil companies operating in Indonesia — Caltex and Stanvac, both of the US — were put under "temporary supervision" of the Indonesian Government in 1965, following Soekarno's new *berdikari* policy. As the country should, according to this principle, "stand on its own feet," all other foreign companies whose governments did not manifest any particular appreciation of Indonesia's international policies, including her withdrawal from the UN and its agencies, were also put under control. US rubber estates owned by two US firms — Goodyear Sumatra Plantations Co (56,000 acres), and United States Rubber (Uniroyal) Sumatra Plantations (54,000 acres) — as well as those of 26 European companies (18 Belgian, four Swiss, three French, one Italian) were placed under the supervision of the Department of Plantations. The total value of these estates was estimated at $29 million. Similarly, five US manufacturing firms — Goodyear (tires), National Cash Register (assembling of office machines), Singer (assembling of sewing machines), Procter & Gamble (margarine and cooking oil), Union Carbide (batteries) — and a US insurance company, American Foreign Insurance Association (AFIA), were put under the management of various departments or official agencies, together with six other foreign, but non-UK, companies: one Australian (Naspro, pharmaceuticals), one Canadian (Bata, shoes), one German (Prodenta, tooth paste), one Belgian (Faroka, cigarettes), one Swiss (Filma, cooking oil), and Heineken (brewing) of the Netherlands, whose Indonesian operation was owned through a Belgian subsidiary.

The disruption of production from these takeovers of plantations and factories was a significant factor in accelerating the decline of the Indonesian economy in these years.

From 1958 through 1964, net domestic product increased by 9.3%, or only 1.5% annually; but in the seven years from 1961 up to the end of 1967, consumer prices rose 1,500 times, and the money supply 310 times. This serious deterioration in the economy contributed to the political events of 1965-1966.

The New Order

The recent political history of Indonesia starts with the abortive coup of Oct. 1, 1965 (the "Gestapu," or September 30th Movement) when the Army Commander-in-chief and five generals were assassinated by a combination of dissident military leaders and youth groups under strong communist influence.

By this time, the military was the only group in the country capable of balancing, to some degree, the power of President Soekarno; and it had for several years wanted to take action against growing communist activity in the country. By 1965, the Communist Party of Indonesia (PKI) was the largest communist party outside the USSR and China. It had close ties with Peking, and China had apparently provided it with some training and supplies. The puzzling aspect of the coup attempt was its timing — or even its occurrence at all. It was clear by 1965 that within another year the PKI would have been in complete control without force. The explanation seems to lie in the PKI's realization that to succeed they needed the blessing of Soekarno.

Soekarno, though not a communist himself, agreed with much of the PKI's philosophy and had done much to foster its growth. He used the PKI, and apparently was increasingly used by it. (Soekarno's actual role, if any, in the attempted coup has never been clarified, but several of his close aides were certainly involved, and it is probable that he at least knew in advance of the plan and did nothing to thwart it.) Soekarno's health

was poor, and he apparently suffered some serious ailment in August 1965. Doctors from Peking apparently reported to the PKI that the President was seriously ill, so in order to ensure that its control would be sanctioned by Soekarno, the PKI decided not to wait for power to come gradually, but to take it by a coup.

The coup was frustrated by the Army, rallied by General Soeharto, who headed the Strategic Reserve Command.

Large-scale massacres — of Communist Party members, Chinese, and others — followed, particularly in Central and East Java and on Bali. Estimates of the number killed range from 50,000 to one million, but the total was probably 300,000-500,000. The Government's latest official figures estimate it at between 100,000 and 200,000. The reasons for the scale of the slaughter are complex and unclear. The Army was partly responsible, but bands of militant youths, usually Islamic, did much of the killing.

The ~~physical~~ destruction of the Communist Party organization through the killing or the arrest of its leaders and cadres did not in itself satisfy the political needs of the Army and its allies. To insure the long-term legality of its action, the Army needed the sanction of Indonesia's foremost national figure and sole charismatic personality, President Soekarno. But a showdown could not be risked at that time. The Army was still too fearful of the ~~potency~~ strength of Soekarno's appeal within its own ranks, as well as among the masses, to risk a confrontation.

Events soon forced a showdown. In mid-December 1965, in a desperate attempt to ~~bridle the~~ curb ~~spiraling~~ inflation ~~that worked politically explosive hardship on Djakarta's swollen population of some four million,~~ Soekarno decreed a currency reform. This caused more confusion than relief. Decrees raising the price of certain commodities and services, particularly gasoline and transportation, bred new areas of dissatisfaction that culminated in January 1966 in massive demonstrations organized by a Student Action Front (KAMI). KAMI, in close alliance with the Army, rapidly emerged as the spearhead of giant street demonstrations that marked the opening of a phase of expanding pressure against the Soekarno regime. Finally, on March 11, 1966, President Soekarno found himself forced to sign an order making General Soeharto Acting President.

On March 12, Soeharto used his new authority to issue a legal ban of the PKI. On March 18, he ordered the arrest of 15 of Soekarno's ministers. There followed on March 30 the installation of a number of new ministers. In late June of the same year Soeharto and the Army convened Indonesia's highest legislative body, the Provisional People's Consultative Assembly (MPRS).

Under the 1945 Constitution, which Soekarno revived in 1959, the MPRS possesses the authority to elect the President and Vice-President. It is also charged with determining the guidelines of state policy on all matters. Purged of its PKI and other leftist members, the decisions of the MPRS gave support to General Soeharto's moves and views.

The most important task of the MPRS was to legitimize the steps already taken by the Army and its ministerial appointees. This involved validation of the March 11 presidential order effectively transferring power to General Soeharto, and the latter's March 12 decree banning the PKI. The MPRS also deprived Soekarno of the title ''President for Life'' that had been given him three years earlier. And it denied him the power to issue further decrees and designated General Soeharto as Acting President.

The Ampera Cabinet

Following the close of the MPRS session, General Soeharto directed the installation of the first cabinet of the quasi-military regime, the Ampera Cabinet. Ampera is an Indonesian acronym referring to the ''Message of the People's Suffering.''

Significantly, Soekarno's influence still affected several key positions in the new Cabinet: of the 24 Ampera ministers, 12 had also held ministerial posts in Soekarno's pre-coup Cabinet. Accordingly, although the Ampera Cabinet's formation undoubtedly marked a further transition from the Old Order of guided democracy dominated by Soekarno to the New Order dominated primarily by the Indonesian Army, much continuity was in evidence amid the flurry of change. It is understandable, though, that Soekarno did—and still does—have supporters; besides being a revolutionary leader, Soekarno played an extremely important role in building the nation psychologically, and was brilliant at political maneuver. In

1966, one year after the unsuccessful putsch, Soekarno was still President, although real power lay with General Soeharto.

The ''Great Leader of the Revolution'' (against colonialism and western imperialism) continued to struggle desperately to oppose the effective government, and it was only in 1967 that any real breakthrough was achieved.

In mid-March the MPRS stated that it would prevent President Soekarno from conducting political activities until the national elections. In April, the matter was clarified by General Soeharto himself, who stated: ''I have fully taken up the responsibilities of the Chief Executive as President of the Republic of Indonesia based on the 1945 Constitution until a President is elected by the MPRS as the result of the coming general elections.'' Finally, the redressing of the Ampera Cabinet, announced by General Soeharto in October 1967, strengthened the position of the General. Four ministers still representing the Old Order were discharged and three new ministers were appointed.

The structure of a Cabinet Presidium, which since March 1966 had initiated major decisions and regulations, was dissolved so that ministers reported directly to President Soeharto. The triumvirate that had been conducting the Government—General Soeharto, Adam Malik as Presidium Minister for Political Affairs and Minister for Foreign Affairs, and Sri Sultan Hamengku Buwono IX as Presidium Minister for Economic Affairs—began to disappear, and authority became more concentrated in the hands of General Soeharto. But the one-man state is now past history for Indonesia; General Soeharto seems to see himself as head of a government responsible to the people.

The Development Cabinet

At the MPRS session in March 1968, Acting President Soeharto was made full President for a five-year term (but with some limits placed on his emergency powers) and the deadline for elections was postponed from July 1968 to July 1971. Most important, the President was instructed to revamp the Cabinet by early July. On June 6th, the new Development Cabinet—replacing the Ampera Cabinet—was announced. It was formed with competence rather than political affiliations or military rank as the major factor. Eight of the

Governmental Leadership in Indonesia

The effectiveness of the New Order has been — and will be — largely determined by its leaders. Here are biographies of the most important ones.

President Soeharto concentrated exclusively on his military career until the attempted communist coup of October 1965. He was born in a Javanese village near Jogjakarta in 1921. After secondary school, he entered the Military Cadre School of the Royal Netherlands Indies Army in 1940. In the Japanese occupation he was sent to officer training school for the Japanese-trained home guard, which became the plotting ground for the post-war fight for independence. When independence was declared in 1945, the home guard became the Indonesian Army, and Soeharto served with guerilla units fighting the Dutch. By 1960 he was a Brigadier General and First Deputy to the Chief of Staff of the Army, and by 1963, Commander of the Strategic Reserve Command of the Indonesian Army. It was from this post that he rallied the Army to crush the communist coup in October 1965.

General Soeharto has proved to be an effective leader with a thorough grasp of the political tensions in his country. By moving slowly and cautiously, and by using strictly constitutional means, he has consolidated the New Order and avoided the pro-Soekarno reaction that might have occurred if Soekarno had been deposed swiftly. His adherence to the Constitution (in many ways, the first time it had been followed since its adoption in 1945) and his belief in constitutional government have overcome most of the initial fears of a military dictatorship or "creeping militarism." Importantly, he quickly became a student of economy, and surrounded himself with able economic advisers. Although he does not have the charisma of his predecessor — a fact deplored by some, but applauded by most — he is considered effective in personal, informal contacts. He made a tour of Asian capitals in the spring of 1968 — the only time he had been out of Indonesia except for a short tour for military contacts in Europe in 1961.

Adam Malik was born in a small town in North Sumatra in 1917 and ran away from a religious school to go into political activity. When only 17, he was already chairman of the "Partai Indonesia" (Partindo) in his native town. He later joined the Gerindo, another left-wing nationalist movement, and the PARI. He established in 1948 the Partai Murba, an anti-fascist, anti-imperialist, anti-capitalist "proletarian party" with Trotskyist leanings. The Murba developed more and more opposition against Soekarno and was banned shortly before the abortive communist coup in 1965. The party has since been reestablished, but Adam Malik officially left in March 1967. His conversion from ideology to pragmatism had occurred some time before. Malik became a member of Parliament in 1956. His foreign service began in 1959 when he was named Indonesia's Ambassador to the USSR and Poland. Later he served as chief delegate to the Indonesian-Dutch negotiations on West Irian and as chief delegate on the United Nations Commission on Trade Developments. He was appointed Minister of Trade in 1963, Minister Coordinator for the Implementation of Guided Economy in 1965, and Foreign Minister in 1966. When the New Order began, he was Presidium Minister for Political Affairs as well as Foreign Minister, and as such was in the triumvirate leading the country. As Foreign Minister, he has been effective through the period of Indonesia's reentry into international organizations, and in developing Indonesia's relations with its Southeast Asian neighbors through such organizations as the Association of Southeast Asian Nations (ASEAN).

SRI Sultan Hamengku Buwono IX was born in the palace of Jogjakarta in 1912. Since his father's death in 1940, he has been considered the traditional leader by the people of Central Java. His great prestige brought a following to the New Order that cut across party lines. During his education at the University of Leiden during colonial days, he was closely connected with Indonesian nationalists and leaders of the democratic Socialist Party. When the revolution began, the Sultan was one of the first outstanding personalities in Jogjakarta to join and help lead it. When, in 1945, the Dutch prevented the Republican Government under President Soekarno from functioning adequately in Djakarta, the Sultan invited them to Jogjakarta. In recognition of his achievements he was made an honorary General of the Army. Out of the 274 Sultans and feudal rulers in Indonesia left by the Dutch colonial administration, only he and his uncle, Prince Pakualam, survived the political revolution. They merged their territory into one Special Territory of Jogjakarta and the Government recognized them as its hereditary heads. The Sultan has served his country as a minister almost without interruption since 1946. During the time of Soekarno's guided democracy, his influence and power were progressively reduced, finally to the level of Head of the National Tourist Council and Chairman of the State Comptroller's Council. Today, as Minister of State for Economic, Financial, and Industrial Affairs, the Sultan coordinates government activity in those fields.

Professor Dr. Soemitro Djojohadikusumo was born in 1917 in Indonesia, and has a Ph.D. in economics from the Netherlands School of Economics in Rotterdam. He also studied philosophy and French literature at the Sorbonne. Following independence he became Assistant to the Prime Minister in 1946, moving the next year into the presidency of the Indonesia Banking Corporation. From 1948-50 he served abroad as Deputy Chief of the Indonesian Mission to the UN, and as Charge d'Affairs of the Embassy in Washington.

He returned to his country in 1950 to serve as a cabinet minister. His first portfolio was Economic Affairs, but his financial ability raised him to the Finance Ministry seat in 1952-53, and again in 1955-56. From 1951 to 1957 he was dean and professor of economics at the University of Indonesia. Many of the current technocrats building Indonesia's industrial and economic future were students of Soemitro during this period.

In 1958 Soemitro left Djakarta to become a leader of the armed rebellion in Sumatra against the regime of President Soekarno. This, together with his decisiveness in government positions, has made him an extremely controversial figure. When other leaders later submitted to signing an amnesty pledge to Soekarno, Soemitro refused, and went into voluntary exile for 10 years. During this period his international reputation spread as the result of his achievements in economic and financial consultancy. He authored several books and numerous essays in these fields, and served government institutions and international corporations.

Soemitro again returned to his homeland in 1967, and together with Mochtar Lubis, founded Indoconsult Associates. General Soeharto brought Soemitro into the Development Cabinet in June 1968. Because of his reputation as a brilliant economist, observers in Indonesia and abroad place great importance on his reentry into government, depending on him to put the economy on its feet.

Professor Dr. Ali Wardhana, Minister of Finance, was born in 1928, and is one of the Soemitro school economists. He received a a doctorate from the Economic Faculty of the University of Indonesia and his M.A. and Ph.D. degrees in economics from the University of California at Berkeley. Since 1962 he has held a number of academic posts, including professor, assistant dean, and dean of the economic faculty at the University of Indonesia, Djakarta. From 1964-68 he was economic advisor to the governor of the central bank, and from 1966-68 served on President Soeharto's Economic Advisory Team. In June 1968, Dr. Wardhana was named Minister of Finance in the Development Cabinet.

Dr. Widjojo Nitisastro, Chairman of the National Development Planning Council (Bappenas), is another of several Soemitro-trained economists in the Government. He received his Ph.D. in economics at the University of California in Berkeley, California. After his return to Indonesia he was appointed professor at the faculty of economics at the University of Indonesia. He became dean of this faculty in 1964, and was simultaneously chief of the National Economic and Social Research Center. In this position and with a group of young professors and other scholars he drafted the basic principles for the present national economic policies being carried out by the Soeharto Government. As a leader of the Indonesian delegation to creditor-country meetings on aid to Indonesia, Widjojo has been most effective in explaining the New Order economic policies and problems, and in general, in speeding the reacceptance of Indonesia in the West. As chief economic adviser to the President and chairman of Bappenas, he is in a position of major responsibility for the future development of Indonesia's economy.

ministers are from political parties, but no political grouping gained important Cabinet posts; six of the ministers are from the armed forces, but several posts formerly held by high-ranking military men are now filled by civilians. Seven Cabinet members are professors. The most notable change was the inclusion as Minister of Trade of Prof. Dr. Soemitro Djojohadikusumo, one of Indonesia's most highly respected economists. This gentleman, however, is a controversial figure, partly because he joined the 1958 Sumatra rebellion. The inclusion of Dr. Soemitro and several other highly regarded economists is evidence that President Soeharto recognizes the critical state of the economy and the importance of improving it by putting Indonesia's best economists in policy-making positions.

The formation of the Development Cabinet also involved the restructuring of several departments to cut down the bureaucracy and smooth the operation of the administrative machinery. For example, the old Department of Estates was merged into the Department of Agriculture, and responsibility for development of power was moved from the Department of Industry to the Department of Public Works.

Changes below the ministerial level were not major at first, but in August 1968 Dr. Soemitro completely revamped the organization and personnel of the Ministry of Trade.

Policies and Problems of the New Order

The New Order has been faced with critical internal problems that demand new directions of policy. The most important of these is the need to arrest the decline in the economy.

By mid-1968, the decline was far from over. Inflation was still running at a rate of close to 100% annually — but the deterioration had slowed immensely. The Government had taken a realistic, pragmatic approach to the problem: foreign debts had been rescheduled, new credits had been negotiated, foreign investment was welcomed, subsidies had been removed, and market forces instead of government controls were playing the dominant role. Despite the vastness of the problems, most observers were in agreement that Indonesia was on its way to eventual economic well-being.

In order to give urgency to several economically — and therefore politically — important areas, President Soeharto in June 1968 established several government projects (see box, below). Each is headed by a cabinet minister, who is charged with coordinating activities relating to the project among the other ministries and agencies involved, and reporting progress to the President. The emphasis on coordination is important, but most significant is that these critical areas will at all times have cabinet level consideration. The projects have no permanent staffs except secretaries; the operations will be handled by the ministries themselves. The projects are basically a statement of priorities. Significantly most of them are economic.

One of the most important assets of the New Order Government is that the ministers and advisers who make economic policy are a team of capable people. They are excellent economists who work extremely well together and have the confidence of the President. Decision-making is not a problem; the serious difficulties are in implementing the decisions.

Corruption

One of the most serious problems that frustrates the best-laid economic plans is corruption. And since the Government has in effect staked its future on economic progress, widespread corruption is potentially a major political problem.

Some of it began because civil servants and military personnel could not live on their salaries, but for many it is now a way of life. Bribes and payoffs are commonly sought at almost every phase of doing business. Foreign investors are sometimes approached by well-connected middlemen asking commissions in exchange for not obstructing normal business transactions. One new investor wanted a telephone for his office, and some official along the way asked for a $2,500 bribe, but generally the amounts are a tiny fraction of that. Bribery often occurs when investors try to procure equipment and facilities. Most notorious are the ports, where customs or military officials can cause infinite delays — or deliver only damaged goods — if the payoffs are not forthcoming.

In seeking bank finance, businessmen are often asked for a "downpayment" (the share of the bank loan, usually 10%), that bank officials demand from customers in return for granting bank

The Government Projects

Numbers	Name of Project	Chairman/responsible officer
1.	Food production	Minister of Agriculture
2.	Supply and distribution of food	Minister of Trade
3.	Clothing	Minister of Industry
4.	Foreign credits	Minister of Finance
5.	Foreign investment	Minister of Mining
6.	Preparation for development	Chairman of Bappenas
7.	Foreign trade	Minister of Trade
8.	Infrastructure	Minister of Public Works and Power
9.	Mental activity, information	Minister of Information
10.	General elections	Minister of the Interior
11.	Restoration and rule of law	Minister of Justice
12.	West Irian	Minister of the Interior
13.	Efficiency of the state economic apparatus and the apparatus of administration	State Minister to Assist the President in Perfecting and Purging the State Apparatus
14.	Restoring order in the implementation of foreign policy	Minister for Foreign Affairs
15.	Rehabilitation of industry (excluding textile industry which is part of Project: Clothing)	Minister of Industry
16.	Transmigration	Minister of Transmigration and Cooperatives
17.	Tourism	Minister of Communications

credits. There are also "private interest rates" — the practice of charging an extra 2% or 3% per month, on top of the official rates at state banks. The central bank is endeavoring to stamp out such practices.

Although these kinds of corruption may be annoying and sometimes costly to business, the more serious corruption for the country is widespread smuggling of imports and exports and various illegal methods of draining the country's foreign exchange. (See chapter on foreign trade.)

General Soeharto established in December 1967 a high-powered anticorruption team to eradicate these and other evils. Headed by the Attorney General, the team has an advisory board comprising the Minister of Justice and commanders of the four military services (Army, Navy, Air Force, Police). Special task force units can be assigned to work from the capital and in different regions.

In one clean-up operation, seven executives (including the director) of the state-owned rubber corporation (BPU Karet) in Atjeh, North Sumatra, were arrested and held under detention on charges of involvement in malpractices that caused the "collapse" of this enterprise, one of the chief foreign exchange revenue earners. These arrests followed the Government's dismissal of 30 officials of the Customs Bureau, seven employees of the State Revenue Office, and nine of the Pension Bureau (the latter for allegedly embezzling pensions of the widows of servicemen). Measures were also taken against several state bank officials: 37 suspended and 34 dismissed.

Many of the worst offenders — often government officials or army officers — have not yet come under fire, however. There are some commanders and president-directors of state enterprises who are ostentatiously wealthy despite public knowledge that their wealth comes solely from corruption. Under a recent crackdown on the privileges of the army, it was made illegal for the army to import most goods tax free and port administration was removed from its hands. But much of the corruption in high places has so far escaped the Government's clean-up campaign.

Military and Civilians

In today's Indonesia, much of the framework of effective power has been provided by the military, although its participation in the Cabinet was weakened by the June 1968 reshuffle.

The Army has long played a significant role in independent Indonesia's history. This role began as early as 1945, with the guerilla warfare against the Dutch. It was enhanced during the 1950's when the Armed Forces put down dissident, separatist movements and thus provided the framework within which the nation established itself. It was increased further when the Army, realizing what Soekarno was up to, began infiltrating the Government and ended up by controlling about 40% of the top official positions. This resulted in the failure of the October 1965 communist coup. Today the armed forces consider themselves both as a protective force for the Republic and as a sociopolitical force to guard and stabilize the state.

Although the projected military expenditure represented only 27.9% of the total 1968 budget, as compared to 70% in 1963, it still indicates the importance of the armed forces in the Indonesian political, administrative, and social structure. The debt position of the country precludes any further acquisition of expensive military equipment, but the present budget planners must take into account the existence of half a million males in the armed forces, representing about a quarter of all government paid personnel.

Relations between the military and the civilians have not always been easy, and civilian fears of creeping militarism have been exacerbated by corruption. In some areas the Army has taken over provincial government down to a low level — a grass-roots political control that could conceivably lead to military dominance on a vast long-lasting scale. Though some appetite for the spoils of power is apparent, there does not seem to be a real desire on the part of the armed forces for a monopoly of power. The military realizes that any kind of regime in Indonesia is doomed unless there is rapid economic expansion, and that a rapidly expanding economy can only be created through a substantial measure of popular support and participation. In any case, the once-strong fears of militarism have diminished somewhat, largely because of President Soeharto's belief in constitutional government and by the addition of civilian technocrats to the Development Cabinet.

The Chinese Problem

Another problem is the question of the Chinese role in the economy. The main problem arises from the dominance of the Chinese in the money economy — they control some 70% of it — and the unwillingness of some Chinese to assimilate into Indonesian society. When anything goes wrong economically, or when illegal practices are discovered, the Chinese provide a handy scapegoat.

But the Government recognizes the importance of the Chinese in the economy, and favors their assimilation into society. It ignores the agreement with Mainland China that stipulates that Overseas Chinese cannot become citizens of Indonesia without permission of Peking; it encourages Chinese to take Indonesian citizenship, and to adopt Indonesian names. Physically it is often difficult to identify the Chinese. Foreign companies generally hire Indonesian citizens — often not knowing whether they are ethnically Chinese or not.

Despite the official push for assimilation, in practice the Chinese find themselves in a difficult situation. Since the attempted coup in 1965, which implicated Peking to an extent, there has been wide suspicion that "all Chinese are communists." The 1959 Regulation PP 10, limiting retail trade in rural areas to Indonesian nationals, has driven the bulk of the Chinese into the crowded urban centers. Though the Government does not want to draw the retail trade line on an ethnic basis, but rather on a citizenship basis, few Chinese feel safe today outside the cities. Though the general policy is lenient, they often find themselves squeezed on an individual basis, because of the prejudice of the specific official administering the laws. The inability of the Central Government to ensure that its policies and regulations are followed in the outer regions makes matters worse.

Thus the Chinese feel insecure, and hesitate to use their considerable wealth in Indonesian investments. Their plight has caused many to enter short-term speculative activities, such as foreign exchange and importing. But in some cases, the old "Ali Baba" system — where Chinese operate with an Indonesian as front man — is now the "Baba Ali" system; where before the Chinese needed the Indonesians, the Indonesians find themselves working for the Chinese. In 1968, however, the Parliament passed a domestic investment law aimed at attracting the investment capital of the Chinese minority. Overall, the Government policy is a pragmatic one. But it must be effectively carried out — in spirit as well as in law — or Chinese capital and skills will be lost to the Indonesian economy.

Regional Differences

The question of regional differences with the Government in Djakarta has long been a problem in Indonesia, but no serious separatist moves are in sight at present. The one danger, in the view of the Government, is that if the 1969 referendum in West Irian should go against remaining a part of Indonesia, separatist moves in other regions might gain strength. It appears likely, however, that the West Irians will vote to stay with Indonesia; and in any case, the Government thinks the danger is less important than its own commitment to hold a referendum.

But other kinds of regional problems exist, too. For example, one area of uncertainty facing a foreign company operating outside Djakarta is how it will be treated by local officials. Though the situation is improving, and President Soeharto is trying to bring the entire archipelago under Djakarta's control, local authority will remain a hazard for several more years. Agreements and concessions by foreign companies are usually negotiated in Djakarta, but the danger remains that though the Government is sincere in its commitments, the regional authorities might interpret agreements differently, to suit their own interests. A major UK food company received permission to establish a branch in Central Java, but found that the local levies (often termed "illegal taxes") were so exorbitant that it dropped the idea. The Government wants to have market forces determine distribution patterns, which theoretically would bring rice from surplus areas into the cities in response to shortages there. But regional officials, fearful of higher prices or future rice shortages in their areas, often prohibit the transport of rice out of the area.

Progress is being made in correcting these uncertainties. The President is placing more of his trusted men in the outer regions and regional conferences have been held with local officials aimed at gaining their confidence and cooperation. To help the financial situation of local government, 10% of export proceeds are returned to the area of origin in foreign exchange. More funds will be allocated to the provinces for infrastructure projects. Improved roads, harbors, and communications will open up these areas, not only boosting their economic growth but allowing better central control.

Foreign Policy

In foreign policy, the change in direction of the New Order was quick and decisive, and problems appear to be few. Indonesia has rejoined the United Nations and its specialized agencies, the International Monetary Fund (IMF), and the World Bank. Both the IMF and the World Bank have sent several missions to Djakarta, and the IMF has a permanent mission there to assist the Central Bank and the Ministry of Finance. By mid-1968, the World Bank was establishing a major permanent mission — the first of its kind in a less developed country — which is providing technical assistance to the Government on project planning and implementation.

Indonesia's overall political stance is one of nonalignment that aims at cooperation with the West and the USSR and Eastern Europe. Unofficially, the Government probably supports the US presence in Asia, as a buffer between China and Indonesia. But in the longer term, Indonesian policy will certainly advocate foreign military power only as a shield against overt foreign agression. Internal subversion — the more likely kind of conflict in Asia — should, in the view of Indonesia, be handled internally.

Indonesia's relations with the US and Western Europe are extremely good. With the USSR, relations are good, if somewhat cooler.

Indonesia's rapprochement with the West, the campaign to eliminate the Indonesian Communist

Party, and the official ban on Marxism by the Provisional People's Consultative Assembly have aroused reactions in the USSR. But the common arch-foe, Peking, has helped prevent relations between Djakarta and Moscow from becoming too strained. At the same time, the fear of giving credibility to the Chinese charges of "Soviet revisionism," apart from the prospect of wasting more rubles in the country, has prevented the USSR from providing further large-scale economic assistance, and accounts for the hard bargaining in the rescheduling of Indonesia's debts to the USSR, its chief creditor (out of Indonesia's total debt of US$2.35 billion, US$990 million is owed to the USSR). Nevertheless, Indonesia has not given up hope for aid from the USSR and may eventually receive some.

While supporting Red China's admission into the UN, the Indonesian Government announced a freeze in its relations with Peking in October 1966, following evidence of Communist China's support in the October 1965 coup. Tensions between Djakarta and Peking increased during August and September 1967, when Indonesia and Taiwan started to establish trade contacts. Diplomatic relations with China are now "suspended" and are not likely to be normalized in the near future. In the meantime, the adventurous "confrontation" against Malaysia was abandoned. Full diplomatic relations between Indonesia and Malaysia were finally restored in August 1967. Soon afterwards, Indonesia-Singapore relations were restored.

A realistic approach is also discernible in Indonesia's relations with Japan. Suspicion still exists that Japan's strength could lead to economic domination, and there is a hangover of resentment from the occupation days. But the Indonesian Government wants to maintain the existing close trade contacts and to attract Japanese capital investment. Significantly, Japan is an important source of foreign aid to Indonesia.

Indonesia has been extremely successful in improving her regional cooperation in Southeast Asia. The Indonesian Government played an important role in setting up in 1967 the Association of Southeast Asian Nations (ASEAN), a regional grouping for economic, social, and cultural cooperation among Indonesia, Malaysia, the Philippines, Thailand, and Singapore. An ASEAN secretariat has been set up in Djakarta, and an ASEAN

ministerial meeting was held there in August of 1968. Increasingly close cooperation in economic fields — communications, tourism, and eventually industry — is a priority in foreign policy.

The Structure of Government

The MPRS (Madjelis Permusjawaratan Rakjat Sementara) is a body unique to Indonesia. As the nation's highest policy-making body, it elects the President and Vice-President for a five-year term, and sets the broad guidelines of national policy. It is composed of the 350 members (representing the political parties) of the "mutual assistance" Parliament (DPR) plus an approximately equal number of additional members representing functional groups and the regions, all of whom have been appointed. For this reason, the MPRS, like the DPR, is called "provisional" until elections are held. The MPRS must meet at least once every five years and has recently held much more frequent sessions under the chairmanship of General Abdul Haris Nasution.

Parliament meets in four sessions yearly; its powers, which were virtually nil under the Soekarno regime, are currently being extended through precedent to include not only legislative, but investigative functions as well, through the DPR's six committees: for general affairs, for law and internal affairs, for defense, security and foreign affairs, for economic and financial affairs, for industry and development affairs, and for people's welfare affairs.

The Supreme Advisory Council is a body of senior statesmen who advise the Government; in practice it has little importance.

The 1945 Constitution, now in effect in Indonesia, thus provides for a strong Presidency not directly responsible to Parliament. (See diagram.)

Although the short and broadly phrased Constitution does not specifically provide for a separation of powers or a system of checks and balances, the present Government has been taking steps to ensure independent authority for the legislative and judicial branches.

Indonesia's judicial system was previously tied very closely to the executive, with the Chairman of the Supreme Court sitting in the Cabinet. In an effort to divorce the judicial from the executive, Soeharto has removed both the Chairman of the Supreme Court and the Attorney General from the

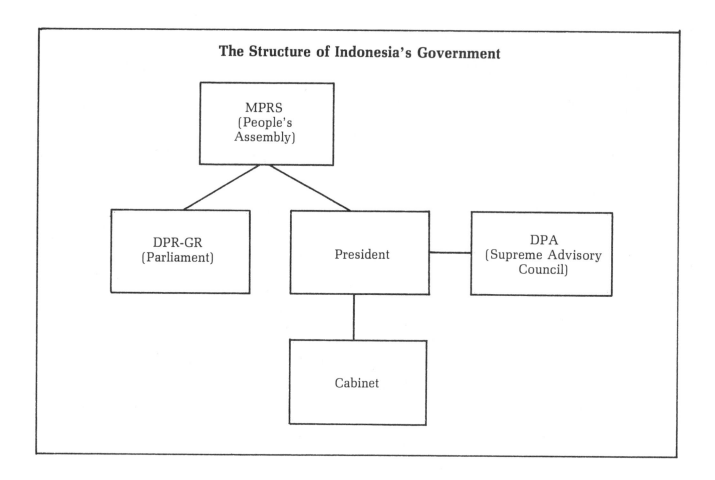

The Structure of Indonesia's Government

- MPRS (People's Assembly)
- DPR-GR (Parliament)
- President
- DPA (Supreme Advisory Council)
- Cabinet

Cabinet. The Supreme Court can neither impeach nor pass on the constitutionality of legislation or decrees. These powers, which are not mentioned in the Constitution, are now exercised by the MPRS.

The Government has also indicated its intention to strengthen local authorities — governors and other appointed high officials in the 25 semiautonomous provinces of Indonesia. But how this can be done without sacrificing efficiency in the use of financial resources still remains to be worked out.

The Civil Service

While Indonesia has a number of able and dedicated public officials, very few have had their responsibilities fixed and been given a description of their job. They are spread through too many ministries and agencies, almost all of which are seriously overstaffed at the lower echelon. The number of government employees grew from 50,-000 in the 1940's to 450,000 in 1957 and to some 1,400,000 today.

Consolidation of ministries and agencies would make it possible to reduce the number of employees and to increase efficiency. Some consolidation has begun. However, the stagnation that has long prevailed in the economy of the country has precluded discharged government workers from finding other permanent jobs. In the meantime, the salaries paid to them — 2,450 rupiahs a month for civil servants of the highest rank (i.e., less than US$10 on the free market) — encourage the current practice of "moonlighting" and contribute to corruption.

Political Parties

Since Indonesia's accession to independence, nearly all political parties have more or less failed, *as political parties.* Most Indonesian parties have not been organizations with positions on national issues, or political objectives. Instead, they repre-

Political Parties in Indonesia

Indonesia's present political parties — and past parties that are still significant — are listed below. The first four are those that proved themselves capable of obtaining the most support in the general election of 1955.

• **The Nationalist Party** (PNI) — the largest party in the 1955 elections, holding 8.4 million votes. It was founded in the 1920's and led by Soekarno. PNI draws most of its support from the tradition-oriented areas in Central and East Java. It became increasingly leftist in the 1960's. When the New Order took over, the PNI was highly suspect because of its close ties with Soekarno and because it was thought to be taking in former communists. In 1967 the regional commander in Sumatra froze all PNI activities, and commanders of other regions demanded that it reform. By the end of 1967, it had changed some of its leadership, repudiated Soekarno, and altered some of its ideology. It is again accepted (partly because the Government would be hesitant to see the dissolution of the only major secular alternative to the strong Moslem parties), but it is internally in an extremely weak state.

• **The Masjumi** — a reformist Moslem party second in the 1955 election (7.9 million votes), banned in 1960 by Soekarno because of the involvement of its leaders in the 1958 Sumatran rebellion. It drew most of its strength from urban trading areas outside Java. President Soeharto has refused to rehabilitate it.

• **The Nahdatul Ulama** (NU), or Moslem Scholars Party — a traditional Moslem Party, third in the 1955 election with 6.9 million votes. Its strength is based in Central and East Java, among the ethnically Javanese. The

NU was once close to Soekarno, but its leadership was anti-Soekarno when the coup came.

• **The Indonesian Communist Party** (PKI) — fourth in the 1955 election (6.1 million votes). The PKI's strength grew substantially after. Its electoral strength was mainly in Central and East Java. The PKI was banned in 1966. Although it may represent a long-term threat, the likelihood of an early effective reemergence is small.

• **The Indonesian Moslem Party** (PMI) — formed in late 1967 and recognized in early 1968, the PMI is basically a replacement for the old Masjumi, and is likely to become a major party. President Soeharto vetoed former Masjumi leaders as PMI leaders, but they could enter the leadership if the party congresses are freely conducted.

• **Socialist Party of Indonesia** (PSI) — a democratic party of intellectuals, with support from senior civil servants, but a small following. It was banned in 1960 by Soekarno because some of its leaders had participated in the 1958 rebellion. Its importance then and now lies in its composition. Many of its one-time members are now strong leaders in the New Order (e.g., Dr. Soemitro, Ambassador Soedjatmoko).

• **PSII** — a Moslem party that tends toward modernism, and is based mainly in West Java.

• **IPKI** — a secular party originally formed by Gen. Nasution as an army party.

• **Catholic Party**

• **Parkindo** — a protestant party, which like the Catholic Party had its principal support in the Outer Islands.

sent the rather static positions of traditional cultural groups, and thus accentuate historic divisions in the society: Moslem *vs* secular, or traditional *vs* modernist Moslem, for example. In addition, some of the major parties have had a small leadership with a mass following — a situation that has not fostered participation of most of the population in political life. As a result, in the early years of the Republic, the parties failed to provide stable, effective coalition governments.

In the late 1950s and early 1960s, the parties increasingly became mere puppets manipulated by Soekarno. (Exceptions were the Masjumi and the Socialist Party, both banned in 1960, and the Murba, banned in 1965.) Many of the leaders cooperated with him rather than maintaining independent positions, and thus forfeited, in some cases, the respect of their followers. In short, the parties' inability or unwillingness to do more than engage in obsolete ideological debate contributed greatly to the decline of parliamentary democracy and of the parties themselves. And when a new opportunity arose during and after the attempted coup in 1965, the parties did not take advantage of it. Student Action Fronts and the military dominated the political scene, while most party leaders sat on the fence.

Yet, although political parties have rarely been very effective, they are important in representing the very deep-rooted cultural groups that must have a place in any representative body. And in any case, the only alternative to parties would appear to be new "fronts" that would cut across old party lines and attempt to deal in practical terms with Indonesia's present problems. But the action fronts that were important in 1966 and 1967 were strong only as long as the anti-Soekarno issue existed; the less emotional economic issues are not enough to hold them together. President Soeharto has given little encouragement to the formation of new parties (although one, the PMI, has been established), but it is not clear whether he feels that there are already too many parties or that the proposed parties are not what the country needs. In public statements, however, he places considerable importance on the role of parties.

The State Role in Industry

As a result of the nationalization of Dutch-owned enterprises (for which compensation has since been paid), the Indonesian Government operates a big complex of industrial, commercial, transportation, and other ventures. State-owned enterprises set up during the Soekarno regime have further swelled the state sector, with the result that today the Government has enterprises operating in almost every economic area, including department stores, plantations, shipping services, sugar mills, fishing, life insurance, banking, and manufacturing enterprises. In mid-1968, the Government was planning to sell off some of these state-owned enterprises, possibly by late 1968 or early 1969, and hoped that foreign investors might enter into joint ventures with others.

Some fields — shipping, electricity, and telecommunications — are closed by law to wholly foreign-owned enterprises, but foreign investment in these fields is allowed in cooperation with the Govern-

ment, or if some provision for government regulation is agreed upon. Investment of foreign capital in the fields of mining, oil, and gas must be carried out in cooperation with the government oil company, Pertamina (the combination of Permina and Pertamin, merged in mid-1968).

As part of the overall economic stabilization program, subsidies for state enterprises (large numbers of which were in the red) are being phased out. Noneconomic prices and charges for many products and services are being corrected, and preferential credit terms ended. Prices of gasoline, diesel oil, natural gas, postal services, electricity, water, telecommunications, ocean shipping, and bus and rail fares are among the charges raised. The aim is to oblige the state enterprises to compete in the market place under the same conditions as private firms.

Nationalization Policy

There need be no fears of nationalization on the part of foreign investors while the present Government remains in power.

The Government of Indonesia guarantees under the Foreign Capital Investment Law not to nationalize any foreign enterprise, nor to revoke ownership rights or reduce rights to control in management unless required by the public interest as determined by a specific act of Parliament.

If nationalization should occur, the Indonesian Government recognizes its obligation to provide compensation in conformity with the principles of international law. If no agreement can be reached between the two parties regarding the amount, type, and procedure of payment of compensation, arbitration will take place which will be binding on both parties. The arbitration board would consist of three persons, one appointed by the Government, another by the owner of the capital, and a third, as chairman, to be selected by the Government and the investor.

Investors who feel that the reference to principles of international law and the procedure established for the determination of the arbitration panel are not sufficiently clear should outline more detailed principles and procedures that they consider important in their applications under the Foreign Capital Investment Law.

The Government of Indonesia

The President under the 1945 Constitution is both head of state and head of the Government. He is elected by the People's Congress for a five-year term and is accountable with regard to government policies before the MPRS; the ministers act as his assistants, and do not have parliamentary responsibility of their own. As head of the Government the President coordinates the activities of the various ministries.

The President: Gen. (TNI) Soeharto.

The Minister of the Interior is in charge of regional administration, autonomy, and development; agrarian affairs; land reform; titles to land; registration, administration, and charting of land holdings; development at the village level with due emphasis on the principle of *gotong royong* (mutual assistance), promotion of small-scale production and financing units in villages; irrigation units at the village level; and general elections.

The Minister of the Interior: Lt. Gen. (TNI) Basuki Rachmat.

The Minister for External Affairs in charge of foreign policy, foreign economic relations, multilateral economic relations, international technical cooperation, bilateral economic cooperation and foreign political and economic intelligence.

The Minister for External Affairs: Hadji Adam Malik.

The Minister for Defense and Security takes care of national defense and security, veterans affairs, coordination of the armed forces for external defense as well as internal stability, training of the armed forces, and logistics and ammunition factories.

The Minister for Defense and Security: Gen. (TNI) Soeharto.

The Minister of Justice is in charge of judicial order in the country, care of delinquents, immigration affairs, supervision of aliens, supervision of border areas, guidance and supervision of legal practices and institutions, civil registration, notary publics, administration of changes in nationality, trade marks, and patents and rights concerning inventions or creative labor.

The Minister of Justice: Prof. Oemar Senoadji S.H.

The Minister of Information is in charge of domestic and external information, publications, audiovisual or mobile information units, development of the press, licenses for publication of newspapers and magazines, supply of newsprint for the local press and graphic industry, radio, television, and films.

The Minister of Information: Rear Adm. (Air Force) Boediardjo.

The Minister of Finance is responsible for monetary policy; analyzing and planning monetary, credit, and foreign exchange policies; preparing the budget; watching the implementation of the budget by other departments; direct and indirect taxes; customs and excise tax; prevention of and fighting against smuggling; increase of government revenue and control over government expenditures; insurance companies; state accounting to control state enterprises; banks, insurance companies and other credit agencies; pawnshops.

The Minister of Finance: Prof. Dr. Ali Wardhana.

The Minister of Trade is in charge of domestic and foreign trade policies, promotion of exports and market expansion for cash crops and handicrafts, interinsular trade, adapting imports to the needs of domestic production, programming exports, fixation and control of export prices, foreign trade relations, commercial intelligence, standardization and normalization, development of marketing institutions, trade fairs, and control of state trading companies.

The Minister of Trade: Prof. Dr. Soemitro Djojohadikusumo.

The Minister of Agriculture is charged with development of agricultural production of food crops as well as cash crops; agricultural extension; charting, planning, investment, supervision, protection, exploitation, export, processing, and marketing of forest products; development, extension, guidance, prevention of diseases in and protection of animal husbandry; development of fishery; promotion of fishers' cooperatives, and foreign investment in fishery; state and private estates; smallholders' cash crops; agricultural research, and promotion of the use of new seeds including "miracle rice"; supervision of special state marketing agencies and/or joint companies for tobacco and other crops; and the Agricultural Research Institute in Bogor.

The Minister of Agriculture: Prof. Dr. Ir. Haj Thojib Hadiwidjaja.

The Minister of Industry is in charge of development of heavy and light industry, textiles and chemical industries, and handicrafts. In all these sectors the emphasis is on the increase of production, improvement of quality, use of local resources, gearing raw material imports to the needs of industry, development of new markets for local industries, research on materials, and training facilities. The Department supervises the great number of industrial projects owned by the state.

The Minister of Industry: Maj. Gen. (TNI) M. Jusuf.

The Minister of Mining is responsible for development of the mining sector; charting, surveying, exploration, vulcanological control, hydrology, and analysis of mining products; control over and issuing of mining licenses; supervision of oil and natural gas production, processing and marketing; supervision of state companies operating in mining for tin, gold, oil, bauxite, etc.

The Minister of Mining: Prof. Ir. Soemantri Brodjonegoro.

The Minister of Public Works and Power is in charge of planning and developing irrigation, use of rivers and marshes, research with regard to water (hydraulics, hydrology), water structures, public housing, city planning, water supply, sewerage, road development, bridges, prevention of natural disasters, generation and distribution of electricity, and such projects as the multipurpose projects at Djatiluhur and Karangkates.

The Minister of Public Works and Power: Ir. Sutami.

The Minister of Communications is charged with coordination of land, sea, and air transport, telecommunications, road transport, railroads, postal services, telegraph and telephone services, civil aviation, meteorology, interisland transport, ocean shipping, and harbors. The Department supervises the state companies operating railroads, telecommunication and postal services, interisland shipping (PELNI), and ocean shipping (Djakarta Lloyd).

The Minister of Communications: Drs. Frans Seda.

The Minister of Education is in charge of basic education, training of teachers, general secondary education, vocational training, adult education, higher education, sports, historical monuments, museums, youth and Boy Scouts. All student scholarships from universities abroad are handled by this department.

The Minister of Education: Mashuri S.H.

The Minister of Health is in charge of public health; operation of hospitals and clinics; mental health (preventive and curative); dental care; nutritional research and improvements; child and mother health; health at schools; prevention of communicable diseases; production of vaccines; quarantine in ports, airports, and border areas; water hygiene and disposal of waste; plant hygiene; pest and mice control; immunization; malaria/framboesia/veneral disease eradication; control over production, importation, supply and distribution of pharmaceuticals; and family planning.

The Minister of Health: Prof. Dr. G. A. Siwabessy.

The Minister of Religion is charged with religious guidance in Islam, Christianity (Roman Catholic and Protestant), Bali Hinduism, and Buddhism; promotion of religious harmony among the various groups; maintenance of houses of worship; research in religious laws; and supplying guidance and facilities for pilgrims.

The Minister of Religion: K. H. Mohammad Dahlan.

The Minister of Manpower is responsible for projections of manpower development and vocational training to meet development requirements, supply and use of manpower, occupational information and counselling, protection and maintenance of health among the labor force, guidance of labor-protection norms (hygiene in industrial plants etc.), mediation in labor disputes, research in rehabilitation of the handicapped, and regulation of the employment of foreign personnel.

The Minister of Manpower: Rear Adm. (Navy) Mursalin.

The Minister of Social Affairs is in charge of support to victims of natural calamities, rehabilitation of victims of disturbances and refugees, licenses to collect funds for charity, rehabilitation of the handicapped and unemployed, care for the aged, and the welfare of pioneers for independence.

The Minister of Social Affairs: Dr. A. M. Tambunan.

The Minister for Transmigration and Cooperatives is in charge of transmigration of population from the densely populated areas in Java to the outer islands; opening of new settlements; guidance and control for production, marketing, and service cooperatives.

The Minister for Transmigration and Cooperatives: Lt. Gen. (TNI) Sarbini.

In addition to ministers who head specific departments, there are five State Ministers without portfolio:

• Sri Sultan Hamengku Buwono IX — Minister of State for Economic, Financial, and Industrial Affairs. The Sultan coordinates the Departments of Trade, Finance, Industry, Agriculture, Mining, Public Works and Power, Communications, and the Central Bank.

• Dr. K. H. Idham Chalid — Minister of State for Public Welfare. He is charged with coordinating the Departments of Education, Health, Social Affairs, and Religion.

• H. Harsono Tjokroaminoto — Minister of State for the Perfection and Purification of the State Apparatus. He is charged not only with reducing corruption, but also with streamlining the state apparatus to make it conform with the Constitution. Under the Soekarno regime, many government agencies were created which were not provided for in the Constitution and were against the spirit of the Constitution; the MPRS has resolved that such agencies must be abolished.

• Prof. Dr. Soenawar Soekowati S.H. — Minister of State for the Supervision of Government Projects. His responsibilities cover the seventeen interministerial projects given priority by the Government (see box page 14).

• H. Mintaredja S.H. — Minister of State for Relations between the Government and the MPRS (Provisional People's Consultative Assembly), the DPR (Parliament) and DPA (Supreme Advisory Council.

Non-Departmental
Supreme State Agencies

1. **Provisional Peoples' Consultative Assembly** (Madjelis Permusjawaratan Rakjat Sementara — MPRS). The MPRS consists of 828 members. It is the highest legislative body in the country, consisting of all members of the DPR (Parliament) plus representatives of the regions and popular groupings. According to the Constitution the members must be elected, but the current MPRS is a continuation of the one appointed by Soekarno. Some of the members — communists or others who were too committed to the Old Order — were replaced. The MPRS formulates the broad outlines of government policy, and elects the President, who is accountable to it.

Speaker: Gen. Abdul Haris Nasution

2. **Parliament** (Dewan Perwakilan Rakjat — DPR). The DPR has 414 members from political and functional groups. The DPR passes legislation in cooperation with the Government. It has the right to question the Govern-

ment, the rights of interpellation, amendment, etc., but it cannot pass a motion of censure against the Government. On the other hand, the DPR cannot be dissolved by the President.

Speaker: K. H. Achmad Sjaichu.

3. **Supreme Advisory Council** (Dewan Pertimbangan Agung — DPA). The DPA has 17 members, elder statesmen appointed in recognition of merit, although some have party affiliations. It renders advice to the Government on any subject it deems urgent or fit. The advice may be requested by the Government or offered at the initiative of the DPA.

Chairman: Dr. Wilopo S.H.

4. **Supreme Court** (Mahkamah Agung). The Supreme Court is the highest court of appeal. It guides the development of legal practice in courts with the stress on the independent position of the judge and the court. This has become more significant under the New Order, since, before the October 1965 coup, the courts had become a mere extension of politics. The Mahkamah Agung has no power of judicial review on the constitutionality of laws.

President: Prof. Dr. Subekti S.H.

5. **National Development Planning Agency** (Badan Perantjang Pembangunan Nasional — Bappenas). Bappenas prepares the development plans for the Government, such as the Five-Year Development Plan beginning in 1969, and the annual development plans. As such, Bappenas cooperates closely with such sources of development aid as the IBRD, IDA, and creditor countries extending development aid to Indonesia. Naturally Bappenas works closely with the various departments.

Chairman: Prof. Dr. Widjojo Nitisastro.

6. **State Audit Bureau** (Badan Pengawas Kenangan — BPK). The State Audit Bureau supervises the implementation of the budget, checking that accountable functionaries spend government funds in accordance with the budget. BPK reports findings on these matters to Parliament.

Chairman: Maj. Gen. Suprajogi.

7. **Indonesian Institute for Sciences** (Lembaga Ilumn Pengetahnan Indonesia — LIPI). LIPI coordinates all research activities. It promotes research, including that done by foreign scholars, and engages in research itself. It also organizes seminars, such as the 1968 Workshop on Food in cooperation with the NAS of the US.

Director: Prof. Dr. Sarwono.

8. **State Secretariat** (Sekretariat Negara) is the center of administration of the nondepartmental government agencies at the central government level. It "assists the President in his capacity as head of state as well as head of government in implementing the power of government whichever involves state and government administration in its widest sense." It consists of three secretariats: the cabinet secretariat, the presidential secretariat, and the military secretariat.

State Secretary: Maj. Gen. Alamsjah.

III—The Economy

AFTER YEARS OF stagnation and decline that led to the brink of disaster, Indonesia's economy is painfully but definitely recovering. During the early 1950's economic advancement was slow, and inflation was already a problem. But the plunging spiral began in the late 1950's with Soekarno's policy of Guided Democracy, the growing dominance of political and ideological purposes over economic principles, and the swelling role of the state in the economy.

The situation that the new regime inherited from Soekarno's Government was little less than economic chaos. Production and overseas sales of several key export products had levelled off or actually declined, and the infrastructure had deteriorated from years of little or no investment. The relationships of economic sectors and industries were seriously distroted by years of economic mismanagement: priority given to prestige projects, protection for inefficient state enterprises, the rapid expansion of the money supply and credit, and inflexible foreign exchange controls. Most serious of all, the country was facing one of the worst cases of hyperinflation the world has ever seen. Indonesia was bankrupt, with its foreign exchange reserves almost depleted, and a foreign debt of $2.4 billion.

In one sense, the economy was in a state of total collapse by 1965, but the population had not really felt the full impact of the decline. This was partly because subsidies had protected the purchasing power of the urban public, but mainly because most of the villagers can live by subsistence agriculture practically untouched by the market economy. However, from 1958 through 1965, real national income increased by only 12.4%, while population (growing at 2.3-2.8% per year) increased by 17.3%. Real per capita income in 1963 was 6.9% below the 1958 level, and by 1965 was still 4.2% below the 1958 level. (See Table 1.)

The New Economic Policies

In a complete reversal from the Soekarno era, the Soeharto Government has given top priority to economic recovery and development. It believes, moreover, that the emphasis should be on market forces, rather than political and administrative pressures, in allocation of resources.

The government's program has three phases— stabilization, rehabilitation, and development. The first two phases were to carry through 1968, in preparation for the start of a five-year plan in 1969. By the end of 1968, a considerable amount of progress had been made, but there was still a long way to go.

Stabilization naturally had first priority. Chronic and growing budget deficits, financed by multiplying the money supply, had brought on galloping inflation. The money supply in 1959 was some seven times higher than in 1951, and in 1964 was

TABLE 1.

Real Growth Rates (%), Net National Product and Per Capita Income, 1959-1967

	1959	1960	1961	1962	1963	1964	1965	1966 [1]	1967 [1]
Net National Product	0.4	0.7	4.2	−0.6	−0.6	4.8	3.0	3.1	4.8
Per Capita Income	−1.9	−1.5	1.8	−2.8	−2.8	2.4	0.5	0.6	2.3

(1) Estimates
Source: Nugroho, **Indonesia Facts and Figures,** 1967

some 20 times higher than in 1959. From Rp675 billion in 1964, it rose to Rp21,000 billion (old rupiahs) in 1966, while the budget deficit grew from Rp398 billion to Rp16,291 billion (old rupiahs). A currency revaluation was introduced in December 1965, under which one new rupiah replaced 1,000 old rupiahs. Bank deposits as a percentage of the money supply dropped from 40% in 1950 to 29% by 1966. (See Table 2.)

The cost-of-living index in Djakarta (1957-58:100) stood at 2,226 by the end of 1963, and had jumped to 36,347 by the end of 1965. (See Appendix I.) Ten liters of rice that had cost about Rp60 in 1960 cost nearly Rp6,000 in 1965 and nearly Rp48,000 in 1966. Inflation reached its peak in 1966, with a rise of 635% in a single year.

The severe inflation and the neglect of Indonesia's growing economic difficulties took their toll on the balance of payments, which has been in deficit since 1961. The deficit was $168 million in 1961 and 1962, and decreased to $142 million and $88 million in 1963 and 1964. It then rose sharply to $235 in 1965. At first the deficit was financed by drawing on foreign assets acquired earlier, but after 1962 short and medium-term credits were increasingly used to finance it. The accumulation of short-term debts, a leveling off of export earnings, and the sharp drop during 1965 in official foreign loans all contributed to a dwindling of foreign exchange reserves. While net reserves stood at $301 million in 1960, gross official gold and foreign exchange holdings were only $21 million at the end of 1965, and foreign exchange liabilities were increasing. (See Appendix II.) By early 1966, Indonesia could no

longer maintain service on its foreign debt, and requested rescheduling of its payment obligations.

The new Government took several strong steps toward stabilization in October 1966, the first being an attempt to balance the budget. Prestige projects were abandoned and other curbs on government expenditures were applied, while efforts were made to boost tax revenues. The success was not complete, but was nevertheless remarkable. Revenues in 1967 amounted to Rp83.7 billion, and expenditures were Rp87.6 billion, leaving a deficit of only Rp3.9 billion, although some current expenditures were covered by foreign aid. In 1968 the Government was trying to finance all current expenditure from domestic revenues, and hoped by 1969 to finance part of the development budget as well from this source.

Other stabilization moves include holding down the expansion of the money supply and credit. Bank lending rates were drastically raised after October 1966 from 9-29% per year, to 6-9% per month, and a selective credit policy was put into effect to channel credits to exports and production. The money supply, which had risen by 746% in 1966, went up by only 147% in 1967. In February 1968, when Indonesia and the International Monetary Fund concluded a Stand-By Agreement providing an IMF line of credit of $52 million, the IMF and Indonesia agreed on quarterly ceilings on the expansion of central bank credit. By late 1968, Indonesia was keeping within these ceilings, which would hold total expansion of the money supply in 1968 to 65%.

Rice is one of the key elements for stabilization. It is by far the most important component in the

TABLE 2.

Indonesia's Money Supply, 1960-1967

(In millions of new rupiahs)

End of Period	Total Money Supply	Currency	Currency as Per Cent Of Total Money Supply	Demand Deposits	Annual Change in Total Money Supply (%)
1960	48	34	71	14	
1961	68	49	72	19	41
1962	135	102	76	33	100
1963	263	175	67	88	95
1964	675	453	67	222	156
1965	2,521	1,933	77	588	278
1966	21,340	15,120	71	6,220	746
1967	52,628	34,355	65	18,273	147

cost of living, and because rice allocations are a significant part of the wages paid to the military, civil servants, and employees of estates or industries, a rise in its price pushes up production costs and government expenditures. Consequently, an adequate rice supply — and adequate distribution facilities — are crucial to holding down inflation. This was dramatically demonstrated in 1967, when a combination of drought, inadequate procurement, and ill-timed foreign aid produced a rice shortage in the cities. There were some areas with rice surpluses, but often transportation was inadequate, or regional authorities prohibited the transfer of rice out of their regions. The result was a drastic increase in prices from September through January 1968, which was aggravated by speculation. It shattered all hopes for staying below the government's targeted inflation rate of 65% in 1967, pushing the rate to 112%. The Government appears determined not to make the same mistakes twice. Rice imports and domestic procurement were both increased sharply in 1968, and rice production and distribution have top priority in the plan that will start in 1969.

Other key elements in the stabilization program have been the liberalization of foreign trade through the BE System (see Chapter 5, *Financing*, and 9, *Trade*), and the reduction of government controls and subsidies. In early 1967, state enterprises were told to meet current expenses from current revenues, and some prices were adjusted to more realistic levels. A major — and politically sensitive — step was taken in April 1968, when prices of petroleum products were sharply hiked. The gasoline price quadrupled and the kerosene price rose by 60%. This in turn pushed up transport and production prices.

These and other stabilization measures have not been enough to meet original expectations, but they have had a remarkable degree of success. The government's targets, after the 635% inflation in 1966, were for inflation of only 65% in 1967 and 30-35% in 1968. The 1967 rate turned out to be 112%, so a new target of 65% inflation in 1968 was set. At the time of writing, the 1968 inflation is expected to be 70-80%, but this really understates the government's achievement. Prices rose by 40% in January 1968 alone, a hangover from the 1967 rice crisis. But in subsequent months the rate averaged between 3% and 5% per month. It appears quite possible that the Government could hold inflation in 1969 to 40-50%, in 1970 and 1971 to 30-40%, and by 1972 to 20-30%.

The Government does face some severe problems in implementing its stabilization and rehabilitation program, however. So far, rehabilitation has mainly meant putting priority on spare parts to get the country back into working order, expanding food production, bringing order into public finance, putting state enterprises on a more businesslike basis, inviting former foreign investors to take back their plantations and plants, passing a foreign investment law, and implementing a selective credit policy. On some even more basic problems, the Government has made a start: an Anti-Corruption Agency, with investigatory and prosecuting authority, has been established; tax collection has been extended somewhat; extortion by the military has been reduced; Djakarta's authority and control over regional authorities has been strengthened, and some local illegal taxes and other barriers to interregional trade have been eliminated; government policy statements have tried to reassure the Chinese minority, concerned over their uncertain status, and a Domestic Investment Law aimed at encouraging investment by the Chinese minority has been passed. In addition, the problem of an oversized and underpaid civil service, which strains government revenues and encourages corruption, has been given some attention. All of these problems are politically sensitive issues that might be difficult to deal with in any country. The solutions to them demand radical, decisive, and enforceable policies, that will go against entrenched interests and deepseated feelings. The Indonesian Government's problem of not wanting to antagonize its supporters is compounded by the traditional Indonesian belief in consensus (*musjawarah*). But it is clear that despite the problems involved, the Government will have to come to terms with these issues even more decisively, or the country's economic development will be severely hindered. Some steps have been taken, but many of the drastic institutional changes required will take time.

Structure of the Economy

Indonesia has a dual economy, with well-defined modern and traditional sectors. The modern sector is mainly a result of Dutch investment in plantations, mining, subsidiary industries, and commerce during the colonial period. Peasant and smallholder agriculture were relatively untouched by modernization. Even today some 70% of the population is largely outside the market economy. But the division is along neither geographical nor product lines. Except for petroleum and minerals, none of the major export products are produced entirely in the modern sector, and in the case of rubber, Indonesia's largest export, smallholder

production is more than double the estate output. Estate agriculture is more important in Sumatra, however, than in Java, and Sumatra produces the largest quantities of such products as rubber and palm oil.

Manufacturing, modern or traditional, is not very well developed. Most industries were established in response to the demands of estates for manufactured equipment and repair facilities. An exception is the textile industry, where some complementarity has developed between the modern and traditional sectors, the former producing piece goods and the latter the well-known batik products.

Manufacturing and mining account for about 12% and 3% respectively of Indonesia's national production, wholesale and retail trade 17%, and agriculture, forestry, and fishing about 52%. The contribution of mining and oil can be expected to increase over the next few years, however. (See Appendix XVIII.)

Agriculture

Over 70% of the population is engaged in agriculture, and it is the complete source of livelihood for 50% of the people. Only about 12% of the land area (0.8 acres per capita) is arable, which is about average for Asian countries. In Java, 70% of the total area is under cultivation, compared to only about 5% in the other islands. Agricultural products, including forestry and fishing, account for 60-70% of the value of Indonesia's exports (the rest comes mainly from petroleum and other minerals). Export taxes on agricultural products produce nearly 20% of the government's non-foreign aid revenues.

Agriculture is divided into two distinct sectors: estates and smallholder operations. Estates, covering less than 10% of the cultivated land area, produce almost entirely for export, but smallholders produce for both export and local consumption (mainly food crops). Except for relatively small amounts of rubber, vegetable oils, hard fibers, and sugar, agriculture supplies few of the raw material needs of Indonesian industry.

Since the nationalization of Dutch and other foreign-owned enterprises, most of the estates are state-owned, but a few large rubber estates were recently returned to their foreign owners. Government-owned units account for 60% of estate production. Both the number and production levels of estates have been generally declining since World War II, but this has been partly offset by increased smallholder production. Estate production and exports, valued at $177 million in 1966, have stagnated in recent years because of the poor financial situation of the industry. Inflation and low earnings (in the case of rubber, partly due to declining world prices), generally brought about by heavy export taxes and unrealistic exchange rates, contributed to the general deterioration of estates.

Exports of smallholder production account for about 40% of total exports, and in 1966 were valued at $220 million. The major commodities are rubber, coffee, copra, and pepper.

Agricultural Production

Agricultural production in 1966 and 1967 was a mixture of good and bad. Production levels in 1966 showed increases in spices (134%), tobacco (28%), corn (26%), coffee (16%), copra (11%), and palm oil (3%), but there were declines in tea (54%), sugar (12%), sweet potatoes, cassava, and rubber. The decline in sugar production was due mainly to a 25% decrease in estate output, brought on by an artificially low price ceiling and increased costs that left no funds for rehabilitation. In 1967, sugar production recovered by 6%, to 1,106 million tons, still far below the prewar level. Palm oil production declined in 1967 by 16%, and copra output by 2%. Tea and tobacco production were up slightly, and spice production increased 9%, but output of corn, sweet potatoes, and cassava declined. (See Appendix III.)

Of cash crops, rubber is by far the most important, and presents the biggest problems. In 1966, production by smallholders decreased by 15,000 tons or 3%, and estate production fell by 5,000 tons (2%). Total rubber production in 1967 was estimated at about 747,000 tons, the same as in 1966. With rubber accounting for about a third of the total value of exports, the decline in production is a serious blow to foreign exchange earnings.

Smallholder production seems unlikely to increase sharply; some 80% of smallholders' rubber needs replanting, and with rubber prices falling and the cost of living rising, smallholders are likely to turn to other crops. Deterioration in the estate sector has lowered yields until over half the estates may not be financially viable. Even if they can be kept in production, sharp increases in output are not likely until after 1970, when the effects of replanting started in 1963 will begin to be felt. In addition, in 1965 and 1966, shortages of spare parts and fertilizers hindered production; in 1967, higher wages, due to the rising price of rice and sharply increased utility costs as subsidies were removed, and to the poor condition of infrastructure, raised production costs. At the same time, of course, world rubber prices were continuing to decline. Many estates are undergoing rehabilitation, but over the long term, some rubber production is likely to give way to other cash crops or to production of rice.

Rice

Milled rice production in 1967 was 9.32 million tons, almost 2% above the 1966 level, but only 7.9% above the 1960-62 average. Rice production has increased by an average of only 1.1% annually since 1959-60, obviously too little to keep up with population growth. In 1961-64, more than one million tons of rice were imported annually. Because of the shortage of foreign exchange, imports in 1965 were slashed to 140,000 tons; the low import level, combined with difficulties of procuring and transporting domestically produced rice from surplus to deficit areas, led to acute shortages. Prices in the cities, which normally get only 6% of the domestically produced rice, went up sharply in the last half of 1965 and the first half of 1966. The Government had planned to import 600,000 tons in 1966, but with limited foreign exchange, it cut back to 235,000 tons. Optimistic about increasing domestic production, and still faced with a scarcity of foreign exchange, the Government kept its import target for 1967 to 265,000 tons. But a long dry season and an unfavorable fertilizer/rice price ratio kept output 20% below the target. Some 400,000 tons were finally imported, but it was too little and too late to prevent rice shortages in the cities that sent prices spiraling after August 1967. In Djakarta, where rice accounts for over 30% of the cost of living, the price of one kg. jumped from Rp30 at the end of September to over Rp86 at the end of January 1968. The Djakarta rice price had fallen 40% by mid-1968, but the dramatic inflation of late 1967 had underlined the political importance of adequate rice supplies to any effort at stabilization.

The Government is already tackling some of the basic problems of rice supply. For 1968, imports were set at 600,000 tons. To build up government stocks for stabilizing the rice price (and for rice allocations for civil servants), procurement by the Bureau of Logistics (BULOG) was increased. A "Farmer's Formula," matching the price of one kg. of rice and one kg. of urea, was put into effect. Good weather conditions helped in 1968; preliminary estimates put the crop at 10.16 million tons, well over the 9.8-million-ton target. The 1969-73 plan emphasizes rehabilitation of the irrigation system, reforestation, and flood control. Several programs for increasing local production through agricultural inputs and technical assistance, such as the arrangement with Ciba of Switzerland (see Chapter 4) are under way.

Past increases in rice production, inadequate as they were, indicate what can be done. They have been mainly the result of the Bimas program ("mass guidance toward self-sufficiency in food production"), an agricultural development program initiated in 1963 and based on a system of expanded agricultural extension work. The aims of the program are improved water control, use of selected seed, use of fertilizers and pesticides, better cultivation methods, and stronger cooperatives. The average rice yield per hectare in Indonesia in 1967 was a very low 1.23 tons, but yields in areas under the Bimas scheme have been 0.9 to 2.0 tons per hectare higher.

Use of the IR-5 and IR-8 miracle rice seeds (called PB-5 and PB-8 in Indonesia) that have brought spectacular gains in the Philippines and elsewhere is expected to increase steadily, but will depend to some extent on the availability of fertilizers and fertilizer credits. Indonesia has one fertilizer plant with an annual capacity of 100,000 tons of urea, and expects to quadruple the plant's capacity. But large imports will still be required. Total fertilizer requirements in 1968-69 were estimated at 401,000 tons (of which 300,000 were for rice), plus 5,100 tons of pesticide and 424,000 sprayers.

Forestry and Fishery

Over 60% (120 million hectares) of the land area is forested, although less than one tenth of the forest area has been evaluated. The output of forestry products, after having fallen by 13% in 1965, rose 7.5% to three million cubic meters in 1966. Forestry, though at present contributing only a negligible amount to exports, is potentially a major source of export revenues. Indonesia could contribute annually around 100 million cubic meters of timber to meet world demand without disrupting its sources. In fact, Indonesian forests have become the object of intense interest on the part of foreign investors now that Indonesia has embarked on a policy of encouraging foreign investment.

The country has immense fishery potential, but fishing is not a flourishing industry. Of the estimated 110,000 small vessels owned exclusively by single operators, less than 1% are motorized. Total fishery production increased by 9% in 1965, and by 11% to almost 1.2 million tons in 1966. The increase during this period was in respect of both inland and sea fisheries, especially the latter. The targeted increase for inland fishery production in 1967 was about 9% to 468,000 tons, owing to the completion of certain reservoirs, while sea fisheries were targeted to show an increase of 8% to 775,000 tons. Foreign investment (particularly from Japan) will be an important factor in future increases.

Mining and Oil

Indonesia is the most important Asian petroleum producer east of the Persian Gulf. Although resources are by no means fully exploited, its annual output is now 186 million barrels, putting it in a class with the lesser Middle East-North African producers. The major oil reserves are in Sumatra, with smaller deposits in Kalimantan; the present emphasis is on off-shore exploration.

Crude oil production in 1965 was 177.0 million barrels, an increase of 4% over the previous year; during 1966, output was 170.5 million barrels, or about 3% less than in 1965. Production in 1967 rose to 186.1 million barrels, an increase of about 8% over 1966. (See Table 3.) The entire increase is attributable to the expansion of Caltex output, which accounted for about 70% of Indonesia's crude production. The application of a more realistic rate of exchange to oil company transactions in February 1968, together with the

TABLE 3.

Indonesian Mineral Production 1962-67

('000 tons)

Mineral	1962	1963	1964	1965	1966 [1]	1967 [2]
Crude petroleum ('000 barrels)	168,209	164,681	189,774	177,006	170,524	186,138
Tin-in-concentrates	17.6	13.1	16.6	14.9	12.8	13.8
Bauxite (crude ore)	461	506	648	688	701	920
Coal	471	591	446	391	320	209
Manganese	6.7	4.8	5.2	7.2	—	—
Nickel	11	46	49	102	117	170

1. Revised estimates
2. Preliminary data
Source: Ministry of Mining

improved environment for foreign enterprises, have stimulated production. A further increase of about 21% was projected for 1968. Crude oil and petroleum products provide about a third of Indonesia's export earnings.

Other mineral deposits are diverse. Tin, bauxite, copper, manganese, some gold and silver, and low-quality coal are significant in terms of current output. Deposits of tin, copper, bauxite, and coal are largely in Sumatra and adjacent smaller islands; manganese, gold, and silver are found in Java. Nickel and iron deposits are also believed to be substantial.

Since the nationalization of Indonesia's mines, tin mining has been in the hands of state enterprises. These were reorganized in 1968 into one state company with four units — Bangka, Billiton, Singkep, and a smelter. Foreign investors are now entering the field. Following a 10% decline in 1965, the production of tin-in-concentrates decreased further by about 14% to 12,770 tons in 1966. Inadequate maintenance, a shortage of skilled labor, management problems (including the inability to retrench surplus unskilled labor), and insufficient working capital were the main factors responsible for the decline. Output in 1967, however, increased by 8.2% over 1966 to 13,818 tons.

Coal production declined sharply to 209,000 tons in 1967, compared to 320,000 tons in the calendar year 1966. Financial difficulties, inadequate supply of spare parts, and marketing problems were mainly responsible for the decline.

Nickel production amounted to 170,000 tons in 1967, compared to 117,000 tons in 1966. Bauxite output in 1967 was 920,000 tons, much higher than the 1966 figure of 701,000 tons.

Manufacturing

Manufacturing is not well developed in Indonesia, as evidenced by its contribution of only 12% to the net national product. Most manufacturing ventures process agricultural products or produce consumer goods or other light manufactures. The textile industry is by far the most important. Many of the large-scale plants in basic industries are state enterprises. An inventory of basic industries in 1966 listed 23 state enterprises, producing, among other things, fertilizer, salt, vehicles and parts, rolling stock, tires, caustic soda, electric equipment, cement, oxygen, glass, paper, and steel products, and there were 14 state-owned plants in basic industries under construction. There are, of course, many more state-owned plants in other fields. Many are now being put on a profit-making basis, some have been turned into joint ventures with private foreign investors, and others may be sold to private interests. Nearly 250 private enterprises in basic industries (including assembly of radio and TV sets and sewing machines) were counted, but in many cases their operations are on a small scale.

Generally, manufacturing operations are heavily dependent on imported equipment, raw materials, and spare parts. Due to government controls over foreign exchange before 1966, acute shortages developed, and both efficiency and production stagnated or declined in many industries. Particularly in the state sector, Indonesian industry has suffered from a lack of management and technical expertise, as well as from a surplus of employees.

By 1967 and 1968, state enterprises were being rationalized and rehabilitated, and imports of spare parts and raw materials allowed some improvement in private industry. But high credit costs and severe competition from imports (both necessary to the stabilization policy), rising costs, and the general low level of economic activity kept many plants operating at only a fraction of their capacity. The problem of dismissing excess labor had not yet been solved, but some progress had been made.

Textiles

Indonesia's textile industry is a combination of traditional handloom production and modern, efficient spinning and weaving operations. It has been operating at 50% of capacity or less, due mainly to dependence on imported raw cotton and competition from low-priced imports from Mainland China via Hong Kong and Singapore. With the increased availability of foreign-aid financed imports of raw cotton and spare parts, textile production in 1967 rose by 12% over the 1966 level to 225 million meters, but this was still 56% lower than the 1965 output. The recession in the textile industry has had serious effects on employment and prices. Tariff protection was increased in April 1968, however, and emphasis is being placed on rehabilitation of the industry to substitute for imports.

Other industries are generally a mixture of some relatively efficient operations and some that operate with ancient equipment or are far below

optimum size. In the engineering field, there are several state enterprises making heavy equipment (generally inefficiently) and small or medium-size private metal-working operations in most cities (55,000 tons annual capacity). In the chemical field, there are many state-owned plants, some of which are considered relatively efficient (e.g., nitrogen, ammonia, oxygen, and carbon dioxide plants). The Palembang fertilizer plant, in contrast to most factories, has been operating at full capacity. There is one modern cement factory at Gresik, (375,000 tons annual capacity) and an old one at Padang (120,000 tons). A near halt in construction activity after 1966 kept them operating at very low levels of capacity, but some pick-up in building construction was occurring by late 1968.

In the transportation field, there are several private car assembly plants with a total capacity of 10,000 cars per year; one of the larger assemblers was the state-owned Gaja Motors (formerly a General Motors plant), but this was about to be liquidated in late 1968. Tires are made by Goodyear and the state-owned PN Intirub, and a new state-owned plant at Palembang was set for production in 1969. A joint venture between Goodyear and the Government was under discussion at the time this report was prepared.

In light industry, there are over 55,000 private establishments producing a variety of goods, but nearly all are on the scale of a small shop. Medium-size private plants (under Indonesia's definitions, medium-scale industries employ five to 49 persons with the use of power, or 10-99 without power) probably number only a few hundred. According to an industrial census taken in 1963, covering both state and private companies, one firm (food) employed more than 2,000 persons, 55 (in chemicals, transport equipment, food, rubber, textiles, printing, nonmetallic mineral products industries) employed 1,000-2,000 persons, 84 (in transport equipment, nonelectric machinery, textiles, nonmetallic mineral products, rubber, leather, printing, wood products, tobacco, beverages, and food) employed between 500 and 1,000 persons, and 461 firms employed 250 to 500. The large majority of manufacturing establishments are in Java, with Sumatra far behind in second place.

Infrastructure

Rehabilitation and improvement of infrastructure

in Indonesia is clearly one of the first essentials for economic development. Lack of adequate transport facilities limits to some degree the size of the market for manufacturing firms, and sometimes results in extremely high transport costs even between different points within Java. This means that imported goods often have significant price advantages in some regions over goods produced inside the country but in other regions.

For example, the cement factory at Gresik in East Java has to apply differential prices for cement used in East Java and cement used in Djakarta. While inadequate transport and communications facilities are costly and frustrating to the businessman, they are even more serious for the Government; the situation hampers distribution of rice, slows exports, and makes complete integration of the country — and control by the central Government — much more difficult.

Transport

Transport facilities in Indonesia have suffered from practically no maintenance for many years. One of the key sectors — since the country has several thousand islands — is ports and shipping.

Ports and port facilities are in poor condition. The dredging fleet is rundown from lack of repairs, spare parts, and above all funds, and there is a backlog of some 40 million square meters of dredging to be done. A large portion of sea transport is state-owned. Less than half the state-owned fleet was operative in 1968. The estimated total effective deadweight tonnage for interinsular shipping was 139,362 dwt and for ocean shipping 302,717 dwt. Until 1967, the state-owned P.N. Pelni was subsidized by the Government, but now it has to cover its costs from revenues. Consequently, shipping rates went up sharply on all but nine basic commodities (and were raised again when fuel prices rose in April 1968). This has pushed up distribution costs for industry.

Air transport is extremely important due to the geography of the country. The major airline is the government-owned Garuda, but several private air taxi services operate, and others are expected to begin in 1969. In 1968 Garuda began operating its Amsterdam route in cooperation with KLM, and equipment was ordered to replace the old and inadequate domestic fleet. Some of the replacement costs were included in the Government's request for $75 million in project aid in 1968.

There are 38 airports where Garuda planes can land, but only three can handle planes as large as DC-8's. Only nine are good for night landings, and most runways need repair.

Another state enterprise in this field is PN Merpati Nusantara which operates 25 planes, mainly in West Irian, but also Kalimantan, Sumatra, and West Nusatenggara.

Railroads are operated by the state railway company PNKA. There are 7,583 km. of track on Java, and 2,174 km. in four separate systems on Sumatra. The other islands have no railways. Most of the track is over 40 years old, and has had little maintenance for the last 25 years. Some two thirds of the rolling stock and 40% of the locomotives are over 40 years old as well. Nevertheless, the railroads are in better condition than most other means of transport. They are important mainly for passenger transport: the number of passenger kilometers is nearly eight times that of goods-ton kilometers.

Roads

The total Indonesian road system is 79,000 km. long; there are 12,000 km. of national roads, of which 50% are in bad condition, 18,000 km. of provincial roads (70% in bad condition), and 49,-000 km. of country roads (90% in bad condition). In addition, the design standards are outdated; more than 75% of the roads are designed for axle loads of only 1.5 to 2 tons, and only 3% is built to carry five-ton loads.

In 1966 there were some 157,000 passenger cars, about 20,000 buses, 84,000 trucks, and 221,000 motorcycles. Government-owned vehicles accounted for about 20% of the cars, 75% of the buses, and over half the trucks. Only about half the total vehicles were in running condition, and by 1968 the situation had not greatly improved, due to the age of the vehicles and spare part difficulties. About 75% of the total motorized vehicles are owned by private individuals or companies operating in the transport industry; two thirds of these are in Java, and a major portion are in Djakarta and surroundings.

Telecommunications

Indonesia's telephone systems cover only 1.5% of the population. Most of the exchanges are very old, but some have been converted to automatic operation. Even with additions and more change-overs to automatic exchanges now under way, the supply will still be far below the demand. International calls are difficult, when not impossible. International telegraph services are generally satisfactory, and telex is available to Tokyo and Amsterdam, but domestic services are poor, especially to and from Djakarta. Some of the problem results from large-scale theft of telegraph wire. A Java-Sumatra microwave link was completed in 1967 and one between Djakarta and Bali is now being built. Ericsson of Sweden, Philips of the Netherlands and Siemens of West Germany are all involved in providing equipment and technical assistance for communications, and ITT of the US is building a satellite ground station.

Electric power

Since 1958, when private foreign electricity suppliers were nationalized, the State Electricity Enterprise (PLN) has administered all publicly owned electricity companies. PLN's actitivies are supervised by the Directorate General of Power and Electricity, which is responsible for major electric power projects. Total installed capacity in 1968 was estimated at 603,254 KW with about 90% in running condition; annual production is estimated at 1,245,000 KW. In 1967, installed capacity was estimated at 5.7 watts per capita and annual production at 15.7 KWH per capita. Java has 78% of the installed capacity, and Sumatra 14%. For all of Indonesia, about 20% of PLN's sales have been to industry in the past few years. Hydroelectric power provided 44% of installed capacity in 1967, steam 20%, diesel 29%, and gas 7%. Private generating equipment (often installed by companies to ensure their own supplies) probably adds 200,000 KW to state-owned capacity. Generating capacity under construction in 1968 would add another 122,170 KW. Through such major projects as the multipurpose Djatiluhur scheme (completed in 1968), generating capacity is expanding relatively steadily, but transmission and distribution networks, particularly in Java, are inadequate.

The Five-Year Economic Plan 1969-73

Indonesia's efforts at planning began in 1952 with the establishment of a State Planning Bureau,

which formulated a five-year plan for 1956-60. The Bureau was abolished in 1958, and the next year a National Planning Council was formed. The Council prepared an eight-year Overall Development Plan for 1961-1968. The first plan produced little, and the eight-year plan produced mainly prestige projects (many still unfinished) and foreign debts.

The new regime reorganized the National Development Planning Agency (Bappenas) under the chairmanship of a cabinet member, and in 1967 assigned it to prepare a five-year plan for 1969-73. The draft plan was to be presented to the Cabinet in November 1968, and the plan would go into effect at the beginning of the budget year in April 1969.

The basic policy is that the Plan should reflect long-term government policy, and would include general five-year targets. But implementation is to be carried out on the basis of detailed annual plans; the draft plan presented in 1968 would consequently contain specific targets and plans for implementation only for 1969, with less de-detailed objectives for 1970. Each year, a revised and detailed plan for the next year will be drawn up on the basis of new experience and information, thus making dynamics a major characteristic of the Plan. Overall, in 1969 and 1970 emphasis will continue to be on rehabilitation rather than new projects.

Although the draft plan was not completed at the time of writing, it appeared that Bappenas was being extremely realistic in its approach. The Plan starts off from a recognition of the major problems inherited from the Old Order, when politics ruled and rational economic principles were completely disregarded. The result, of course, was deterioration of facilities in nearly every sector. There is so much to be done that, as one planner half-jokingly put it, the Plan could start anywhere. But priorities have been carefully chosen, and the planners recognize that what can actually be done will depend to a great extent on the availability of foreign aid.

The Priorities

Agriculture — mainly rice production — has top priority under the Plan, with a goal of self-sufficiency in rice by 1973. This will require a five-year increase of approximately 50% over the

1968 production level to about 15.4 million tons. The methods will include expansion of the Bimas Baru (using "miracle rice" seeds) scheme, the Inmas program (providing inputs of fertilizer, pesticides, etc., but without the extension and credit facilities of Bimas), and expansion of acreage by swamp recovery. The Farmers' Formula relating rice prices to fertilizer, and the government's rice purchase price will be set to encourage production.

The Asian Development Bank is providing technical assistance on food production and has conducted a survey on agricultural credit. Crucial to the success of the programs will be the government's procurement of fertilizer and other agricultural inputs. Some $45 million was expected to be available in 1969 for purchasing fertilizers, pesticides, and equipment; needs in 1970 are estimated at about $60 million. For other kinds of food production, the Plan will cover only projected development in order to estimate input requirements. The overall food target is 2,100 calories per capita per day including 55 grams of protein by 1972, compared to the 1968 level of 1,700 calories with 35 grams of protein.

The emphasis on rice production dictates several other priorities. Irrigation (for which the World Bank has granted Indonesia a $4-million loan) must be rehabilitated and extended if the new seed varieties and fertilizers are to be effective. The emphasis in transport development will also be agriculture-linked. Road development will concentrate on "rice roads" to link production and consumption centers, and "export roads" to get cash crops to the ports. But road development will be mainly rehabilitation (20,000 km) or upgrading (2,500 km of main roads). The largest new project is expected to be 250 km of roads in Kalimantan.

Foreign exchange earners in the agricultural field will get strong support. Forestry and fisheries are expected to be rapidly developed, mainly by foreign investors. It is hoped that rubber production can be boosted enough to provide $440 million in exchange earnings by 1973, up from an estimated $352 in 1968.

Industrial Priorities

Priorities in the industrial sector will go to agriculture-linked (inputs or processing) produc-tion, export producers and import savers, and labor intensive industries. On this basis, the Plan will emphasize nine sectors: manufacture of food, beverages, and tobacco; textiles; timber production and processing, paper and printing; chemicals (especially agricultural); machinery and equipment, again with emphasis on agricultural needs; construction; small-scale industry and handicrafts; and oil and mining, including domestic processing.

Oil and Mining

The output of petroleum was 520,000 barrels per day in 1967. This is expected to rise to a million daily by 1973. Two new refineries are planned, one in Dumai with a capacity of 100,000 brl/day expandable to 200,000 brl/day, and another somewhere in Java. (See Table 4.)

Tin output is expected to rise from 14,000 tons in 1969 to 17,600 tons by 1973, but this will partly depend on the amount of project aid available. Production of bauxite can be boosted quite easily from 800,000 tons to 1,200,000 but so far only Japan has shown interest in purchasing Indonesian bauxite. In March 1968 (effective 1969) a 10-year contract was signed with Showa Denko and Sumitomo Chemical for the sale of 800,000 tons annually for the first two years, then 1 million tons annually, from the Bintan area. The price is to be fixed by both parties every two years, but will start at $5.60 per ton. Output of tin, nickel, and copper should all show increases in 1972—the year Billiton Mij, INCO, and Freeport Sulphur are all slated to start production.

After agriculture, the Plan will concentrate on

TABLE 4.
Projected Earnings from Petroleum
($ million)

	Exports	Gross Revenue from Exports
1969	358	153
1970	458	225
1971	485	231
1972	475	244
1973	587	284

Source: Ministry of Mining

infrastructure. But some observers fear too little weight will be placed on this area, particularly transport and port development, since the Plan does not go far beyond rehabilitation of existing facilities. The targets may be raised, of course, if finance is available. One extremely hopeful sign is the World Bank's permanent mission in Indonesia — the first of its kind in a developing country — which will provide technical assistance in planning and programming development projects. And the World Bank is undertaking a survey financed by the United Nations Development Program (UNDP), of the road transport system.

Restoring Railroads, Airports, Communications

Rehabilitation for railroads during 1969-73 will involve a total of $35 million plus some Rp11.4 billion according to plans of the Department of Public Works. The major item will be tracks and buildings ($13.1 million plus Rp7.4 billion), followed by rolling stock and maintenance shops ($11.6 million).

Navigational aids for 19 airports are to be improved, and airstrips at 16 airports will be repaired and upgraded. Lights and meteorological installations are to be added at 30 airports. With improved facilities, flight frequencies will be increased and more feeder lines established. These improvements, as well as construction of hotels, etc., are linked to tourism development, of which Bali will be the center.

Rehabilitation and expansion in telecommunications is expected to involve about $17.5 million and Rp4.4 billion, and equipment for this work is high on the list for project aid from creditor nations. The major items are to be modernization of the telephone system of Surabaja, and a link from Malang to Surabaja to Djakarta. These are estimated to cost $4.2 million.

Bappenas has indicated that family planning should have priority in the health field, but indications are that the Government will merely encourage and provide some facilities for private groups, rather than making it a national program. In education, more emphasis will go to vocational training. Some regional development possibilities are to be formulated, but it will be up to regional authorities to implement any regional projects from their own resources.

Foreign Aid

Soekarno's famous "to hell with your aid" policy was rapidly reversed by Indonesia's new regime.

Conferences between Indonesia and her main Western creditors (the US, West Germany, France, Italy, Great Britain, the Netherlands, and also Japan) have been successively held in Tokyo (September 1966), Paris (December 1966), Amsterdam (February 1967), Scheveningen (April 1968). These conferences, also attended by representatives of Canada, Australia, Switzerland, and New Zealand, were supported by the IMF and the World Bank. They resulted in the consolidation and rescheduling of Indonesia's foreign debts to Japan and Western countries (known as the Intergovernmental Group on Indonesia, or IGGI).

At the Tokyo meeting and the first Paris meeting, Western creditor nations agreed to a rescheduling of Indonesian debts falling due in 1967, as well as arrears of payments ($530 million) due in 1966. (Finally, in mid-1968, Indonesia and the USSR ratified a two-year protocol on the rescheduling of Indonesia's debt to the Soviet Union; at $990 million, the USSR debt was Indonesia's largest single obligation.) Rescheduling of Indonesian debt service payments falling due in 1968 was arranged at the second Paris meeting. Rescheduling covered the entire sum of debts plus interest falling due up to Dec. 31, 1968, covering both short-term debts (181-720 days) and medium and long-term ones. Those of less than 181 days and other debts not backed by a government or state bank guarantee were not included in the reschedulings (but see Chapter 5 on the DICS-Rupiah Scheme). Indonesia was given a grace period of three years from 1967; the first installment of rescheduled debt is to be repaid over eight years, with the moratorium interest (the interest falling due during the grace period) fixed bilaterally with each of the participating countries. It was clear by late 1968 that further rescheduling would be required (see Appendices IV and V).

The first steps to organize fresh aid to Indonesia were taken at the Amsterdam and Scheveningen meetings. Among the Western creditors, the US played an energetic, though publicly restrained role.

At the Amsterdam meeting, the US Government and the other country members of IGGI accepted the Indonesian-IMF estimate of foreign aid needs during calendar year 1967 in the neighborhood of $200 million. The US separately pledged its intention to provide about one third of this amount ($65 million) provided other donors met the remaining requirements, and provided also that the economic performance of the Indonesian Government, as assessed by the IMF, continued to be acceptable. These conditions were met. The US assistance was made available in support of the stabilization and rehabilitation program, rather than for specific projects. It was composed of AID dollar commodity loans made in 1967 for financing purchases of US commodities on the Government of Indonesia's "Bonus Export" list of essential imports ($37.5 million), and of agricultural commodities under PL480 ($27.8 million — made up of $8 million in cotton and $19.8 million in rice). It was agreed at the Amsterdam meeting of February 1967 that loans would be made on soft terms: an interest rate of 3% per annum with 25 years to pay back, including a grace period of seven years. The US extended even softer conditions: 40 years to pay back, including a 10-year grace period, and 1% interest per annum during the grace period and 2.5% afterwards.

Another IGGI meeting was held in Amsterdam in November 1967 in order to assess the Indonesian request for external assistance of $325 million to cover the estimated balance-of-payments gap ($250 million) and to finance some projects ($75 million) in 1968. The representatives agreed at this meeting that the loans would be granted on the same soft conditions as those extended in 1967. It was also agreed that another meeting in Rotterdam in April 1968, would finalize Japanese and Western commitments in response to Indonesia's request for assistance in 1968.

The US again promised to provide a third of the total, on the condition that Japan and Western Europe would each supply another third. Japan balked at increasing its aid, at first, but finally agreed to provide $80 million in stabilization credits in 1968, and $30 million in project assistance spread over a longer period.

By mid-1968, aid commitments to Indonesia totaled $268.2 million. Of this, $180.6 million was stabilization aid, $42.7 million was for project assistance and $9.9 million was in the form of grants. Commitments were from the US ($65 million in stabilization aid, mainly in the form of PL480 agricultural commodity agreements; $10 million for project aid), Japan ($65 million in credits for imports, $10 million in project aid, and $5 million in a food grant), the Netherlands ($14.5 million for imports, $6.8 million for projects, and $4.9 million as a stabilization grant), West Germany ($12.6 million for stabilization, $6.8 million for projects), Australia ($12.6 million and $1.6 million), France ($8.1 million and $4.0 million), the UK ($2.4 million), Belgium ($0.4 million), and the International Development Agency of the World Bank ($4.5 million for projects). By late 1968 it appeared that the $325 million request would be more than met; total 1968 aid seemed likely to come close to $400 million.

Prospects for future aid to Indonesia are also quite good, despite the overall decline in foreign assistance from industrialized countries to less developed countries. Indonesia is one of the countries that will be least affected in the immediate future by the drastic cuts made by the US Congress in the US fiscal year 1969 aid bill; because Indonesia's present needs are for stabilization, commodity agreements under PL480 are as useful as development loans. But Indonesia's needs will be increasingly for project loans. In addition, Indonesia appears likely to retain a priority place in future years for the aid that is available from industrialized nations. This idea has recently been reinforced by the World Bank's decision to establish a permanent mission in Indonesia.

Another IGGI meeting was to be held in Europe in October 1968 to consider Indonesia's aid request for 1969, and possibly to discuss further debt rescheduling. The size of the aid request was not known at the time of writing, but was expected to be in the neighborhood of $500 million. The degree of success Indonesia will have in meeting even the rather meager (though realistic) goals of the Five-Year Plan will depend on whether IGGI nations are willing to extend this level of aid for 1969 — and probably higher levels of aid in later years.

IV—Investing and Organizing

INDONESIA IS IMPATIENT to see rapid growth of foreign investments and movement of more of the foreign investments approved from the drawing board to the operational stage, but the country nevertheless can feel some satisfaction at the amount of foreign investor interest so far displayed. In the 21 months through September 1968, since the Foreign Investment Law was passed, 84 projects with a total value of $342.13 million (excluding oil exploration contracts) had been sanctioned by the Indonesian Government. Of these, 61 had received final approval from the cabinet, and 23 had been approved by the Foreign Investment Board and were awaiting final government approval.

Seen against the background of Indonesia's present economic problems and the great difficulties of operating a business there, the figure of $342 million is impressive. As rough measure it can be set against the fact that the historic total of direct foreign investment in Pakistan (which has a population slightly smaller than Indonesia's) was only $400 million in 1966; and that average annual direct foreign investment inflow into India in recent years has only been in the $50-$60-million range. It is true that Indonesia is experiencing a backlog of capital inflow after the years of Soekarno's rule, but there is also evidence that the present rush of international companies to invest there has by no means spent itself. Foreign investment proposals still in the preliminary stages of discussions with ministries could represent outlays by foreign companies of another several hundred million in the next few years. This is far more direct investment inflow than many countries that are much more affluent and that have far higher ratings for economic and political stability may expect.

Yet the mention of $342 million in foreign investment is in some ways misleading, and probably overstates the confidence of foreign investors in the country. It includes the totals of planned investments, some of which will take several years to come to fruition, and some of which could be abandoned. Some of the inflow will be in the form of reinvested profits over a period of years, and some will be loan capital, rather than equity investment. (Actual inflow in 1968 was probably well below $100 million.) Most of the $342 million is accounted for by resource-based investments; these have been given far more encouragement by the Government (e.g., lower taxes for mining companies) than have manufacturing ventures, and as major foreign exchange earners, these investments will be somewhat protected against exchange and other risks. Nearly half of the total represents only three projects — the Freeport Sulphur copper mining venture in West Irian (potentially $76.5 million), the International Nickel (INCO) contract for nickel mining (potentially $75 million), and N.V. Billiton's $7 million in a tin mining venture. Another

$70 million is in forestry projects (see Appendix VI C).

Nevertheless, there is nearly $70 million of approved investment in manufacturing. Part of this is investment to rehabilitate or expand plants released from government control and returned to the owners, but a great deal of it comes from new investors whose products already have a market in Indonesia, or who want to get a start now for the Indonesian market they think will develop. If the mining and oil contracts start to pay off in a few years, the market could begin to develop fairly rapidly.

US companies account for $114.6 million of the total approved investment. Canada is second, due to the INCO contract, and a $48.5-million forestry project puts South Korea third. Then come the Netherlands with $19.4 million and Japan with $17.5 million. Japanese companies, already dismayed at their small total and at having missed out on several major projects (especially in mining and forestry), are expected to increase their investments substantially in the next year or so.

This foreign investor interest in Indonesia is the result of a dramatic reversal in policy: from nationalization and government control of foreign enterprises during the Soekarno period, to restoring companies to their foreign owners and welcoming new foreign investment since the New Order came to power in 1966. For some people, both in the Government and out, the new policy reflects their philosophy — a respect for the free enterprise system and a belief in an open economy — as well as having practical value. For many others, the policy is desirable on purely pragmatic grounds: Indonesia simply does not possess the capital, technological, and managerial resources necessary to develop its economy, so foreign investment is necessary. In either case, though, the welcome for foreign investment by the higher echelons of the Government is sincere, and a radical change of attitude is improbable. The same is true of much of the press, a large part of the business community, and most informed public opinion.

Indonesia's encouragement for foreign investment, though sincere, is not without conditions. Nationalism is a strong force, and most Indonesians would probably prefer that the country's resources were developed by Indonesians, if that were possible.

Some distrust of foreign investors is a natural result of 300 years of colonial rule, and nearly a decade of Soekarno's anti-foreign oratory. There are also some present and potential vested interests that are critical. The armed forces, which own plants in a variety of industries, or a provincial governor with interests in an industry in his province may sometimes oppose foreign investment to protect their own sources of privilege or income. Indigenous businessmen worry that they will be unable to compete if there is too much foreign investment in small manufacturing operations. The presence of these kinds of attitudes has resulted in certain restrictions and obligations being imposed on foreign investors, and may sometimes create temporary obstacles to certain foreign investments, but they are not likely to prevent investment. Some of the fears that foreign investment might be a new form of colonialism may disappear after a few years of experience. On the other hand, there is the possibility that as economic conditions in Indonesia improve, and as Indonesian companies develop greater capability, a reaction against foreign investment could develop; but even if this should occur, it will not mean a return to Soekarno-style policies.

The Government's policy is meant to encourage foreign investment, particularly in fields where Indonesian capital and technical or managerial expertise is insufficient. The Government hopes that the presence of foreign enterprises will act as a catalyst for modernizing production and improving business techniques, but wants foreign investment to be complementary to domestic investment rather than in competition with it. Consequently, the laws and regulations give preference to joint ventures, emphasize Indonesianization of personnel and provide for eventual local participation in ownership.

The Foreign Capital Investment Law

The outlines of Indonesia's policy on foreign investment are laid down in Law No. 1/1967, the Foreign Capital Investment Law. It sets out the conditions under which foreign capital is permitted entry into Indonesia, and the manner in which it will be allowed to operate; and provides guarantees and incentives as a counterpoise to certain limitations and obligations imposed upon foreign investors.

The Law allows foreign investment in all fields except those vital to national defense (e.g., production of arms, ammunition, explosives). Transport, communications, power, water, and mass media are closed to ventures in which foreign investors exercise full control, but foreign companies may invest in these fields in cooperation with private domestic capital or with the Government. Investments in mining and oil are only allowed on a contracting basis, since constitutionally, minerals are the property of the state. All other fields are open to foreign investment on either a joint venture or a wholly owned basis. Priorities are to be determined by the Five-Year Plan (See Chapter 3), but in general, investments in non-priority fields are welcome too, though perhaps with fewer incentives. The Government's priorities are for industries that earn or save foreign exchange or that are quick-yielding, increase employment, introduce new technology or techniques to increase productivity, or use modern equipment that increases productivity or lowers production costs. In addition, there are several retarded projects that the Government cannot now complete, which are open to foreign investors. Granite City Steel of the U.S. was considering in late 1968 an investment in one of these — an unfinished steel mill at Tjilegon begun with USSR credits — probably in a joint venture with the Government.

Investments may be made in the form of foreign exchange that does not form part of the foreign exchange reserves of Indonesia (or with rupiahs that carry the benefits of foreign exchange, under the DICS-Rupiah scheme — see Chapter 5), or in the form of equipment, patents, spare parts, or raw materials. Reinvested profits are also eligible for benefits given under the Law. The investment — in whatever form — must be registered with the Foreign Exchange Bureau (BLLD, which is to be merged into the central bank), to be eligible for incentives and to ensure future repatriation. The BLLD must be supplied with a copy of the proposed document of incorporation and a copy of the foreign investment contract or permit. If the investment is in foreign exchange, a debit/credit note must be submitted to the BLLD; if in equipment or raw materials, shipping documents are required. An investment in the form of patents requires approval from the Ministry concerned and from the BLLD. If foreign exchange or goods are used to pay for services, a written statement may be requested from the BLLD stating whether the foreign exchange or goods will be recognized as invested capital.

Guarantees on Nationalization

The Government of Indonesia guarantees under the Foreign Capital Investment Law not to nationalize any foreign enterprise, nor to revoke ownership rights or reduce rights to control in management unless required by the public interest as determined by a specific Act of Parliament.

If nationalization should occur, the Indonesian Government recognizes its obligation to provide compensation in conformity with the principles of international law. If no agreement can be reached between the two parties regarding the amount, type, and procedure of payment of compensation, arbitration will take place which will be binding on both parties. The arbitration board would consist of three persons, one appointed by the Government, the other by the owner of the capital, and a third person as chairman, to be selected jointly by the Government and the investor. Indonesia became a party to the Convention on the Settlement of Investment Disputes in February, 1968.

Investors who feel that the reference to principles of international law and the procedure established for the determination of the arbitration panel are not sufficiently clear, should outline more detailed principles and procedures that they consider important in their applications under the Foreign Capital Investment Law.

Guarantees on Remittances

Law No. 1/1967 guarantees foreign investors the right to transfer, in the currency of the original investment at the prevailing exchange rate, all current after-tax profits, certain costs, depreciation of capital assets, and compensation in case of nationalization. Transfers are conducted through the BE system if the investment was originally made through BE. Companies whose investments are not allowed through the BE system (mainly service firms), make inward and outward transfers through DP. (See Chapter 5.)

Transfer of profits is normally at the prevailing

BE rate, after approval is obtained from the BLLD. The company submits an application for transfer (stated in rupiahs), a balance sheet and profit and loss statement, and a tax clearance certificate or tax exemption certificate for firms with tax holidays. The BLLD approval is more or less automatic. The only difficulty in transferring profits is that since a tax clearance is required, there may be a delay of several weeks or even months between the time when the profits were earned and when they are remitted; with a rising BE rate, the final remittance could shrink considerably. Although there has been little experience so far with profit remittances, firms operating in Indonesia report no difficulties.

Transfers for patents, copyrights, royalties, survey fees, and management fees must be approved by the BLLD, and the agreements setting such royalties or fees must have been approved by the Investment Board or the Ministry concerned. Transfers for depreciation must be approved by the Foreign Capital Investment Council and the BLLD. This is meant to guard against disguised capital flight, as standards for depreciation are not yet well developed; but depreciation designed to finance plant improvements and replacements will be assured of conversion rights. Expatriate personnel are allowed to remit up to 20% of taxable salary with a ceiling of $400 per month. No additional amounts may be transferred for fringe benefits, except for home leave travel expenses once every two years.

The Government allows transfers for amortization and interest payments on loan capital as expenses. Normally, interest payments are approved automatically by the BLLD, but remittances for repayment of principal are not permitted during a company's tax holiday period. The principal may, of course, be repaid out of a firm's remitted profits, and after the tax holiday ends, remittances for repayment of principal would be allowed. The terms and conditions of a loan, and a provision for remittance of interest and principal, should be included in any agreements the foreign investor enters into with the Government for carrying out a project, or written into the investment permit issued to the investor under the Foreign Capital Investment Law.

Repatriation of capital is not allowed while the investor is enjoying tax incentives. Capital is not normally guaranteed the right of conversion to the currency of the original investment, but it is the clear intent of the Government not to prevent such conversion without reason. The present regulations stipulate that in the original registration of invested capital with the BLLD, the investment capital may be stated in foreign currency (in addition to a requirement that the capital be stated in rupiahs) for the determination of future repatriation of capital. If a foreign investor sells shares locally after a few years, the proceeds of such sale are guaranteed conversion and repatriation rights.

The United States Agency for International Development (AID), in January 1967, signed an investment guarantee agreement with Indonesia providing guarantees against specific risks (inconvertibility, expropriation, and war, revolution or insurrection) and against some commercial risks (the extended risk program). By June 30, 1968, over 60 companies had made preliminary requests to AID for guarantees on potential investments of more than $900 million. Many, if not most, of these companies may never actually apply for a guarantee, however.

To date, only four actual applications for AID guarantees have been approved. Chase Manhattan Bank, Freeport Sulphur, and Petroleum Helicopters had been granted specific risk guarantees, and International Telephone and Telegraph (ITT) had been awarded both specific and extended-risk coverage for its $7.2-million project to build a satellite ground station. The ITT agreement provides that under the extended-risk guarantee program, AID will guarantee repayments of 75% ($4.1 million) of a $5.5-million loan from the Bank of America and a group of co-lenders (Connecticut General Life Insurance Co., North Atlantic Life Insurance Co. of America, First National Bank of St. Paul, and the National Shawmut Bank of Boston). The remaining $1.4 million of the loan and ITT's $1.7-million equity investment are covered against losses from war, revolution, insurrection, expropriation, and currency inconvertibility. The terms of the loan are unusual in that the grace period is not based on the construction period of the ground station, but on the completion of the entire satellite communications system. The payout will be somewhere in the 10-15-year range, depending on the profitability of the system. The part of the $5.5-million loan not covered by AID will be guaranteed by ITT.

Investment guarantee agreements with Indonesia have also been signed by Denmark and the Netherlands, and one with West Germany has been concluded but not ratified. A guarantee under the Danish program has been granted to East Asiatic Co. Ltd., which is investing $1 million in a wholly owned plant to make pharmaceuticals under the "Dumex" brand, already widely known in Southeast Asia.

Incentives

In addition to basic guarantees on remittance rights and against nationalization, the Foreign Capital Investment Law seeks to attract foreign investment by providing incentives. The major incentive is a two to five-year tax holiday from corporate and dividend taxes, and the possibility of reduced taxes for up to five years more. The basic requirement — intended to reserve the small-scale manufacturing sector to local firms or joint ventures — is that the foreign investor either invests $2.5 million in the first two years, or invests in a joint enterprise with an Indonesian company. Foreign investors are also exempted from the capital stamp tax. (For details on tax incentives, see Chapter 7.) The Law provides the framework for the tax exemptions, but the $2.5-million limit and other eligibility requirements are set out in a Cabinet Decree of January 27, 1967. The Government is aware that for many potential investors, the $2.5-million minimum is too high. Exceptions to the rule have been allowed, and it is possible that the figure may be lowered.

The Law also provides exemption for foreign investors from import duties on basic equipment and supplies needed for the investment. A Ministry of Finance decree of August 3, 1967, amplified the provision to allow exemption from import duties on machinery and equipment for the investment, and on raw materials, semi-finished and finished goods to be processed by the enterprise within a two-year period, which may be extended. Tariff exemptions are also available on means of transport for movement of goods, on used personal effects belonging to foreign personnel, and on imported consumption goods for foreign personnel up to a maximum of $50 f.o.b. per person or $100 per family per month.

Application may be made for import duty exemption on office equipment, furniture, motor vehicles (except sedans) to be used for transportation of personnel, and construction and building materials for factories, offices, housing, hospitals or places of worship needed by the company. Subsequent regulations and interpretations of old laws have put severe limits on these exemptions, however. (See Chapter 9.)

Other incentives may also be negotiated, including tariff protection. In several cases, prospective investors have asked for protection against additional investments in their field for a period of time (generally about three years) or at least that they be warned, and so have the opportunity to expand, before further investment permits were granted. Grounds for such requests were generally the need for economies of scale (and therefore a project large enough that the needs of the market would be met, in theory, at least), a need for time to develop marketing facilities and publicize the product before the venture could happily withstand competition, or that there was already too much competition for the enterprise's products from legitimate or smuggled imports. In a couple of cases, the Government at first accepted the principle of closing an industry to additional investment for a time, but when other investors applied to enter it, the Government changed its mind. There is some disagreement on the question within the Government itself, but it appears likely that in special cases, protection against additional investments will be granted. In the 1968 negotiations between Goodyear and the Government for establishment of a joint venture, Goodyear was asking for three years without new competition.

Ownership Restrictions

Under the Foreign Capital Investment Law, foreign investors are expected to provide for local participation, either by entering a joint venture or by selling shares of the enterprise to local citizens sometime in the future. As mentioned, ventures of less than $2.5 million are normally closed to foreign investors, unless the investment is in a joint venture. If the proposed investment is in a high-technology industry or produces solely for export — and thus is not competing with local firms — the Government is likely to be more lenient on this point.

Joint ventures are also eligible for an additional year of tax exemption (but with a five-year limit on the total tax holiday), and have the benefit of being able to operate in sectors closed to enterprises that are wholly foreign controlled. In addition, investment applications for joint ventures with Indonesian capital receive priority consideration. The Domestic Investment Law passed in 1968 excludes the possibility of a joint venture between a foreign investor and a non-Indonesian (read alien Chinese) resident of Indonesia.

Of the 84 foreign investment projects (excluding oil ventures), approved by the Indonesian Cabinet or recommended by the Investment Board for final approval through September, 1968, 58 were joint ventures with Indonesian partners. Several of those were with state enterprises, and a few directly with the Government. There are no requirements regarding the equity share of the local partner, since the Government recognizes that local capital is scarce. In many instances of joint ventures with private Indonesian companies, the Indonesian partner holds 15% or less of the equity, and its contribution is often in the form of physical assets.

Two ventures in manufacturing are by Dutch firms that have formed joint ventures with their former Indonesian subsidiaries after these were nationalized in the late 1950's. (In Indonesian legal parlance, US, UK, and other European businesses were merely brought under government "control" or "supervision," but Dutch businesses were definitely nationalized.) One of these Dutch firms, Van Swaay NV, will join with the Indonesian government enterprise, PN Metrika, to make electrical equipment in Djakarta, using some facilities once owned by Van Swaay.

The other firm, Philips NV, formed its joint venture under an agreement with the then Department of Basic and Light Industry and Power. The agreement provides for a joint venture under the name of PT Philips-Ralin Electronic, with Philips holding 60% equity and the Indonesian Government the balance. The firm, with headquarters in Djakarta, will make electronic components in Bandung and light bulbs in Surabaja. Production, which was scheduled to start in February, 1968, will initially be solely for the Indonesian market. Exports will be made later if the opportunity and demand arise.

Philips contributed its share of the joint venture's capital (which is equivalent to NFl17.5 mil-

lion) in the form of machinery and equipment. The Indonesian Government's contribution is in the form of the assets of the state-owned "Ralin" factories. A capital increase up to NFl25 million is envisaged over the next five years.

Philips was given the right to appoint the initial management, and it was agreed that this would include two Indonesians, as well as two Dutch citizens. There is an understanding that this management arrangement will last for five years, although no specific limit is indicated in the agreement. After that, the top management will be nominated by a Supervisory Board on which Philips and the Indonesian Government will have equal representation.

Goodyear Tire and Rubber of the US was negotiating with the Government of Indonesia in late 1968 to establish a joint venture. Under the proposal, Goodyear, which has a tire plant at Bogor, would acquire two government-owned plants (PN Intirub, and a plant under construction at Palembang) in exchange for shares of Goodyear's Indonesian company.

There is a general requirement in the law that wholly foreign-owned ventures must provide the possibility of local participation at some time in the future. Again, the Government recognizes that only small amounts of domestic capital will be available in the near future. Consequently, no hard and fast rules have been set regarding the percentage of the equity that should be offered locally; and there is no stipulation that there be participation of local capital by any particular date, but only that the opportunity be provided.

As guidelines for future local share offerings by manufacturing or service companies, a 30% offering within five years has been mentioned, and in forestry undertakings, 50% of the shares within five years. There is little chance that there will be enough local capital available in five years to take up such offerings, however. In the meantime, the percentage to be offered and the period of time are negotiable, and prospective investors should make their own proposals in their applications for investment permits. Normally, the share offerings would be at market value, but there are no rules on how market value should be determined. These, too, might be included in the investment proposal. As mentioned above, proceeds from such sales are guaranteed conversion rights.

Thirty-Year Limitation

The length of time during which a permit under the Foreign Capital Investment Law is valid is 30 years. It is recognized, however, that many companies might be concerned about the disposition to be made of their operation as the 30-year period comes to a close. The Indonesian Government has expressed willingness to discuss operations beyond the 30-year period within two years of the end of the first 30 years. The Government is also prepared to discuss standards which can be examined at periodic intervals during the 30 years, with the understanding that if these standards are met, the 30-year period can be renewed at periodic intervals, so that a foreign company may continue to have before it a full 30-year period of assured operations. These standards might relate to the company's compliance with such policies as Indonesianization of personnel and capital.

Many firms have sought more definite assurances that their permits would be renewed on reasonable operating terms, or have asked for immediate extensions of the original permit. Uniroyal, for example, requested a 30-year extension (for a total of 60 years), and the INCO nickel mining contract provides that INCO could form a new company in 30 years (when the present contract runs out) that would be eligible for another 30-year agreement. Some firms have asked that 30-year permits be automatically extended to a full 30-year period whenever the company expands, or if profits are reinvested. The Government is looking for formulas to ease this 30-year restriction, but so far is reluctant to grant any automatic extension that would not require Government review and approval.

Indonesianization

The Foreign Capital Investment Law and other policies of the Government put considerable stress on the need for Indonesianization of personnel, including managerial staff. There are no fixed requirements, however, and the Government recognizes that in many cases foreign managers and technicians will be required for some time. The Law grants the foreign investor full authority to appoint the management of the enterprise in which his capital is invested, and to recruit and employ foreign managers and technicians for positions that cannot yet be filled by Indonesian nationals. (For details of the regulations, see Chapter 6.) But the investor is required to provide training facilities in Indonesia or abroad for Indonesian employees so they can eventually replace expatriates. The company's intention to Indonesianize its staff at all levels should be clear. A prospective investor should include a plan for training and replacement of expatriates in the investment application.

Obtaining Land

The land laws of Indonesia make it impossible for a foreign enterprise to own the land for its investment site. The laws divide land rights into the right of ownership, the right of exploitation, the right of building, and the right of use — all of which may be separately held and regulated. In addition to these primary rights, a set of subordinate rights are recognized, including the right to lease land for building, the rights to collect forest products or breed or catch fish, the right to air space, and rights relating to religious or social purposes. But only a citizen of Indonesia may hold the hereditary right of "ownership" — the most comprehensive set of rights. The Foreign Capital Investment Law altered the rights of foreign investors to allow them to have the right of exploitation, the right of building, and the right of use, as well as subordinate rights, according to the needs of the investment. The Law also provides that the 30-year investment permit extends any limitations of less than 30 years that may exist under the Land Law. The effect of the land laws and the Foreign Capital Investment Law is that a foreign investor may "buy" (i.e., lease) land for up to 30 years, or for a longer period if the lease is extended, but may not actually own the land. The Government is aware that this poses problems for the foreign investor, but the very complicated land laws (with much land outside the cities under the ancient customary law, rather than a system of land registration) probably cannot be changed in the near future. The Government intends to establish industrial estates, where sites could eventually be obtained at concessional rates, but the plans will take some time to materialize. Because of the Government's own need for funds to develop such sites and the present lack of infrastructure, the lease prices are not likely to be particularly attractive for some years. The Government of Djakarta—where the large majority of foreign investors site their plants—has set aside four areas to be used as industrial estates, as a part of the overall city and regional planning for the Djakarta area. Eventually each area is to contain industries, housing, hotels and shopping centers, and social and welfare facilities with the Government providing the basic infrastructure. As these areas are just getting under way, however, only a main road is included at present. Accessory roads and power and water supplies would have to be provided by each investor. Tentative lease prices are $1 per square meter for a year lease (paid in advance) in three of the areas—Pulo Mas, Tjempaka Putih, and Pluit. For sites in the first two, groundfilling of one half to one meter would normally be necessary. The best of the areas, and the one furthest along in development, is Project Antjol, a 560-hectare area on the harbor, next to the ocean port. Because the land does not require groundfilling, and because of the availability of port facilities, the tentative price for 30 years is $3 per square meter, paid in advance. Project Antjol is planned to contain 128 hectares for industry, 98 hectares for housing, 137 hectares for recreation facilities, 19 hectares for neighborhood facilities, 18 hectares for town facilities, and 160 hectares of roads and parks. The projects are the responsibility of the Project Officer for Foreign Investment in Djakarta (POFID) of the Djakarta municipal government (called DCI Djakarta). Each project has a manager, who can issue a license for the land, although formally the license is issued on behalf of the DCI Djakarta government by the chief of Agrarian Affairs.

At present, investors generally have to resort to the private local market, where the prices and the conditions of sites vary widely. Land in Djakarta that is reasonably ready for construction—and without the complication of its being in use—is priced at around $8 per square meter for a 30-year lease (payable in dollars in advance). A rice paddy a few kilometers outside Djakarta, where the land would require filling and where the various rights may be held by several different persons, may be priced as low as Rp250 per square meter (payable in rupiahs). Several investors have conceded that the possible saving may not be worth the trouble of improving the land and as-

suring the necessary rights.

Investors seeking sites for plants must take into consideration the local and regional development plans. In most areas, plans do not yet exist, but land in the Djakarta area has been zoned. When a company has located a possible site, it must check with the Djakarta municipal authorities (since land-use maps have not been reproduced) as to whether the site may be used for industry or whether it has been reserved for residential areas, a green belt, and so on.

Special Investment Fields

Since the Foreign Capital Investment Law was passed, many government departments have issued policies on foreign investment in the areas under their jurisdiction. In many cases, these "policies" simply indicate priorities, or possibilities for investment by foreign companies in a particular field; they are not comprehensive lists, however, and other proposals are welcomed. In some areas (e.g., forestry), the ministry's policy on investment goes beyond the Foreign Capital Investment Law by stipulating certain conditions on which investment will be approved. In mining and oil, where foreign investment is on the basis of a contract of work or some other form of cooperation with the Government, special procedures apply. Foreign investment has been designated a "Government Project," with the Minister of Mining heading a project group made up of ministers or representatives of the various departments. In addition to reporting periodically to the President on progress in foreign investment, this group is charged with coordinating foreign investment policies among the various ministries.

Industry

In addition to the government's general list of priorities for foreign investment (e.g., export-producing, import-saving), the Ministry of Industry lists as priority industries those supporting food production, textile production and related chemicals, and infrastructure, as well as retarded projects and rehabilitation of existing industries. Its policy statement on investment includes long lists of types of industries and specific industrial projects open to foreign investors. As a general guideline, in projects involving less than $2.5 million, at least 10% of the equity should be in the hands of the local partner within five years; for joint ventures with state enterprises, the equity split should generally be 50/50.

The investment policy statement of the Ministry of Health emphasizes the need for production of nearly every kind of pharmaceuticals, and suggests extraction of medicinal and essential oils, manufacture of medical instruments, assembly of X-ray apparatus and other electronic medical instruments, X-ray film, and glass manufacture, among others. The Ministry of Agriculture suggests development of industries that process estate products.

Among the foreign investors in manufacturing ventures is F. A. Peter Cremer of West Germany, which has joined with PT Lokon and C.V. Adang & Sons to make upgraded cattle fodder for export at Tjirebon on the northern coast of central Java, with an investment of $250,000. Australia's government-sponsored Dairy Produce Board is investing $1.35 million in a condensed milk plant in joint venture with an Indonesian firm, PT Marison; the plant will produce one million cans of sweetened condensed milk, and will require 4,500 tons of skim milk powder and 16,000 tons of butterfat from Australia (but sugar will be obtained from Indonesian refiners). Among the many other joint ventures in manufacturing approved by the Government of Indonesia are a $1.7-million venture to produce zinc plates, with equity to be shared by Toyo Menka of Japan and PT Tumbak Mas of Djakarta; a $2-million joint venture between C. Itoh & Co and Kawasaki Steel of Japan and PT Zigzag of Indonesia for the manufacture of galvanized iron sheets in Medan; a $1-million food flavoring project in which Stuckert Trading Co of West Germany and an Indonesian partner, Tan Siong Kie, will share the equity; a NFl2-million joint venture between NV Chemische Fabriek Naarden and PT Mantrust of Indonesia to produce essences; a US$5-million venture to assemble and manufacture motor scooters and three-wheelers, with joint investment by Carl Hansen of the US and PT Lambretta Service of Indonesia; a Dm6.5-million pharmaceutical investment by Farbwerke Hoechst of West Germany and Zainal Abidin; and a $1.2-million pharmaceutical investment by Farbenfabrieken Bayer AG of West Germany and PT Djawa Maluku of Indonesia.

Approved investments in wholly foreign-owned manufacturing ventures are mainly new investments by companies whose assets and plant facilities were returned to them after several years of government control (see below). In addition to these are some "straight" (i.e., wholly owned) investments by Kiwi International of Australia (a $200,000 boot polish factory in Djakarta), East Asiatic's $1-million pharmaceutical plant, and a $250,000 wig factory owned by R & D Products Co of Hong Kong.

Agribusiness

The Ministry of Agriculture stresses the urgency of investments in fertilizer plants, production of pesticides (probably starting with a formulating plant for insecticides), and assembly of sprayers, as well as infrastructure equipment and technical assistance for the government's programs of intensifying agricultural production. At least one international company has already entered the field of technical assistance and supply of agricultural inputs.

Ciba Ltd of Switzerland has been engaged by the Government to treat 300,000 hectares of rice-growing land in East, Central, and West Java with pesticides and fertilizers over a period of five years. The initial contract, signed in May 1968, covers only the wet seasons of 1968-69 and 1969-70. Ciba will be paid $40 per hectare by the Indonesian Government for supplies and services rendered in the first of these seasons. The agreement provides that the total sum of $12 million would be paid to Ciba in three installments — $2.4 million (20%) on September 20, 1968; $2.4 million (20%) on January 20, 1969; and the balance of $7.2 million (60%) on June 30, 1969. Ciba has agreed to purchase suitable fertilizers for the program from sources in Indonesia — if and when they are available — instead of importing them from abroad. Payments for such materials would be made in the same three installments and on the same dates as the Government's payments to the foreign company. Ciba will pay the prices charged by competitive sources for fertilizers of comparable quality. The agreement for 1969-70 contains similar provisions except that the land area is increased to 400,000 hectares.

Transportation, Communications, and Power

While foreign investors exercising full control are excluded from transportation, communications, and power fields, there is considerably more flexibility in the limitation than first appears. Foreign participation is not necessarily limited to a venture that involves the enlistment of local capital. A project may be feasible even when wholly foreign-owned, provided the Indonesian Government has some other form of control. For example, arrangements might be worked out in the form of sale and lease-back of plant and equipment, by means of a management agreement involving a sharing of the profits with a governmental body, or by sharing ownership between the foreign investor and a Government unit through agreement that land or some right be regarded as a contribution of capital. Also, if a venture involves the establishment of controls by the Indonesian Government to assure that the cost and quality of a service to be provided will be regulated in the public interest, the Government is prepared to permit 100% foreign ownership.

International Telephone & Telegraph Corp of the US has concluded an agreement with the Indonesian Department of Communications to set up the country's first international satellite communications system, with provisions for telephone, telex, and television channels. The station is to be constructed from US materials and equipment and will be built and managed by PT Indonesian Satellite Corp (INDOSAT), a wholly owned subsidiary of ITT, under a 20-year contract signed with the Indonesian Government. The latter will own the station but will lease it to INDOSAT for 20 years in return for a share of the net profits.

In the field of air communications — scheduled or nonscheduled feeder lines — investment may be wholly foreign-owned or on a joint venture basis. In order to operate on trunk lines or semi-trunk lines, a company would have to be in a joint venture with one of the two national airlines, Garuda and Nusantara Merpati. Several proposals by foreign firms have been approved. Schreiner Air Transport NV of the Netherlands is entering a joint venture capitalized at NFl500,000, to operate an air taxi service out of Djakarta. PT Bristow Masayu, a joint venture with Bristow Helicopters of the UK as the foreign partner, operates a helicopter service, mainly in Sumatra.

Mining

Taking into account Indonesia's broad economic priorities, the importance of its mineral wealth, the present state of its mining industry, and the contribution that it can make to the national economy, the extractive industries are among the most promising sectors in which foreign capital can operate. Besides setting up ancillary facilities necessary for the improvement of the country's infrastructure, mining ventures can achieve a substantial and rapid increase in Indonesia's exports.

At present, although almost the whole of Indonesia's mineral output is exported, its value represents only 5-7% of the total of Indonesian sales abroad. Mineral exports, therefore, need to be stimulated, if only to replace traditional exports of agricultural products, such as rubber, which no longer command good prices on world markets.

Tin still occupies the foremost place among Indonesian mineral products and exports. The total export value for all other minerals, such as nickel, copper, and bauxite, represents only about 10% of the export returns from tin. Mining of these minerals needs to be developed, if only to keep pace with the growth of world consumption of such metals as nickel (8% per annum) and copper (3% per annum). Mining is therefore likely to be a main target for foreign investors.

In fact, the Indonesian Government is trying to direct foreign investment towards the mining sector, which is destined to become a key sector of the country's economy. It is also one that requires large amounts of capital and the ability to take financial risks, which the Indonesian Government at present cannot shoulder alone.

Roughly a year and a half after the Foreign Capital Investment Law was passed, these were the main developments in mining:

Copper: Freeport Sulphur of the US had signed a contract of work with the Indonesian Government to explore for copper deposits in West Irian, in an estimated potential investment of $76.5 million. By mid-1968, the existence of high-grade deposits was reportedly proved, and production was targeted to begin in 1972.

Nickel: After international bidding, International Nickel Co of Canada (INCO) was granted the right to negotiate a contract with the Government for exploration and development of nickel on Sulawesi. The contract, signed in July 1968, calls for INCO to spend $1.5 million in an exploration program lasting up to five years and to go into production within 11 years, with a stipulated investment of $75 million if the exploration is successful. INCO expects to be in production by 1972. Estimates of the eventual size of the project are in the $100-150-million range. Some of this would go for harbor and power facilities, a processing plant, and roads and buildings. The contract is for 30 years from the start of production, and it gives some assurance that another 30-year contract could be signed when the first runs out. In addition, the contract, seen as a precedent-setting agreement by the Government, gives INCO "most-favored-company" treatment.

Negotiations were also under way with Pacific Nickel (Netherlands and US) and Sumitomo Metal Mining of Japan.

Tin: NV Billiton Maatschappij of the Netherlands entered into a 30-year contract with the Government in July 1968, for exploration of tin areas off Sumatra. Seven years are allowed for exploration, but production is targeted to be at 1-2,000 tons per year in 1972-73. Under the agreement, NV Billiton owns 50% of the shares, directly or indirectly; each year the company will offer at least 2.5% of its shares to local investors. Two consortia of foreign firms—one made up of Rio Tinto Zinc Corp and Bethlehem Steel, the other including Ocean Science & Engineering Inc, Amerada Petroleum, Kathleen Investment (Australia) Ltd, Dillingham Overseas Corp, and Signal Oil and Gas—were also negotiating contracts with the Government for tin exploration.

Bauxite: Alcoa has been negotiating with the Government of Indonesia for rights to survey bauxite deposits throughout Indonesia outside the Bintan area, and was discussing the establishment of an integrated aluminum plant. Kaiser Aluminum has discussed the possibility of setting up an aluminum smelter, probably using imported alumina at first.

Rare metals: Ocean Mining AG has signed a letter of intent for offshore prospecting for these minerals.

Late in 1967, Indonesia's Minister of Mines issued a general invitation to foreign and domestic mining operators to bid for exploration rights on 53 blocks of potentially mineral-bearing land, each block about 1.1 million hectares or 2.75 million acres, situated throughout the country: 15 in Sumatra, 18 in Kalimantan, one in Java, eight in Sulawesi, 10 in West Irian, and one in the Lesser Sunda Islands. Several companies, including Kath-

leen Investment (Australia) Ltd, OMRD of Japan, and Kennecott Exploration (Australia) Pty Ltd have already applied for exploration blocks.

In exchange for exclusive exploration rights for one or more of these areas, successful bidders must submit to the Indonesian Government at the end of the two-year exploration period a geological map (scale 1 inch:250,000 hectares) of all blocks for which rights are granted. The Ministry further states that companies wishing to "have a look" around the unallocated block areas may do so before undertaking the full obligation of the agreement, but on the understanding that the Government will not be obliged to grant exclusive exploration rights until the company contracts for one or more of the blocks.

When a company submits an application for exclusive exploration and development rights for any of the 53 blocks, the Ministry will take 90 days to consider it. During this 90-day period, the Government will continue to accept applications for the same areas from other companies. All applications submitted within this period are weighed by the Committee of Foreign Investments in the Ministry, which will negotiate a contract with the company making the best offer.

Further clarifying the general procedures, the Mining Ministry announced the requirement of a $50,000 performance bond for each exploration block, payable within 30 days of signing the agreement, 50% of which will be refunded with the submittal of four consecutive quarterly progress reports that satisfy the performance demands of the Ministry of Mining. The remaining 50% of the bond will be refunded upon submission and approval of the above-mentioned geological map. Failure to fulfill the terms of the agreements will lead to forfeiture of the bond. An acceptable alternative is a $50,000 bank guarantee agreed upon by the company and the Ministry.

Foreign companies interested in mining in Indonesia must enter into a "contract of work" (*kontrak karya*) with the Government, or with an Indonesian person or private firm already holding an "authorization to mine" (*kuasa pertambangan*) granted by the Government (Law No. 11/67 of December, 1967).

The principle underlying this system is that the foreign party will be conducting all stages of operation, including general surveys, exploration, exploitation, refining and processing, transport, and marketing and sales of mineral products for and on behalf of the Indonesian Government. The minerals, as natural resources, remain the inalienable property of the state, and the mining rights remain in the hands of the Government (or state enterprise). The foreign firm retains the status of contractor, bearing all risks and costs, and is compensated by the products mined or the foreign currency resulting from their sale. The Government and the foreign contractor have to agree upon the division of net operating income between them; provision has to be made for the Government minimum profit or share from the operation. Tools, equipment, and installations are recognized as contractor's property.

A "contract of work" for mining has to be signed by the foreign firm following consultations with the Technical Committee for Foreign Investment in Mining (Djalan Menteng, 3, Djakarta). The functions of this body are to discuss all problems related to foreign investment in mining, to hold negotiations with prospective investors, and to prepare agreements on cooperation between the Government and foreign parties.

Under a "contract of work," which consists of a basic agreement on exploration and possible mining development, a foreign company gains exclusive contractorship to carry out general geological and mineral surveys in the area as set out in the contract. The duration of the exploration period is usually three years, with a possible extension of one or two years. In case exploration leads to the discovery of commercially exploitable mineral deposits, the company also has an exclusive contractorship to develop those deposits in accordance with principles set out in the basic agreement. The company, with the Indonesian Government's consent, can introduce a third party to develop the deposits if it is not prepared to do so itself. The effect is that a mining company may have an investment permit for as much as 41 years instead of the normal 30-year operating permit: two years for a general survey, three or four (sometimes five) years for exploration, one or two years for a feasibility study and design of a processing plant, and three years for construction, to a maximum preparation period of eleven years.

For mining projects in general, a foreign company has to pay land rent and royalties. For land rent during the survey, exploration, and exploitation stages, the charges are respectively $0.005 per hectare/year, $0.10 per hectare/year and $2.00 per hectare/year. The amount of royalty depends on the type of mineral and the type of product (raw ore, concentrate, or refined product), and is calculated in relation to the export value of the raw product.

Exemptions from import duties are granted to foreign contractors for the import of machinery and parts, working tools, and instruments needed to prospect, explore, and exploit mineral deposits, and possibly construction materials. Because mineral resources are unrenewable, the Government does not grant tax holidays to mining companies. But special tax concessions — more generous than those for other types of investment — are granted (see Chapter 7). Mining companies must agree that 75% of their personnel will be Indonesian within the first five years of the operating period.

Oil and Natural Gas

The actual and potential importance of oil and gas can be seen from a comparison of its total annual export value to the country's total exports. In 1966, exports of oil and natural gas amounted to $300 million (of which $220 million came from foreign oil companies and $80 million from Indonesian state enterprises), while exports of all other products together in 1966 totaled $475 million. Indonesia's *net* foreign exchange earnings from the exports of petroleum products will increase by 13.6% from $98 million in 1967 to $272 million in 1975.

Oil and natural gas, as parts of the national wealth, are the property of the state, whose rights include exploration, exploitation, refining and processing, transportation, and sale of all deposits of oil, asphalt, ozokerite, all kinds of bitumen in both solid and liquid form, and of all natural gas and derived products.

These rights can be entrusted only to state enterprises specifically nominated as "mining authorities," and not to foreign companies. However, in view of the lack of experience, capital, and modern technology, a mining company is allowed to enter into a production-sharing agreement, with a foreign company operating as a contractor, for the exploration and extraction of oil and natural gas.

The determination of the agreement is left entirely to the consideration of the Indonesian Government, which is represented in these matters by the Director-General of Oil and Natural Gas. The latter is assisted by the Technical Committee for Petroleum and Natural Gas.

The items covered in an agreement usually include the following: responsibility of the contractor, location and duration of the operation; share in crude oil; sale of crude oil by the contractor and payment arrangements for the sale of the "mining authority's" share of crude oil by the contractor; expenditures for exploration and investment; taxes and foreign exchange arrangements; bookkeeping; auditing; domestic sales; imports and exports; specific rights and obligations; and arbitration of disputes. The agreement also provides for employment and training of Indonesian personnel for all job classifications. Employment of foreign technical personnel is subject to requirements determined by the Department of Mining.

Maximum periods for exploration and exploitation by foreign companies are 10 years and 20 years respectively. The state enterprise retains an overall management authority, but management of operations is handled by the foreign company. The contracting foreign company carries the risk of all operations costs. Under the production-sharing scheme applied to recent contracts, foreign companies that have received concessions take a flat 40% of any oil production that flows from the contract area to meet all their costs. The balance of 60% of output is split in the ratio of 65:35 (or 67.5:32.5) between the Government and the foreign company concerned. Thus, the Government gets 39% (65% of 60%) of the total production.

The Oil Companies

The "temporary supervision" that the Soekarno regime placed over two US oil companies, Caltex and Stanvac, under his *berdikari* policy, was unilaterally withdrawn by the Indonesian Government in April 1967. Under the Soekarno regime there had been some abortive talks designed to enable Indonesia to purchase the local installations of the two companies, but these had not yielded any agreement. Under Stanvac's original agreement with the Government of Indonesia, the Government has an option to buy Stanvac's refinery in 1973 or to obtain it for nothing in 1978. Stanvac would then be out of the refining business in

Indonesia, but not out of the country, since it has a large exploration block in Central Sumatra. The entire local Shell operation was sold to the Indonesian Government in December 1965. Payments on the purchase price ($110 million) are phased over the period 1966-70, and have been made on schedule.

By September 1968, 13 contracts (in addition to the Caltex and Stanvac contracts) had been signed between international oil companies and the government-owned oil company, PN Pertamina, for onshore and offshore exploration. The first contract, with US-based Independent-Indonesia-American Petroleum Co (IIAPCO) and Sinclair, was signed in early 1967, and operations were under way in 1968. Other contracts are with Japex (a consortium of the Mitsubishi, Mitsui, Sumitomo, and Fuji groups) and Kyushu, both of Japan; Cities Service, Continental, Union, International Oil, Phillips and Superior, Indotex (a group of US independents), Virginia International and Huffington, and IIAPCO (this time by itself), all US firms; CFP of France, and Italy's Agip. There were seven contract areas left — several of them in the South China Sea. Among the companies interested in them were Continental, Gulf, Frontier, Mobil, Esso, and Shell.

The agreements differ somewhat, of course, but the basic outlines are closely similar. The contract signed by PN Pertamina and CFP on July 8, 1968, provided for a 30-year contract, and commits CFP to a minimum investment of six years of exploratory work. CFP has also agreed to supply the domestic market at $0.20 per barrel after operational costs have been paid, and to invest in refining and petrochemical industries. At first, the production split will be 65% for Pertamina and 35% for CFP, but the ratio will become 67.5:32.5 when production reaches 75,000 barrels a day. If after eight years no oil is discovered, onshore or offshore on Djambi, the contract automatically lapses. The agreement marks the entrance of French firms into an Indonesian industry formerly the exclusive investment domain of Japanese and American firms. It is also the first major nonplantation investment by a private French company.

Forestry

One of the sources of Indonesia's natural wealth is forestry. Out of a total area of 120 million hectares, forests that are easily accessible either by sea or by navigable river extend over 24 million hectares.

All forests within the territory of the Republic of Indonesia, including the natural wealth contained therein, are under the administration of the state. But Law No. 5 of 1967 allows wholly foreign-owned firms or joint enterprises between local capital and foreign partners to operate in forestry. Forestry lands have been specifically earmarked by the Indonesian Government for foreign investment.

Logging concession rights cover 20-year periods and may be extended once or twice. The contract for cutting rights must include an industrial development plan providing for necessary infrastructure and for the addition of processing operations, preferably in three to five years. The investor is obliged to use and train Indonesian labor, and to contribute to the economic development of the region concerned by providing social insurance and establishing hospitals and schools for employees and their families.

Foreign investors first apply for exploitation rights to the Director General for Forestry Affairs of the Department of Agriculture. A survey must be made of the forest area allocated to the prospective foreign investor. This survey is financed by the applicant, and should cover an area larger than the one to be exploited; the results must be handed over to the Director General for Forestry Affairs. (By mid-1968, some 20 or 30 companies were conducting these preliminary surveys.) An agreement must then be reached on the area to be exploited between the foreign applicant and the Indonesian authorities concerned — and also between the latter and the Indonesian counterpart in the case of a joint venture. This agreement must be approved by the Investment Board and the Foreign Capital Investment Council. Following this approval, the Minister of Agriculture will issue an order for the implementation of the project. Finally, the Director General for Forestry Affairs grants the license for cutting rights.

Holders of such rights pay to the Indonesian Government an annual fee of $0.05 for every hectare that is exploited, and royalties of $0.50 to $7.00 (payable in rupiahs) for every cubic meter of timber (1 cubic meter=35.3 cubic feet).

Nine projects involving total investments of $70 million for the exploitation of Indonesia's timber resources had been approved by the cabinet by September 1968, and another four involving $9.5 million had Investment Board sanction. A breakdown reveals that more than half of the proposed investment is accounted for by the $48.5-million project of the Korea Development Company of South Korea. An outlay of $2.5 million will be made in concert by Cicofrance, the Societe Commerciale d'Affrements et de Combustibles (SCAC), both of France, and the Scieries Modernes du Grand Lahou (SMGL) of the Ivory Coast, for logging more than 750,000 acres and sawmilling in north and west Djambi, Riau and Sumatra. This is the first time that these companies have operated anywhere in Asia. They are interested in diversifying their sources of mahogany, usually drawn from Africa. The incentives offered by the Indonesian Government were an attraction to them, as is the nearby Japanese market, which is expected to absorb about 90% of their production. Two other large investments in forestry are being made by Valgosons of the Philippines ($5 million) and Sealog Ltd of Hong Kong ($6 million). Three of the approved projects are Japanese investments, three are Philippine, and two are by Malaysian-based funds. No US investments had been approved and only one from Europe — My de Fijnhouthandel NV in a $1.5-million joint venture. Several major US firms, including Weyerhaeuser and Boise Cascade, were discussing investment projects in 1968.

Scores of applications from foreign companies for forestry projects had been received since the passage of the Foreign Capital Investment Law, and the available survey and exploitation areas were rapidly dwindling by mid-1968.

Fisheries

The Department of Agriculture prefers joint ventures in fishery, with at least 10% of the capital in the hands of the Indonesian partner, where possible. Within 10 years a wholly foreign-owned company is to offer shares to local investors, and the Ministry suggests that par value of the shares be used if purchased by the Government. Within two years, 80% of the workers in a fishery venture must be Indonesian, and within three years, 80% of the experts as well.

By September, 1968, seven overseas investments based on Indonesia's resources had been sanctioned by the cabinet. Toyo Menka of Japan has approval for a $2.5-million, 100%-owned shrimping project to operate in the Straits of Kalimantan (west and south); Arafura Pearls Ltd of Japan is in a $1-million joint venture with PT Cora-Cora for cultivation of pearls in the Moluccas; Fincon of the Philippines is investing $1 million in a shrimp and fish project in East Kalimantan; the Gulf Fishery Co of Kuwait and an Indonesian partner, PT Minapaja, have formed a $2.5-million fishing venture to operate off North Sumatra in the Molucca Straits; a Norwegian firm, Skips A/S Norkar Norwegia, has formed a joint venture with an Indonesian firm to exploit shrimp and fish in Sulawesi, capitalized at $1 million; Toho Bussan Kaisha of Japan and PT Pelindo, its Indonesian partner, are investing $2 million to tap fish and, more especially, shrimp resources off South Sumatra; and finally, Nihon Kinkai Hogei, also of Japan, is the foreign partner in a $1-million joint venture with an Indonesian firm, PT Yalamina, to gather fish and shrimp off the northern part of East Kalimantan.

These fishing ventures represent a total investment of $11.5 million, and all will be engaged in canning and processing marine products, as well as in harvesting them. Several other fisheries ventures have been sanctioned by the Indonesian Department of Maritime Affairs and are awaiting Cabinet approval.

Returned Investors

In addition to preparing a welcome mat for new foreign investors by passing the Foreign Capital Investment Law, Indonesia has tried to make amends to old foreign investors whose ventures were seized or placed under government "supervision" by the Soekarno regime. In December 1966, all Ministries concerned were instructed to return to their owners all foreign enterprises that had been brought under their control, either as a result of the "confrontation" policy against Malaysia in the case of UK enterprises or the berdikari policy in the case of US and European firms. An interdepartmental committee, the Assistance Team for the Return of Foreign Companies, was set up to handle the return of these enterprises and to negotiate any problems between the returning owners and the ministries or agencies that had been operating them.

The December 1966 decision did not include Dutch assets in Indonesia. These were subject to a separate agreement between the Governments of the Netherlands and Indonesia, concluded in September 1966, under which Indonesia agreed to make a payment of $167 million as compensation. At the time of their nationalization, Dutch investments in Indonesia had an estimated value of $1 billion.

During 1967, the owners of most of the major foreign investments in manufacturing, plus some in plantations, accepted the invitation to resume operation of their ventures. Such companies as Unilever, British-American Tobacco Co Ltd, Bata, Heineken, Nicholas Aspro, Prodenta, Singer, National Cash Register, and Goodyear resumed control of their plants in Indonesia. So did some major plantation owners, including Goodyear and Uniroyal, and the UK-based Harrison & Crossfield Co. Others returned in 1968, among them the Dunlop Tyre Co, Union Carbide, and International Flavors and Fragrances (IFF).

At the end of 1967, however, the Indonesian authorities noted that some owners of foreign enterprises, chiefly plantations, had not responded to the offer for the return of their property. It set April 30, 1968, as the ultimate date for these owners to conclude agreements over their property; otherwise the Government would assume that the owners were unwilling to take their enterprises back. In such cases, compensation would be fixed in conformity with the terms reached between Indonesia and its creditors at the Paris meeting of December 1966. For technical reasons the deadline was postponed until June 15, 1968. Settlements have been reached with all of the plantation owners that claimed their rights.

The conditions for the return of the properties have been fairly standard, and are in some ways similar to conditions for new investments.

Generally, returning investors have been obliged to agree to restore and if possible expand their plants beyond present capacity. They have agreed to train Indonesians for all positions, with the aim of Indonesianization of management. Reinvestment of part of the profits of the enterprise has been another condition; during the first three years after a business has been returned to its former owners, no more than 50% of net profits after taxes may be transferred abroad. Thereafter, all profits may be remitted. Most of the agreements under which foreign businesses have been returned include reference to some equity going either to private Indonesians or to the Government, but in no case has this condition yet been fulfilled. Operating permits for returned foreign investments have been granted for periods in the 15-30-year range, depending on the length of time the business has already operated in Indonesia. Two years before the expiration of the permit, the Government will confer with the foreign owners regarding future operating options.

The Government has extended to old investors who are modernizing, expanding, or rehabilitating their enterprises, tax incentives and other benefits similar to those given to new foreign investors under the Foreign Capital Investment Law, but with a maximum tax holiday of three years. The $2.5-million investment minimum has been waived for returned investors. By agreeing to make a fresh investment of only £56,000, the British-American Tobacco Co Ltd obtained an exemption from corporate and dividend taxes on profits paid to shareholders in 1968, 1969, and 1970. Another returned investor, Belgian-owned Faroka, also got a three-year tax holiday when it agreed to make a new investment of only $230,500 in its Indonesian cigarette factory. Repatriation of capital following the return of foreign enterprise is not permitted during the period in which tax concessions are being received.

Most of the international companies that have regained their Indonesian assets have agreed to expand their operations there. This includes firms with plantations, such as Uniroyal, which will invest the equivalent of $10 million over a 20-year period in its subsidiary, United States Rubber Sumatra Plantation; and manufacturing firms, such as Unilever, which is investing another $1.5 million for modernization of its existing plants and to add a synthetic detergent plant. Goodyear of the US has agreed to put fresh capital into Goodyear Sumatra Plantations, as well as its tire factory.

The agreement between Indonesia's then Ministry of Basic Light Industries and Power and the Swiss firm Indeur SA of Geneva covering the return of PT Filma illustrates the conditions under which many other foreign ventures have been returned. The agreement, signed on December 2, 1967, provided that the owners would accept the business of Filma as it stood, and that the agreement would be effective from the day it was signed. Other salient points were:

• Indeur's agreement to maintain the Indonesianization of middle management and to carry out Indonesianization of top management as soon as possible. Limited numbers of foreign experts were permitted to enter Indonesia "for a limited time" to carry out rehabilitation of the factory — and to train future Indonesian managers.

• An undertaking by Indeur to avoid creating any unrest among Filma's labor force as a consequence of resuming ownership, and to maintain, as far as possible, existing staff relationships. This involved respecting promotions and appointments made during the period of Indonesian control, unless the persons concerned showed themselves incompatible with the smooth and efficient operation of the business. No persons involved in the communist coup attempt were to be employed.

• A promise by Indeur to rehabilitate the factory as soon as possible and to present to the Indonesian foreign investment authorities a plan for its modernization and expansion no later than the end of April 1968. The rehabilitation and expansion program is to cost approximately $250,000.

The agreement under which PT Dunlop Indonesia was returned to its UK owners was signed on May 31, 1968, after a transition period of 30 days, and with the transfer to be fully effective only after a further transition of 30 days, during which the government supervisory body worked in conjunction with managers from the parent company. As in the case of Filma, the agreement laid heavy emphasis on Indonesianization, and on not creating unrest among the Indonesian labor force. Specifically, Dunlop agreed that at least two Indonesians would be involved in top management and that some would be trained for research and development work. But the clauses relating to expansion of the plant were less specific than in the case of Filma; Dunlop merely agreed to expand its operations under provisions of the Foreign Capital Investment Law if the market in Indonesia proved favorable, and no specific capital investment was mentioned.

Uniroyal's negotiations for the return of its plantations, covering 54,000 acres in Sumatra, lasted almost a year. The plantations came under direct control of Indonesia's Rubber General Directorate (BPU Karet) in 1965 following the *berdikari* policy. Three US managers, in a situation of grave personal danger at times, remained on the estates during the takeover period, partly because Uniroyal was continuing to buy latex from the now government-operated plantations. Moreover, Uniroyal refused to consider the takeover as valid and definitive until some kind of formal agreement had been reached with the Indonesian Government.

Eventually, Uniroyal agreed to a politically enforced sale of the plantations to the Indonesian Government, and contracts had been drawn up when negotiations for the return of the property were started in December, 1966. Uniroyal decided it would be better to resume ownership and operations under the new regime than to accept the balance of the compensation offered. The latter was rather a grim alternative, since the company would have received only $4.5 million for assets valued at $18 million. Moreover, under the Paris agreement of 1966, the payments would have been spread over an eight-year period after 1972, with the outstanding sum carrying a very low interest rate.

The Managing Director of Uniroyal's Plantation Division, who had previously been General Manager of Uniroyal Malaysian & Indonesian Plantations, represented the company during the negotiations with what was then the Department of Estates (now merged with the Department of Agriculture).

Uniroyal regained full management of the plantations on November 1, 1967. Nine expatriates found themselves in charge of 7,500 local employees, compared to 6,000 when Indonesia took control of the estates. Due to social and political factors, Uniroyal has not yet been able to trim this vastly inflated labor force. Moreover, to help cope with its unemployment problems, the Indonesian Government has since asked Uniroyal to put another 350 people on its payroll. These were all ex-communists, about to be released from jail. The request is in strange contrast to the agreements obliging other foreign companies (such as Indeur, mentioned above) not to employ persons involved in the 1965 attempted coup by the communists. Uniroyal considered that these 350 new employees would swell the ranks of the potential agitators among its labor force, possibly numbering 25% of the total.

The remaining 75% of the labor force was overtly pleased to see Uniroyal resume control of the plantations. For one thing, it meant that they would once again receive the rice and other commodities that are the most prized part of wages in Indonesia and which had only been fitfully distributed when BPU Karet ran the estates. At present, Uniroyal distributes 400 tons of rice monthly to its 7,500 employees and their families, as well as 50 tons of salt fish, and 5,000 square yards of textiles. The company is now planning to invest $500,000 in food crop estates over a three-year period. These estates will supply 4,000 tons of rice annually, which will be distributed to the rubber plantation workers. These, together with their families living on the plantations, total about 30,000 persons.

The $500,000 for rice production is part of the $10 million equivalent that Uniroyal will invest in the next 20 years for rehabilitation and improvement of its plantations. In discussions with the Indonesian authorities on the incentives that would apply to its new investments in Indonesia, Uniroyal was asking for an additional 30-year extension to its present 30-year concession (making a total of 60 years), a five-year tax holiday instead of three years, and exemption of duties on imported machinery and equipment.

Unilever has a three-year holiday, effective from April 6, 1967, the day on which the plants were returned to their owner. Unilever has an oil mill and a soap and margarine factory in Djakarta, and a factory making soaps and toilet preparations in Surabaja, together employing about 3,300 people, and is adding a synthetic detergent plant in Djakarta. Unilever Indonesia, the new company formed to carry out a "recovery program" on Unilever's regained property, is wholly owned by Unilever. The rehabilitation program involves sending to Indonesia foreign specialists in organization, accounting, production, sales, and marketing who will transfer expertise to Indonesians in the organization. Experts in packaging, detergents, edible oils, and toilet preparations are also booked to go to Indonesia to advise on technical problems.

While probably the vast majority of plants operated under state aegis during the Soekarno regime finished up in a sadly run-down state, this did not always happen. Nicholas Aspro reported that its Naspro pharmaceutical plant was in good condition when it resumed ownership in 1967; the company had left one of its Australian managers there as a watchdog during the period of Indonesian control. Singer's sewing machine assembly plant in Surabaja was also relatively well operated and kept in good condition during the period of Indonesian control, although its 50 employees were pleased to see Singer return. Singer, for its part, was happy that the key personnel had remained and that its capital assets had been protected throughout the turmoil. The plant had been under supervision of an Army colonel — possibly an advantage, in light of the experience of other corporations whose plants were civilian-controlled.

Singer has invested another $100,000 to improve its marketing organization. For these supplementary funds it is anticipating receiving some tax benefits. Singer is considering setting up a manufacturing plant in Djakarta, at a cost of $600,000-$1 million, to produce sewing machines for the local market.

Union Carbide's company, National Carbon Co (Java) Ltd, was returned on May 2, 1968, but the plant was in such run-down condition that Union Carbide decided to start with a new one. In September (but retroactive to May) the Government issued a license to Union Carbide to invest $2.7 million (50% equity, 50% loan) in a new wholly owned dry cell plant.

Ownership of some distributive and service business has also been resumed by foreign companies. One is the UK firm, United Molasses, which specializes in storage and export of molasses. An agreement for the return of American Foreign Insurance Association assets in Indonesia has also been signed. Two of the foreign banks that opened branches in Indonesia in mid-1968 — the Chartered Bank of the UK and the Hongkong and Shanghai Banking Corp — had operated in Djakarta for many years before confrontation came.

The Investment Approval Process

Proposals for investment must receive three approvals — by the ministry concerned, the Investment Board, and the Foreign Capital Investment Council. Although the system of triple approvals might suggest a rigid, cumbersome, and time-consuming process similar to the multilayered approval machinery set up by India, in practice it is much more flexible. Before a formal application is submitted, letters of intent and memoranda of agreement may be used as preliminary and non-binding indications of intent to proceed further in exploring a project or an agreement in principle with the Government. This gives the prospective investor time to prepare his project and conduct further studies and surveys. And when the application is submitted, the potential investor often finds that many more things are negotiable than the Foreign Capital Investment Law suggests.

The would-be investor generally begins by approaching the ministry responsible for the field of investment in which his proposal falls. At the same time, it is wise to call on the Investment Board, and to keep it apprised of investment intentions. In fact, an investor may go first to the Board, which can then arrange meetings between the company and the ministry concerned.

Nearly all proposed manufacturing investments come under the Ministry of Industry. Other ministries that are involved in first-stage negotiations and screening of foreign investment proposals are the Ministries of Agriculture, Mining, Communications, and sometimes Trade, Finance, or Public Works. The first discussions or negotiations are generally held with the Secretary General of the ministry (the first official below the minister) or with the Director General (next rank) in charge of the specific industry. In the Ministry of Industry, for example, there are Directors General for Basic Industries, Chemical Industries, Light Industries, and so on. Some proposed investments — generally major industrial projects — may involve more than one ministry; one project under discussion in 1968, for example, concerned the Ministries of Industry, Mining, and Public Works (power). In such cases, a special interministerial team is set up, ad hoc, to negotiate the particular proposal.

Much of the hard work of evaluation and negotiation is done at the ministerial level. After this, the second-stage approval by the Investment Board often requires only a few weeks. Important policy questions (e.g., how many foreign firms to approve in a particular field, or whether assembly as opposed to full manufacturing is acceptable) are often decided by the departments. The negotiations cover all the technical aspects of the proposal, and generally some matters of incentives and obligations of the investing company. But in judging a proposed investment the ministry often seeks the help of the Investment Board.

The Investment Board

The Foreign Investment Board (or Technical Team for Foreign Capital Investment) operates as a staff group for the Stabilization Council — the President and his economic ministers — in the field of foreign investment. It is chaired by Prof. Dr. Mohammad Sadli, a US-trained economist, and its members include officials from the State Ministry for Economy, Finance, and Industry, the Ministries of Finance, Trade, Industry, Manpower, Internal Affairs, and Foreign Affairs, and Bappenas and Bank Indonesia. Its offices and secretariat are at Tjut Mutiah 7, Djakarta.

In late 1968 the Foreign Investment Board's responsibility was extended to cover investment under the 1968 Domestic (i.e., rupiah) Investment Law, and coordination of domestic and foreign investment. Now called simply the Investment Board, it is headed by Prof. Sadli, with Drs. Surjo Sediono (Vice-Chairman of the original Foreign Investment Board, and an official of the Department of Industry) in charge of foreign investment, and S. Pamungkas of Bapindo and the Department of Finance, as head of the domestic investment side.

The Board is responsible for coordinating action by various ministries on investment proposals, and to some degree coordinates proposals with the goals of the Five-Year Plan. It acts as expediter in negotiations, and although it technically has no role once an application has final approval, it can and does assist in implementation of investment projects. It has, for example, helped investors get through red-tape roadblocks that were preventing the clearance of goods through customs, and in at least one case it stepped in when a foreign investor was quoted an exorbitant price for land. Its specific role in the approval process is to review investment agreements initialed by the departments; if necessary, renegotiate some points with the would-be investor; and approve or reject the proposal. In considering a proposal, the Board reviews its conformity to the Foreign Capital Investment Law, and may accept or reject (or attach conditions to) proposed special incentives or exceptions from the general regulations. It scrutinizes applications carefully in the light of the project's ability to save or earn — or use — foreign exchange. As a general policy it encourages higher stages of industries (e.g., from logging to processing, from assembly to manufacture).

Proposed ownership certainly falls within the purview of the Board because of the stipulations of the Law, but the Board neither seeks joint-venture partners for potential foreign investors nor does it enter into negotiations between foreign and local joint-venture partners. The Board does not, at present, usually judge purely business aspects of the proposal (e.g., royalty rates, fees, rates of return) in any great detail, and beyond checking company backgrounds to try to eliminate carpet-baggers and fly-by-night operators, it does not judge the viability of a proposed investment. Its attention to the business aspects of proposals will increase, however, as more experience gives the Board better criteria on which to judge them.

Investment Council

When an investment application has been initialed by the relevant ministry and approved by the Investment Board, it passes on to the cabinet-level Foreign Capital Investment Council with a recommendation that approval be granted. The Council is chaired by President Soeharto, and includes as members the State Minister for Economy, Finance, and Industry, the Minister of Finance, the Minister of Trade, the Minister of Industry, the Minister of Foreign Affairs, the Governor of the Central Bank, and the Chairman of Bappenas. Generally, proposals approved by the Investment Board are given Council sanction unchanged, but the Council can and sometimes does propose certain changes in agreements. When final approval has been granted at cabinet level, the Council issues an investment permit and the Ministry that first approved the application executes the agreement.

Establishing a Company

The Foreign Capital Investment Law provides that an enterprise operated wholly or for the most part in Indonesia as a separate business unit must be a legal entity organized under Indonesian Law and have its domicile in Indonesia. For the Freeport Sulphur copper mining investment, however, the US firm was granted permission to establish a company domiciled in Indonesia, but established under the laws of the state of Delaware. This required special sanction from Parliament. Other companies have proposed the same arrangement. In order to allow more flexibility — as long as problems are not created for Indonesia in the process—and to eliminate the need for special parliamentary approvals, the Investment Board is considering requesting an amendment to the Law. Under the Law, some firms—mainly banks or other service companies—may establish branches rather than organizing Indonesian corporations, but they are generally eligible for fewer incentives than are locally incorporated firms. The company law itself, still based on the old Netherlands Commercial Code, is likely to be changed within the next few years.

Companies in Indonesia must be legally registered under one of the following forms: (1) *firma*, in which the owners are fully responsible for liabilities of the company—this form is usually limited to small operations; (2) *commanditaire vennootschap* (CV), including one or several partners (*commanditaire venoot*), whose liabilities go only as far as the amount of capital they have put into the company, while the managing partner(s) remain(s) fully responsible for the firm's liabilities; (3) cooperatives; and (4) limited liability company, or *perseroan terbatas* (PT). For foreign investment, the limited liability company is in fact the only relevant form, as specified in Announcement No. 3, of Jan. 24, 1968, of the Indonesian Foreign Exchange Bureau, supplementing Article 3 of the Foreign Capital Investment Law.

A limited liability company may be formed by foreigners alone, or by foreigners jointly with Indonesian nationals. A minimum of two persons are to be involved in the founding of a PT. Consequently, for legal purposes foreign investors without local partners sometimes officially form a PT jointly with one of their own representatives.

The first step in setting up a PT is to make a draft Act of Formation, or Act of Incorporation, to be submitted to the Minister of Justice with a request to examine the draft so submitted. It is advisable to start by consulting a lawyer, and since the Code requires a Notarial Act for the establishment of a company, to have a notary draw up the document in order to hasten and facilitate legalization by the Minister of Justice. This notarial instrument, which must be written in Indonesian, is an absolute requirement for the validity of a company. Names of notaries public may be obtained from the Department of Justice. Other legal help is available in Indonesia, though sometimes hard to find.

As to the contents of the Act of Formation, the Department of Justice should be first approached to discover whether there are any objections to the proposed name of the company. It is not permitted to use the name of one of the members, but the name may show the corporate objective. Further, the words *perseroan terbatas,* or the abbreviation "PT," must be incorporated in the name.

Besides the name of the company, the draft Act must set out the purpose, location, and management rules of the company, in accordance with the provisions of the Foreign Capital Investment Law.

The Department of Justice also requires documents giving written agreement to the formation of the company concerned from the government department(s) in charge of the industry in which the company will operate.

When the draft Act has been examined by the Department of Justice, it is returned to those concerned. Every person who is to receive documents and other written decisions concerning limited liability companies other than the notary concerned should hold a written reference from the notary stating that the said person has authority to receive documents and written communications relating to the company concerned.

The draft Act returned by the Department of Justice may contain recommendations for alterations, and advice to make the Act of Formation before a notary public. This allows any problems to be worked out before formal filing and helps avoid the need for complicated amendments later. The draft must also be approved by the Investment Board and BLLD. When the necessary approvals have been obtained, the notary will submit a request for legalization, or registration of the document by the Minister of Justice. All this normally takes two to three months.

Cost of Registration

Fees paid to notaries public vary from .01% to 0.5% of the company's authorized capital. Lawyers ask for 1%. In addition, there is a service tax equal to 20% of the fee. Foreign investments are exempted from the stamp tax, amounting to 5% of the paid-in capital. The fee for compulsory publication of the details of new companies in the State Gazette (*Berita Negara*) is Rp17,500, but foreign investors are exempt from this as well.

Capital Requirements

The registration, or incorporation, of the company will be refused if the founders of the company have failed to subscribe at least 10% of the authorized capital. Evidence of this must be obtained in information, or a receipt from the BLLD. This should be forwarded to the Department of Justice together with the company's Act of Incorporation. The articles of incorporation will also be refused if together the original founders do not represent 20% of the nominal capital. The nominal capital is the amount indicated in the memorandum of association, or draft of the Act of Formation, and determined at the time of incorporation of the limited company. It cannot be changed.

These articles must also indicate the period within which the unpaid balance of the issued capital will be paid. No bearer shares can be issued as long as the full amount for them has not been deposited to the account of the company.

The capital of a company incorporated in Indonesia must be denoted in rupiahs, but for purposes of future capital repatriation may be denoted in foreign currency as well. The equity capital owned by foreign shareholders must equal the countervalue in rupiahs of the government-approved foreign investment, calculated at the BE rate prevailing on the date of the investment permit issued by the Foreign Capital Investment Council. If the limited company is a joint enterprise, the assets of the Indonesian partner should be valued.

Management

The highest power and the highest management of the company are vested in the shareholders, who make decisions at periodic general meetings. Decisions are made by a majority vote.

Under the antiquated Dutch law in use, no shareholder may have more than six votes, regardless of the number of shares he holds (and not more than three votes, if the company has fewer than 100 shares). The limitation on votes can, however, be quite easily circumvented by issuing nonvoting shares, or by stipulating in the articles of association that each, say, 100 profit shares represent one voting share.

The Department of Justice is considering a new draft corporation law, which would eliminate the vote limitation and update the law to match those applied in other countries. In addition to voting and nonvoting shares, both common and preference shares may be issued. Preference shares may generally be sold only to other holders of preference shares, however.

When directors receive remuneration, they are servants and representatives of the company under Indonesian law. Managers are appointed, subject to recall, by the members of the board, or by the shareholders. They may be under, or independent of, the control of the directors.

If the activities of the directors are restricted exclusively to the supervision of the managers, and they, therefore, do not participate in any act of management, they may be authorized by the articles of incorporation to examine and approve the managers' accounts. If the directors are not so authorized, the inspection and approval must be made by persons appointed for this purpose by the articles of incorporation. The managers are obliged to submit a statement of profits and losses to the directors once a year.

Bookkeeping

It is obligatory for everyone operating a business in Indonesia to maintain records. It is therefore required that the manager annually draw up a balance sheet in accordance with the requirements of his company. The balance sheet must be signed by him personally within the first six months of every calendar year. The books and balance sheets must be retained for 30 years, while letters and telegrams received and copies of outgoing correspondence must be retained for a period of 10 years.

Books may be kept in foreign currency. In that case, expenditures in rupiahs are to be calculated at the current exchange rate of the day. Profits, however, must be indicated in rupiahs, since they are subject to local taxation. The Tax Directorate has yet to give clear-cut guidelines as to how this is to be done.

Dissolution of a Company

As soon as the managers become aware that the nominal capital of a company has sustained a loss of 50%, they are obliged to report this to the office of the court of justice, as well as in the official gazette.

In case the loss amounts to 75%, the company is dissolved, and the managers are personally and severally responsible for funds due to third parties arising from obligations undertaken after they were, or should have been, aware of the 75% loss.

To prevent the dissolution, the articles of incorporation may contain provisions that a reserve fund be formed from which the deficiency may be met.

Licensing

Very few international firms have entered straight licensing arrangements in Indonesia, but this approach could have advantages for firms that want to get their products known but are not yet ready to make an equity investment. To date, most licensing of patents, trademarks, or know-how has been associated with investments by foreign firms.

If the rights licensed to a partly or wholly foreign-owned subsidiary constitute part of the equity investment, the arrangement must be approved by the Department concerned and BLLD. If the agreement calls for the licensee to pay royalties or fees abroad, it should form part of the investment proposal and must be approved by the relevant Ministry or the Investment Board (generally both) and the BLLD. As long as royalties or fees proposed are reasonable, approval is granted. There are no guidelines or set restrictions on the amounts. In both Government and business circles, however, there is not always a clear appreciation of the value of patents, trademarks, and know-how, and what these represent. In some instances, no royalties at all are paid for the use of trademarks. In many cases, the arrangement has been for the licensee to pay royalties or fees annually, generally in a fixed lump-sum payment (i.e., not based on sales), for a number of years. The number of years of payment varies considerably. Reasonable royalties or fees are generally deductible by the licensee. There are at present no withholding taxes on royalties and fees remitted abroad, but it is likely that a tax may be imposed in the next few years.

There is very little protection for patents and trademarks. Indonesia is a member of the Paris convention on patents, adhering to the London text of 1934, but not the 1958 version. It is also a signatory to the Hague arrangement of 1925 (as amended in 1934) and the Neuchatel arrangement of 1947 relating to designs and models. But, there are few Indonesian laws to provide a framework for protection of industrial property, and during the years of the Soekarno regime, the administration of patent, trademark, and related matters broke down. What regulations existed were not enforced.

For patents, the existing regulations provide only for depositing requests for patents (announcement of the Ministry of Justice No. 9, Aug. 28, 1953). There has been some preparatory work for a patent law, and a bill was submitted in 1964, but there are no real prospects for a patent law being passed in the near future. The advantage of applying for a patent is that under the Paris Union for the Protection of Industrial Property, the applicant can get priority if he has registered the patent in another country; but this depends on national laws of the countries concerned. Since 1953, a few hundred requests for patents have been deposited. The application fee is Rp1,000 and a certificate of application costs Rp100. In theory, at least, any conflicts over product imitation can be taken to court, but in the absence of any basis in law, firms that have encountered the problem have felt they had little recourse. Patent infringement is apparently not too serious a problem in most industries, but some pharmaceutical companies have had their products imitated.

The law on trademarks (Law No. 21/1961) is based on the principle of the first user. It provides for registration of trademarks, as acknowledgement that the person who registers the mark is the first user, but since use is the criterion of right, registration is not required. To register a trademark, the owner submits an application to the Directorate for Patents of the Department of Justice, annexing labels (10 copies), a block, and a description of the item. If the owner of the trademark is domiciled abroad, he must appoint an attorney in Indonesia to act on his behalf. The Directorate checks for similarity against previously registered marks, and if there is no conflict, registration of the mark is approved, and the trademark is published in the State Gazette. Copies of each registration are published in a Public Register, which is open to everyone. During the following nine months, others may oppose registration of the trademark, and file suit against it. After nine months have lapsed, someone may still file opposition at court, but he must prove that he is the actual first user. Opposition after the nine-month period has never occurred in Indonesia, even though some 90,000 trademarks have been registered since 1912. The fee, payable on application for registration of a trademark, is Rp5,250 (as from August 1, 1968), comprising an application fee of Rp2,500, an examination fee of Rp250, and a registration fee of Rp2,500; if the application is rejected, Rp2,500 is returned to the applicant. For a transfer of trademark rights, the fee is Rp2,250. For a check on similarity to registered marks, the fee is Rp750. For either information on contents of the Public Register or copies from the Public Register on one trademark, the fee is Rp250.

Contract Manufacturing

Several companies have set up contract manufacturing in Indonesia. Two methods are commonly used. In one, the foreign company provides raw materials to its affiliate in Indonesia on a consignment basis (through the *barang kiriman* system — through the DP market, and without a letter of credit). The local manufacturer takes title to the raw materials, manufactures the product, and distributes it. The foreign firm makes its profit on the f.o.b. price at which it sells the raw materials, and (almost invariably) by a royalty or fee for the rights to manufacture its product, or for know-how or technical assistance. The contractor company working under this type of arrangement generally has a very high margin on sales, because it must eventually pay the raw material supplier in DP. Costing must therefore be on the basis of an estimated future DP rate.

Under the second method, the foreign company supplies the raw materials (but retains title to them), pays the local company a manufacturing fee, then distributes the product through its own distribution network. Several foreign firms, especially pharmaceutical and chemical companies, are already using this system. Glaxo of the UK, through its Allen & Hanburys division, began contracting in 1968 for manufacture of throat lozenges under the first scheme. Glaxo supplies granules and packaging materials. The Indonesian company, Industri Kimia & Pharmasi BETA, pays a royalty of 10% as payment for supervisory expenses. In nearly all cases, quality control is handled by sending samples abroad for testing.

V — Financing

MORE THAN A DECADE of inflation, and particularly Indonesia's soaring inflation rates of the past few years, has made financing a serious problem for both private investors and the Government. Largely as a result of past government policies, financial institutions have operated through excessive and indiscriminate lending, instead of promoting savings and sound private finance. The official lightheartedness toward inflation during the Soekarno era combined with a lack of banking expertise after the Dutch banks were nationalized, led to a severe decline in the efficiency and the reliability of the banking system. The Government pumped money into the indigenous banks through subscriptions to capital, government loans, and advances from the central bank, until Indonesian banks acted virtually as government credit agencies. This led to a lack of coordination among financial institutions, excessive issue of credit, anomalies in interest rates, and inadequate scrutiny of applications for funds and supervision of their use. The result was that after 1959, large accumulations of liquid funds were sporadically dissipated, while very little was channeled into productive investments.

It is obvious that the present Government intends to reverse this situation; some progress has already been made, but mobilizing domestic capital is a sizable task. The certainty that the value of the rupiah will decline has taught the public to put its money into goods, land, or better still, into foreign currency in a Hong Kong or Singapore bank. Savings are only about 5% of national income. Yet it is estimated that Indonesians own some $500 million in banks abroad; little will return permanently to Indonesia until the prospects for economic stabilization are better.

In addition, the combination of inflation and high taxes on money earnings encourages payment in kind. This practice slows the complete entry of much of the population into the money economy, and consequently inhibits development of private savings.

The lack of confidence in the rupiah is nearly matched by a lack of confidence in the banking system. The result is that only 30-35% of the money supply is deposited in banks. This, combined with the tight money policy that forms part of the government's stabilization program, means that rupiahs available for lending are scarce and expensive.

As long as the country is plagued by severe inflation, little improvement in financing conditions can be expected. But in 1967 and 1968, the budget almost ceased to be a source of inflation. And the prospect of increasingly adequate rice supplies means that rice prices — the most important factor in overall price increases — may be stabilized soon. One major problem remaining is the Government's credit policy. While in general the Government has followed a tight money line to reduce inflation, the state banks' lending rates have been kept artificially low in an effort to boost exports and production. The effects are twofold: Low rates on loans — actually negative interest rates — have obliged the central bank to subsidize the state banks, thus adding to the inflation problem. At the same time, low lending rates have meant low deposit rates, and consequently the state banks have been able to attract few deposits. Private "mushroom banks," whose owners are often little more than black marketeers, have sprung up, offering high interest on deposits and lending (mostly for speculation) at rates as high as 15% per month. But many have closed as fast as they have opened, while the owners skipped out with the funds — a situation that has added considerably to the public's distrust of private banking.

So the depositor has faced the choice of putting his money into a state bank where the interest on deposits is not enough to match the rate of inflation, or into a private one that might not exist next week. There are, of course, other options, and these seem to be widening. Some private banks pay interest high enough to cover inflation, and are reliable. Foreign banks can attract some rupiah deposits, largely because of their good names (though low interest rates limit their appeal).

In September 1968, the Government embarked on a campaign to attract deposits by sharply increasing state bank interest rates. Significantly, the Government promised that no questions would be asked about where deposits came from, promised no taxes on them or the interest, and promised that the "banking secret" regulations would be observed (i.e., that tax authorities would not have access to the banks' records). Lending rates were raised slightly, but not to market levels; this, with higher deposit rates, will oblige the central bank to continue subsidizing the state banks. The overall rate structure of the state banks can be expected to move to market levels in the fairly near future, however.

As inflation is brought under control, the shortage of rupiah finance will certainly lessen, and a capital market will eventually start to develop. For the present, however, local funds are simply inadequate to provide a source of working capital, and foreign investors should expect to work mainly with their own financial resources, at least for the next few years.

Very little protection against exchange risks is available at present. Foreign companies may keep their accounts in foreign currency, but the main usefulness of this is only in helping maintain the value of assets. In addition, companies may keep funds in a freely transferable foreign exchange account in Indonesia, converting them into working capital only as needed. The establishment of a forward exchange market is under discussion, although the central bank is somewhat reluctant, on the ground that a futures market might produce adverse psychological effects that would accelerate the deterioration of the value of the rupiah. The central bank is also exploring the possibility of establishing a market for hard currency-rupiah swaps. Some steps toward the development of both a futures market and a swap system are likely to be taken in the near future, but it will be some time before either is very strong. A team was appointed to make recommendations to the central bank by the end of 1968 on means of developing a money and capital market.

The rupiah has had an unfortunate history in recent years. Chronic budget deficits — worsening year by year until, in 1965, expenditures were almost twice revenues — were financed mainly by the printing press. There were successive devaluations, and in December 1965 there was a revaluation when one new rupiah replaced 1,000 old rupiahs. Since then nearly balanced budgets have helped, but the money supply has continued to climb (though at a progressively slower rate) from Rp 5.8 billion in the first quarter of 1966 to Rp 22.6 billion in the fourth quarter of 1966, to Rp 52.6 billion in the last quarter of 1967, and to Rp 84 billion by September 1968. A rice crisis in the last quarter of 1967 seriously aggravated the already severe inflation. The nine-commodity cost-of-living index for Djakarta (September 1966:100) rose from 145 in January 1967 to 395 in January 1968, and stood at 475 in July.

The October 3 Regulations

Until the new economic policy of Oct. 3, 1966, Indonesia operated under a system of multiple, officially fixed foreign exchange rates, strict foreign exchange control, and a system of foreign exchange allocation by the Government. The October 3 regulations were designed to put more reliance on market forces and reduce government control over the economy. The mechanism introduced was the Bonus Export (BE) System. Its major aim is to decontrol foreign trade and payments by moving toward a free foreign exchange market with a single exchange rate. Because of Indonesia's severe foreign exchange famine, the Government established an exchange rate system aimed at channeling foreign exchange to essential imports. A BE import list was established, consisting of essential and semiessential goods importable with BE certificates — or foreign exchange earned or purchased at the free-floating BE exchange rate. Luxury imports and invisible transfers were allowed only with free foreign exchange ("complementary" foreign exchange, or Devisa Pelengkap — DP). BE, like DP, was allowed to find its own market level, but since its use is restricted, its rate is naturally lower than DP. Because it is used for most imports, and exporters' proceeds are mainly in BE, the BE rate has become the most important exchange rate of Indonesia.

After October 1966, the exchange rate structure included, in addition to the floating DP and BE rates, several fixed, periodically adjusted rates. Most of them were left over from the old system and operated as taxes, mainly on trade. (For a full explanation of the BE System as it relates to trade, and a chart of exchange rates applicable to trade transactions, see Chapter 9.) Some of these exchange rates have disappeared since October 1966, and more are likely to be abolished. A more significant change has been that the BE rate is no longer a completely free market rate. Regulations announced in May 1968 required that BE acquired through export proceeds be sold immediately to a foreign exchange bank, which then offers the BE for sale on the Foreign Exchange Bourse. Consequently, all trade in BE is conducted through the Bourse. Three times a week there is a BE "call," when the central bank, after comparing bids and tenders, sets a "call" rate at the point where supply and demand are nearly equal. While supply and demand are still the main determinants of the rate, the central bank can influence it by its own offers of BE. In early 1968 the central bank announced its intention to intervene in the BE market, and it began to influence the market strongly in June 1968. A similar trade in DP is conducted at the Bourse, but since DP is freely traded outside the Bourse, the rate is little affected. It is possible that sometime in 1969 or 1970 the Government will abolish the BE

system and move to a single exchange rate system with import licensing. For the movement of BE and DP rates since 1966, see Table 1.

For purposes of investment and financing, the relevant exchange rates in mid-September 1968 were (in rupiahs per US dollar):

DP Rate (fluctuating) — 430
Applies to capital transfers connected with foreign investment in services; im-

TABLE 1
Indonesia's BE and DP Exchange Rates, 1966-68

End of	General BE Rp. per $	DP[1] Rp. per $
1966		
March	—	56.5
June	—	110.0
September	82.0[2]	143.0
December	84.0	122.0
1967		
March	97.0	122.5
June	137.5	157.0
September	148.0	171.0
December	235.0[3]	290.0[3]
1968		
January	266.0[3]	297.5
February	260.0	293.0
March	267.0	305.0
April	286.0	340.0
May	300.0	345.0
June	302.0[4]	360.0
July	306.0	390.0
August	310.0	410.0

(1) Rates given are Djakarta free market rates. Rates for DP trading at the Foreign Exchange Bourse sometimes differ from free market rates, but usually not significantly.

(2) The rate is for October, when the BE System was instituted.

(3) The sharp rises reflect the rice crisis of September 1967-January 1968, and considerable speculation in the BE market.

(4) The stability of the BE rate in the summer of 1968 was due to intervention by the central bank to hold the rate steady near the 300 mark.

ports on the DP list and all other imports not prohibited; all invisible receipts and other invisibles to which the BE rate does not apply; private loans from abroad and interest and principal remitted abroad on such loans, unless the loan is brought in as part of the original approved investment.

BE Rate (fluctuating) — 317

Applies to capital transfers and invisibles connected with most approved foreign investments; conversion of DICS-rupiahs; imports on the BE list; invisibles connected with trade and certain other invisibles; all government imports and invisibles.

Oil Rate (adjusted periodically) — 240

Applies to foreign exchange receipts and payments of oil companies.

West Irian exchange rate — 10

The official rate in West Irian, but many transfers are made at other rates.

The essential rule is that funds transferred *to* Indonesia may be remitted *abroad* under the same rate system (at the rate prevailing on the day of the transfer). Thus if loan money from abroad is brought in at the DP rate, interest and principal on the loan remitted abroad will also be at the DP rate.

Exchange controls affecting borrowing from abroad are minimal. If a foreign investor includes loan capital in his approved investment, and the loan funds are consequently brought into Indonesia at the BE rate, he will not be granted permission to buy BE for repayment of the principal while he is benefiting from a tax holiday. A firm may, however, purchase BE for remittance of interest on the loan during its tax holiday, with routine permission from the Foreign Exchange Bureau (BLLD). After the tax holiday, again with permission from the BLLD, it may buy BE for repayment of the principal. It can, of course, repay the loan during the tax holiday if it chooses to use transferred profits for that purpose. Loans from abroad, for, say, working capital, brought into Indonesia at the DP rate, are not subject to any exchange control. There is at present no tax on interest remitted abroad.

Because the Government wants to avoid strain on its meager exchange reserves from an outflow of interest payments and principal on loans, it strongly prefers that foreign investors have a high equity:debt ratio in their original investment (and in some cases the Foreign Investment Board may be reluctant to approve an investment that includes a high portion of debt capital). Only transfers through the BE system are considered to have any effect on the balance of payments, since DP transfers are completely free and unrecorded by the Government. Consequently, funds brought into Indonesia through the DP system are not affected by this policy.

The Monetary System

Bank Negara Indonesia (BNI) Unit I is the central bank. It supervises the banking system, issues banknotes, watches the stability of the rupiah, sometimes intervenes in the BE market to stabilize the BE rate, administers the foreign exchange reserves, and is the lender of last resort. The central bank and most of the rest of the state banks came into existence with the nationalization of the major Dutch banks in 1958-60. The Soekarno regime tried to integrate the state banks into a system in which each bank became a "unit" of the Bank Negara Indonesia. Under this system — which has never been fully effective — the central bank (Unit I) carried out some, though not all, of the functions of a central bank, and simultaneously acted as a commercial bank. A series of banking laws expected to be passed sometime late in 1968 would abolish this integrated system. The proposed law on the central bank, to be known as Bank Indonesia, restores its function as a true central bank with adequate powers, and removes it from commercial banking. The central bank was already shedding some of its commercial banking operations in mid-1968, but it is expected that there will be a transition period of about two years before it is completely out of commercial banking. The law will also decide the degree of autonomy of the central bank *vis-a-vis* the Government; at the time of writing there was some concern that the bank would not have enough independence to effectively perform its duties.

Even without the new law, Bank Indonesia has considerable powers to control credit and regulate banking activity. One of the most important is the minimum reserve requirement, now at 30% for both state and private commercial banks. The requirement has not always been enforced, however, at least before August 1967. Eased trade credit regulations announced in July 1967 led a number of private banks (and reportedly, one state bank) to extend credit not only in excess of the reserve requirements, but also beyond normal bank safety margins. When the central bank required the banks to cover their clearing debits within a week, 22 private banks proved unable to do so and were suspended. Although the banks involved accounted for only a fraction of the total bank credit, the crisis was in danger of spreading to other banks. The central bank took several measures to right the situation, including granting emergency credits to restore the liquidity of the suspended banks. It was authorized to reduce the minimum reserve requirement for private banks from 30% to 10% for a three-month period, but did not do so. Presumably the central bank has kept a closer watch on the banks' adherence to reserve requirements since that time.

Another credit control mechanism of the Bank Indonesia is its rediscount rate. Interest rates on discounts and advances to the state commercial banks are 50% of the maximum lending rates of the state banks; thus on state bank rates of 3-7% per month, the rediscount rates are 1.5-3.5% per month. Rediscounting for fertilizer and pesticide credits is at a preferential rate. Because the state bank lending rates are set by the central bank, and have actually been negative interest rates, the state banks are in effect forced to turn to the central bank for credits regardless of the rediscount rate. After the 1967 private banking crisis, the central bank was authorized to extend ordinary credits to private banks on the same conditions that it extends credits to state banks, i.e., at 50% of the private bank's lending rates for the export and production sectors.

The central bank also has two means of affecting the direction of credit, through guidelines on credit to economic sectors, and through interest rates. Under present policy, the "A" sector of the economy — exports and production — is to receive 90% of total bank credit, and the "B" sector (anything not in the A sector, except imports) is to receive the other 10%. Before the regulations of Oct. 3, 1966, there was also an allocation of credit to the Government (60%) and

to private borrowers (40%), but the new economic policies abolished this distinction. The economic sector rule applies only to the state banks, but these account for 80% of total credit. In addition, since import credit is prohibited, private bank credit probably fits into the 90-10% split.

Crucial to the central bank's selective credit policy is the interest rate structure of the state banks. It is designed to give priority to exports and essential industries (see Table 3). For some cyclical kinds of credit (e.g., fertilizers, irrigation) the central bank lends directly at preferential rates. The central bank is likely to move state bank lending rates up by stages, eventually to market levels (which would now be 7-8% per month), but the priority sectors of the selective credit policy are likely to remain much the same for the next couple of years.

On a more passive level, the central bank can have some effect on credit policies of commercial banks by requiring weekly or monthly reports from banks to which it has granted credits, or by making on-the-spot investigations. Bank Indonesia has already begun to improve the overall administration of the banking system, and to encourage sounder banking practices.

In addition, the central bank has fairly wide responsibility for regulating banking activities. A Basic Banking Law was passed in December 1967, covering, in general, the activities of state and private commercial banks, savings banks, development banks, and branches of foreign banks. But like many Indonesian laws, it leaves wide scope for interpretation, and charges other bodies (e.g., the central bank, the Ministry of Finance) with issuing implementing regulations. This, combined with a flurry of directives to banks connected with changed trade regulations, meant that new central bank regulations were being issued very frequently in 1968.

Short-Term Credit

Short-term credit is nearly the only credit available in Indonesia. Commercial banks (state, private Indonesian, or foreign) may extend loans for up to one year, but because of the rapid inflation of the rupiah, most loans are for three or six months.

An overdraft is technically not permitted, since a written agreement covering the amount and duration of the loan is required (but term loans are often referred to as overdrafts). At present there is neither a bill market nor any other kind of discounting. Short-term credits can generally be rolled over, but with some exceptions the loan must be repaid when the term is up; this depends on the relationship between the bank and the customer.

All credits must, by law, be secured. Collateral is defined in the Basic Banking Law as either primary (related to the kind of credit, e.g., if industrial credit, the factory or inventory; if export credit, the export stocks) or secondary (movable or fixed assets unrelated to the type of credit; guarantees by third parties). In practice, state banks require secondary collateral to equal 100% of the amount of the credit, even where part of the credit is covered by primary collateral. Credit from state banks to exporters is normally limited to 75% of the value of their export stocks.

The State Banks

In addition to the central bank there are five state banks, four of which are commercial; Unit V is a savings bank. All but one of the commercial banks (Unit III) are former Dutch banks that were nationalized. In the system of integrating the state banks into units of the Bank Negara Indonesia, each was to specialize in a particular field (e.g., rural credits, foreign trade), although all were to provide general commercial banking services. The specializations have not been retained to any great extent.

One of the banking bills before Parliament in 1968 was meant to revamp the state bank system, providing substantial increases in capital for each bank, restoring their specializations, and eliminating the unit system of names. (See Table 2.)

The state commercial banks lend at rates of 3%, 4%, 5%, or 7% monthly, depending on the purpose of the credit (see Table 3). In principle, the 3-7% per month is "all-in" interest. It is normally charged on a discounted basis, so that a borrower of Rp1,000 at 5% gets Rp950; while commissions are sometimes charged, they are one-time fees, charged only for the first month, and only on the amount drawn. For loans in the

---

TABLE 2.

The State Banks

Name	Assets June 30, 1968 (in Rp billion)	To be called	Specialization
BNI (Bank Negara Indonesia) Unit I	—	Bank Indonesia	Central bank
BNI Unit II [1]	11.97	Bank Rahjat Indonesia Bank Ekspor Impor	Rural credits Foreign trade
BNI Unit III	20.66	Bank Negara Indonesia 1946	Trade, including foreign trade
BNI Unit IV	18.93 [2]	Bank Bumi Daja	Estate production and exports
BNI Unit V	—	Bank Tabungan Negara	Savings bank
Bank Dagang Negara [3]	6.83	Bank Dagang Negara	Trade, industry

(1) Unit II will be split into two banks
(2) March 31, 1968
(3) Although it had no unit number, it is a state commercial bank and is considered to have maintained the soundest banking practices.

TABLE 3.

State Commercial Bank Lending Rates, 1965-68

Effective from:	Annual interest (%)	Economic Sectors	Commission on loan to [1] Gov't.	Private
August 19, 1965	9	Vital production	3/4%	1%
	15	Other production, exports	1%	1¼%
	24	Other (distribution, imports)	1½%	2%
June 13, 1966	14	Vital production	3/4%	1%
	20	Other production, exports	1%	1¼%
	29	Other (distribution, imports)	1½%	2%

	Monthly interest (%)			
December 1, 1966 for loans to private borrowers; January 1, 1967 for loans to government enterprises & cooperatives	6	Food production		
	7	Exports and production of export products Clothing production Transportation Other production		
	9	Other sectors, especially distribution of the nine basic commodities, domestic production		
February 1, 1967	6	Group IA: a) production & distribution of 9 basic commodities, including production & distribution of 1) food industries (rice mills, sugar factories, salt and baking oil factories) and 2) clothing industry (spinning, weaving, etc.)		
		b) agriculture, animal husbandry		
		c) production of export goods		
		d) exports		
		e) production & distribution of pharmaceuticals		
		f) transport industries, distribution of spare parts		
		g) maritime industry		
	7	Group IB: a) clothing and food industries not in group IA		
		b) paper industry		
		c) handicraft industries		
		d) mining		
		e) other production		
	9	Group II: Trading and services not in Groups IA or IB		
April 16, 1967	4	Group IA, as above		
	5	Group IB, as above		
	7	Group II, as above		
July 1, 1967	3	Groups IA and IB as above		
	4	Group II, as above		
	5	Group III: Activities not included in categories I and II, but excluding credits for imports		

State Commercial Bank Lending Rates, 1965-68 (continued)

Effective from:	Monthly interest (%)	Economic Sectors
September 19, 1968	3	Production of food and textiles
	4	Exports and certain industries, including
		1) medicines and pharmaceuticals
		2) transportation vehicles
		3) transportation companies
		4) paper
		5) handicrafts
		6) mining
		7) building materials
	5	Other industries
	7	Other sectors

(1) Commissions still exist, but are on a different basis. See section on short-term credit.

3% per month category, the maximum commission is 1%; for loans at 4% or 5% per month, the maximum commission is 2%. Sometimes additional "fees" must be paid in order to get a loan, but such payoffs are growing less common.

Lending rates were increased in September 1968 when deposit rates were sharply hiked in an effort to attract deposits. Deposits rates are 1.5% per month for deposits of less than three months, 4% per month for three months, 5% per month for six months, and 6% per month for deposits of one year.

The state banks normally account for 80-90% of total bank credit outstanding. In the first quarter of 1968, of a total of Rp37 billion of credit outstanding, the state banks accounted for Rp32 billion (Rp17 billion to the government sector and Rp15 billion to the private sector). Of the Rp37 billion total, Rp18 billion were credits for production, Rp7 billion for exports. Total outstanding bank credits at the end of June 1968 amounted to Rp58.5 billion, about 90% of it coming from state banks. The government sector received Rp33 billion, or 56% of the total, largely through credits to state-owned enterprises and Rp16 billion for rice procurement. The private sector received Rp26 billion (44%). Of the total, Rp23 billion in credits was granted for production (including Rp5.2 billion for sugar, Rp0.7 billion for estates, Rp2.2 billion for agriculture, and Rp3.3 for fertilizers), and Rp8.9 went to finance exports.

The Private Banks

In May 1968 there were 123 private banks in Indonesia with 145 additional branches; Djakarta was the headquarters of 54 private banks that had 25 additional branches. Most of the private banks are commercial banks, while about a dozen are savings banks. Sometimes a private bank forms the nucleus of a group of trading companies, and most of its credit goes to them. Most private bank lending is for short-term trade credits or working capital loans (with import credits prohibited; however, some loans sought for working capital are actually used to finance imports). Six months is the longest term, and most lending is for three. The private banks pay 5% per month at the least, and generally 6-8% per month on three-month deposits; their interest charges on loans consequently start at 7-8% per month, and are often higher.

Foreign Banks

By October 1968, eight foreign banks — American Express, Bank of America, Chase Manhattan, and First National City Bank, all of the US; the Chartered Bank and the Hongkong and Shanghai Banking Corporation, both British; the Bangkok Bank; and the Bank of Tokyo — had opened branches in Djakarta. Algemene Bank Nederland was planning to open a branch within a few months, and the Deutsche Asiatische Bank, and

Dresdner Bank were considering doing the same. Pierson, Heldring, & Pierson of the Netherlands had already established a representative office, and several other Dutch banks were planning to. Nederlandse Overzee Bank had a representative in Djakarta, and four banks — Amsterdam Rotterdam Bank NV, Deutsche Bank, Barclays Bank, and Societe Generale — were establishing one joint representative there.

The regulations on foreign commercial bank branches stipulate that, for the present, they may be established only in Djakarta. They may not accept savings deposits, but may receive time deposits. Their loans, like those of other commercial banks, may be only for one year or less; longer term loans are allowed only with special permission from the central bank. In practice, loans are generally for no more than three months, and for six at the outside. Collateral is often fixed assets, inventory, export stocks, deposits or other security abroad, or, in the case of a joint venture, a guarantee from the foreign partner. Several foreign banks were considering providing warehouse financing.

Foreign banks generally follow the fixed interest rates of the state banks (3-7% per month, depending on the economic sector) but some charge one or two percentage points more. On dollar loans, the rates would range between 7.5% and 12% per year, but would generally be at least 2% above the rates prevailing in the US and Europe. In the fall of 1968, however, it was unclear whether the foreign banks would be permitted to lend foreign currencies.

Foreign Exchange Banks

The state commercial banks, the foreign banks, and three private banks are licensed as foreign exchange banks. The private banks are P.T. Bank Dagang Nasional Indonesia (headquartered in Medan, with 10 branches), P.T. Bank Persatuan Dagang Indonesia (in Djakarta with three branches), and Bank Umum Nasional P.T. (in Djakarta with 10 branches).

Medium and Long-Term Credit

At present, medium and long-term credit is almost nonexistent in Indonesia. Only development banks may grant credits of over one year, and under present inflationary conditions, even development bank loans are often for one year or less. There are, however, several potential sources of longer term funds.

The main source is the state-owned BAPINDO (Bank Pembangunan Indonesia, or Development Bank of Indonesia). It was originally established by the Government in 1951 as Bank Industri Negara (BIN) to operate as an investment bank for the private sector. In 1960, it was merged into the newly created BAPINDO, and its activities were limited to the Government sector. In 1961, the shares in private enterprises acquired by BIN were transferred to government ministries — thus creating some 50 enterprises of which the state owned all or a majority of shares. By 1967, with no development funds available, BAPINDO was authorized to extend short-term loans to state-owned and private industries; but by 1968, efforts were under way to make it a true development bank.

BAPINDO, now 100% government-financed, is capitalized at Rp110 million, of which Rp60 million has been paid in. In 1968 the Government granted it a no-interest loan of Rp7 billion, to be used to finance government projects and enterprises. As soon as a law on BAPINDO is passed, the institution's capital is to be increased to Rp20 billion. Under the plan, 40% of the voting shares (two out of a total of five, each worth Rp200 million) would be offered to private, including foreign, investors. This Rp1 billion would be paid up in 1970. Non-voting shares (totalling Rp19 billion) could be in any proportion of government:private, and would be paid up at the rate of Rp2 billion annually.

Talks have been held with the International Finance Corporation, the IBRD, and West Germany's Kreditanstalt fuer Wiederaufbau, and BAPINDO is hoping for investments from foreign banks. BAPINDO is likely to take equity in state-owned enterprises, and may make equity investments in private firms, in addition to normal medium and long-term financing.

BAPINDO loans in 1968 have been for working capital or rehabilitation. Working capital loans are generally one-year credits, and interest is 3% per month. Rehabilitation loans are for a maximum of three years, at 1.25% per month. With inflation of 3-5% per month, these loans are basically a subsidy. Loans to private enterprise are generally limited to three years, but loans to the Government may extend to five or ten years. All industries are eligible for BAPINDO loans, with priority going to industries important in the new five-year plan.

BAPINDO credits in 1967 and the first half of 1968 totaled Rp2.34 billion, of which Rp1.51 billion went to private enterprise. Of the private sector loans, Rp114 million went to food production, Rp265 million to the textile industry, Rp176 million to transportation, and Rp956 million to various industries including soap, rubber, and furniture factories, and construction.

In mid-1968, BAPINDO extended a one-year, 3% per month, working capital loan to Philips-Ralin, the joint venture in electrical and electronic goods production between Philips NV and the state-owned Ralin Electronics. Another 3% per month loan went to PT Air, a small private Indonesian steel mill, for importing pig-iron from Australia. Loans to the government sector were mainly to finance retarded projects; these included companies producing cement, paper, tires, and soda; spinning mills; a shipyard; and a coal mine. The credits were for five to ten years with a two to three-year grace period and interest of 15% annually.

Indover (N.V. De Indonesische Overzeese Bank) —an Amsterdam affiliate of Indonesia's central bank—and the Nederland Overzeese Financieringsmaatschappij (NOF) have proposed a joint venture development bank for Indonesia in Amsterdam. The proposed Ontwikkelingsbank voor Indonesia (OBI) would be formed to attract European capital to finance capital goods for industry in Indonesia. BAPINDO would act as agent in Djakarta. A private Indonesian firm granted a loan would receive the rupiah component from BAPINDO and the foreign exchange component from the OBI. In addition, BAPINDO would have access to cash loans from the OBI to be converted into rupiahs if necessary.

Regional Development Banks

BAPINDO has branches in the provinces, but in addition, there is one provincial development bank in each province. Many of them are now in extremely poor condition, but a few (such as those in West Java and South Sulawesi) have possibilities of becoming sources of medium and long-term finance within a few years. Some of their funds

come from the budget through the Department of Internal Affairs, and some from deposits (which they can more easily attract, since the inflation rate is lower outside the major cities). Most provincial development bank lending has been for three or six months.

Other sources of medium or long-term funds are few. The prospects of US Cooley funds becoming available are quite slim, and if any do become available the amounts will be small, and will probably go to small investments. There are several insurance companies, but they are not now a source of finance, and unlikely to be for some years. There is one private development bank, the Bank Pembangunan Swasta, but because of government controls and inflation, it has not been active. There is no stock or bond financing and none is likely to develop in the near future.

The DICS-Rupiah Scheme

A source of investment funds that has been important for some foreign companies is the Debt Investment Conversion Scheme (DICS). Under this plan, announced by the Government in May 1967, foreign exchange debt claims against Indonesia from private creditors not guaranteed by a foreign government could be settled by conversion of the debt into DICS-Rupiahs to be used for investments in Indonesia. A company with a debt claim against Indonesia informs the central bank of its desire to convert the claim to DICS-Rupiahs, then either uses the DICS-Rupiahs itself as a part of an investment in the country, or sells the DICS-Rupiahs to another investor in Indonesia. Conversion of such claims is at the BE rate.

DICS-Rupiahs are treated as if they were foreign capital investment, and carry all the rights of profit transfer and other privileges under the Foreign Capital Investment Law. For the creditor, the scheme allows repayment of his claim (which, given Indonesia's heavy foreign debt, would not have been possible for years), though in rupiahs or (if he sells the DICS-Rupiahs to another foreign investor) at something less than the full value of the claim. The scheme is attractive to new foreign investors because they can buy DICS-Rupiahs from a creditor at a 30-40% discount.

Under the original regulations, DICS-Rupiahs could be used 1) for investing in a new or existing enterprise in Indonesia, 2) as working capital for an investment, and 3) by converting the DICS-Rupiahs into BE or DP foreign exchange, for imports of equipment and raw materials for an investment in Indonesia. Subsequent regulations (in July and September of 1968) have put some limitations on the use of DICS-Rupiahs, however. DICS-Rupiahs may now be used for imports (3, above) only by an original creditor or its affiliate. In the case of a joint venture between an original creditor (or its affiliate) and a local partner, DICS-Rupiahs may be used for imports only up to the amount of the foreign partner's equity. Companies that buy DICS-Rupiahs, but who are not original owners, may use them only for local expenses. DICS-Rupiahs owned by Indonesian nationals may now be used only for investments in joint ventures that fall under the Foreign Investment Law, and may be used for importing only if the Indonesian national is the original owner of the DICS-Rupiahs. There are also certain limita-

tions on the use of BE bought with DICS-Rupiahs (BE ex-DICS-Rupiahs). The 1968 regulations also stipulate that the central bank may allow conversion into DICS-Rupiahs in stages, or restrict the amount to be converted if the monetary situation warrants.

A total of some $60 million worth of DICS-Rupiahs could become available. Of this amount, an estimated $16.8 million had been converted into DICS-Rupiahs by the end of the third quarter of 1968. Most of the debt claims were from one-year deferred credits that were to fall due in 1967. By 1969 or 1970 all such claims should have fallen due, and much of the DICS-Rupiahs created will probably have been used. Some 20% of foreign investors have used DICS-Rupiahs. Freeport Sulphur has used small amounts, and such companies as ITT, Philips NV, Van Swaay, Toyo Menka, Siemens, and Pfizer have used DICS-Rupiahs or are considering using the scheme.

VI—Labor

INDONESIA HAS A GREAT overabundance of labor, both in its cities and in rural areas. The active labor force, comprising some 36% of the population, was estimated at 42 million in 1968. Some 28 million of these are male. The Department of Manpower estimates that the labor force is increasing by 1.2-1.3 million annually, and will total about 44.5 million in 1970. And at present, there are no signs that the growth in the labor force will slow down. Not only is the population growing by around 2.8% per year, but in addition, the 1961 census showed a striking increase in the 5-9-year age group and in younger groups; even if a family-planning program were undertaken on a massive scale, the effects would not be felt for several years. This all means that labor will probably be in oversupply for years to come.

According to the 1961 census, 71.9% of the labor force was engaged in agriculture, 0.3% in mining, 5.75% in industry, 1% in construction, 6.7% in trade, banking, and insurance, 2.1% in communications and transport, 9.5% in services (including government officials), 0.3% in gas and water, and 1.5% in other sectors. From 1930 to 1960, only 0.5% of the population shifted out of the agricultural sector, while the percentage of the labor force employed in industry dropped from 11.5% and in mining from 0.5%. These trends should reverse in the next decade or so, however, if the Five-Year Plan results in increased produc-tivity in agriculture, and as investment in forestry, mining, and manufacturing increases.

Much of the labor supply is unskilled, but there are also skilled workers and even highly educated and trained workers (engineers, for example) who are unemployed or underemployed. Total unemployment is estimated at 2.5-3.5 million, mainly in the cities, and rural underemployment is put at 12 to 15 million. Naturally enough, one of the goals of the Soeharto Government is to alleviate the unemployment problem—for political, economic, and social reasons.

The problem is aggravated by the distribution of the population. The great majority of the labor force—and of the unemployed—is in Java and Madura, and there are sometimes manpower shortages in the outer islands. Yet transmigration schemes have so far had very little effect.

The basic education system, although inadequate, offers some potential for improving the labor force. Overall, about 47% of the population is literate, but among the younger strata, the figure is much higher. Of males in the 10-19 age group, over 76% can read and write; and in the 20-34 group, more than 60%. But as in many less developed countries, the value system of the society favors white collar jobs to manual labor. As a result, vocational education—crucial to the development of the economy—has been neglected, and there is considerable "intellectual unemployment." From 1960 to 1967, the number of pupils in elementary schools went up by 50% to about 13 million. Yet in junior and senior technical high schools the number of pupils decreased by 35% from 1964 to 160,000 in 1967, and in commercial schools, by 10% to 101,000. In 1967, about 9,000 university graduates came into the labor force, and the figure was expected to double in 1968. Slightly over half are in nontechnical and nonteaching fields. To try to remedy the shortage of skilled and trained workers, the major emphasis on education under the Five-Year Plan will be on increasing vocational training.

The Department of Manpower has made some progress in this field on its own. It maintains vocational training centers for commercial administration, woodworking, construction, metal trades, welding and diesel repair, radio/TV, horticulture, and auto mechanics. But these programs train only 1-2,000 workers annually.

Indonesianization

As a part of the policy of using and developing Indonesian manpower, the Government strongly encourages Indonesianization of personnel by foreign investors. The Foreign Capital Investment Law provides that foreign-owned enterprises must use Indonesian workers in all types of jobs if and when qualified Indonesians are available. But the policy is not a rigid one. The Government recognizes that local personnel are often not qualified for technical and managerial positions, and knows that the country needs the technical and managerial expertise that foreign investors can bring. Consequently no specific rules have been set for Indonesianization. Some ministries have issued guidelines as to what percentage of a firm's employees should be Indonesian within a specified period (see Chapter 4), however, and investors are expected to indicate some plan for Indonesianization in their investment applications.

New investors naturally begin with a higher percentage of expatriates, but many of the returned investors already have very few non-Indonesians. Unilever, for example, had only seven expatriates in 1968, out of a total managerial staff of 120, and a total work force of 3,300. The ratio of expatriates to local employees at British-American Tobacco is still lower.

Many companies find that Indonesian nationals are good workers—pleasant and eager, and as capable as Europeans after training. They also find, though, that Indonesians are better suited to work as technicians, rather than as sales or trading personnel—fields dominated by the ethnic Chinese. Other firms have apparently been less fortunate; they find that the culture and the society have not taught most Indonesians to be industrious, and that many do not make the most of the training they receive.

Some foreign companies in Indonesia prefer to have ethnic Chinese (but citizens of Indonesia) on their staff. All six of the salesmen for one US pharmaceutical company are Chinese, and the local manager says he would not hire anyone else. But other foreign companies hesitate to hire any more Chinese; because of anti-Chinese discrimination (and in some cases, because of higher costs of educating their children since the Chinese schools were closed), many Chinese finally give up and emigrate to Singapore, Hong Kong, or Taiwan. One such company recently lost five Chinese line managers; and the Chinese top sales engineer for a US business equipment company—after many years of intensive training—arranged a transfer to the Singapore branch "to give his family a more secure future."

The Law also requires that foreign investors organize regular and systematic training and educational programs, either in Indonesia or abroad, to train their employees, in order that expatriates can eventually be replaced. The legal requirement was probably unnecessary, both because so many international firms provide training as a matter of policy, and because most of the new investors in Indonesia have found training absolutely essential. Even recruits with past experience in the same field are often not trained to the standards of foreign investors. Most companies provide on-the-job training in Indonesia, and some have sent Indonesians to company installations in the Philippines, Australia, Europe, or the US for training. A graduate-level Management Training Institute was started in Djakarta in early 1968, providing a two-year curriculum for a limited number of students with university degrees and preferably some business experience. Within two years, the Institute intends to provide special "contract training" courses on request from foreign investors, and to provide some consultancy services.

Recruiting

The Department of Manpower maintains about 100 employment offices throughout the country where jobseekers and employers seeking workers may register. Most of the registrants seeking work are unskilled and unexperienced, but most have at least elementary school education, and some have high school training. Registers (incomplete) of engineers and other technicians are available at the Department of Manpower. But most recruiting is done by advertisements in newspapers or by word-of-mouth. A single advertisement for a secretarial post is likely to bring 50 or more applicants, many of them not at the level of competence sought. In such cases, where only one or a few employees are needed, it can be more effective to ask present employees (or employees of other companies) if they have qualified friends.

Recruiting manual labor in the outer islands can be a problem, and sometimes workers must be brought from Java for jobs in these areas.

Trade Unions

Some 40% of Indonesia's labor force is unionized. Most unions are industrial unions affiliated with national trade union federations. They seem to operate, however, more like fragmented company unions. In any one major plant (say, company X) there will be at least three or four unions, each including various types of workers, and each known as the "company X" section of one of the federations. For purposes of collective bargaining, each of the unions in the company appoints a representative, and the several representatives bargain with management as if, generally, they represented one union.

The trade union movement has also been fragmented on political lines, and in recent years some of the federations have become mere appendages of political parties. In addition, they are poorly financed and not strongly organized. Some union federation leaders, however, are endeavoring to reduce the emphasis on politics and ideology, and make the unions into more effective forces working for higher wages, training, and welfare of workers. Since the communist party was banned in 1966 (and with it, SOBSI, the communist union federation that in 1964 had 26% of the unionized labor force), the major source of militancy and strike-making in the labor movement has gone. Strikes are not now a problem and do not appear to be a potential danger for the next few years. However, when investors have regained property

TABLE 1.

Indonesia's Labor Union Federations

Federation	Membership, 1967	% of Total Unionized Workers
1. Gasbiindo (Islamic)	3,078,119	17
2. KBM (affiliated with PNI)	2,800,000	15
3. Sarbumusi (Islamic, affiliated with NU)	2,500,000	14
4. IKM	2,000,000	12
5. KBKI	1,259,205	7
6. KBIM	1,200,000	7
7. Kubu Pantjasila	1,200,000	7
8. SOB Pantjasila (Christian)	1,105,605	6
9. Porbisi	1,030,000	6
10. Kong Karbu SOKSI	893,093	4
11. Kespekri (Catholic)	512,045	3
12. Gobsi Indonesia	254,446	0.5
13. KBSI	194,000	0.5
14. SOBRI (affiliated with Murba Party)	125,000	0.5
15. Gerbumi	50,000	0.5

seized under the Soekarno regime, the Government has stressed the importance of their maintaining harmonious relations with their work forces. This was clearly considered a sensitive matter, at least in some regions and some plants and plantations. The reason is probably that the Government was concerned over the attitude to foreign investors among some sections of the labor force, who had been subjected to years of antiforeign and anticapitalist propaganda during the Soekarno period. In practice, however, most workers were apparently happy to see the foreign owners return. In fact, reactions of the labor movement against policies of employers have been mostly directed against the Government itself and its state enterprises; the unions have objected strongly to mass dismissals in state-owned plants, which were necessary to put faltering enterprises back on their feet, and in some cases the unions seem to have won.

Collective bargaining is the major method of determining wages, fringe benefits, and working conditions. Collective labor agreements are negotiated to cover a maximum of two years, with a possible extension of not more than one year.

Settling Disputes

In case of labor disputes, a system of compulsory arbitration is applied. The parties must first call in a government mediator, and if the case can still not be settled, it is submitted to a tripartite Regional Labor Court (P4D). This Court's decision may be appealed to the tripartite Central Labor Court (P4P), whose decision is binding unless the

---

TABLE 2.

Minimum Monthly Wages in Indonesian Industries, June 1967 [1]

(for a laborer with wife and 2 children)

Sector/Firm/Industry	Wages in Cash	in Kind
1. Estates (Java)	Rp 90	Rp 528
(Sumatra)	90	1,028
2. Mining (Stanvac)	1,062	2,099
(Caltex)	3,408	2,121
3. B.A.T. (cigarette industry)	1,743	163
4. Unilever	1,347	1,282
5. Can factory "Indonesia"	975	300
6. Daha Motor (Fiat)	1,105	591
7. "Sriwidjaja" fertilizer plant (Palembang)	422	2,384
8. "Gunung Sahari" printing plant	222	225
9. ASRI contractors (for buildings)	750	—
10. PN Hutama Karya (state owned building contractors)	440	567
11. PT Ampera (electrical engineers)	1,238	—
12. BNI Unit I (Central Bank)	2,128	670
13. Bank Parniagaan Indonesia (private bank)	1,072	828
14. Toko Sinar Matahari (private department store)	711	—
15. Garuda Indonesian Airways	651	1,050
16. Hotel Indonesia	1,178	748
17. Hotel Duta Indonesia	295	1,040
18. Government official	213	450

Source: Directorate of Supply and Employment of Labor (Department of Manpower)
(1) These are actual minimums, as there is no legal minimum wage. Wages or allowances have risen since June 1967 with increases in the cost of living.

Minister of Manpower considers it contrary to the public interest. (The Minister has never annulled a decision of the Court, however.) The Central Labor Court also has the right to settle an important labor dispute itself, rather than leaving it to a government mediator or the regional court. It functions somewhat as a general labor relations board, and labor contracts in some industries must be approved by it to be binding. Voluntary arbitration is possible if the parties agree to submit the case to an independent arbitrator or board of arbitration. The arbitrator's award must then be approved by the Central Labor Court.

Working Hours

The Labor Law of 1948 provides for a 40-hour workweek, with a maximum of seven hours a day. After four hours of work, there must be a break of at least 30 minutes. Plants generally work - on a 7 a.m. to 2:30 p.m. schedule Monday through Thursday, close at 11:30 or 12 on Friday (the Moslem religious day), and sometimes close an hour or two early on Saturday. Shift work is allowed. Offices generally open at 7:30 or 8 a.m. Most foreign investors would prefer longer working hours Monday through Thursday and a two-day weekend, but because local companies generally do not want to provide lunches and because many workers have second jobs, the working hours are difficult to change. More serious is the 40-hour workweek — a luxury few developing countries feel they can afford. By law, overtime must be paid at a minimum of 150% of the normal hourly wage.

Wages and Fringe Benefits

The high rate of inflation in recent years has led to widespread payment of wages in kind (rice and other essential goods) and to the growth of fringe benefits. The variation in the composition of wages (money plus payment in kind) is very wide. Overall, wages are extremely low, but there are wide differences among industries and among plants in the same industry. There is no minimum wage (but for minimums paid in various enterprises in mid-1967, see Table 2). The Department of Manpower view is that wages should be paid according to the work. It prefers that wages not be paid all in money, but that they be partly payment in kind. The tax system, too, is set up

to encourage payment in kind and plenty of fringe benefits (see Chapter 7).

The Manpower Department suggests that basic wages (in money and kind) may be fixed, but that extra allowances should be flexible to adjust to rises in the cost of living. In general, the Ministry is only concerned that the total take-home pay should meet the minimum physical needs of the employee. While there are no actual wage-reporting requirements for companies, the Ministry tries to maintain reasonable minimums by making recommendations to employers. The Ministry has stated that a minimum wage equal to US$35-40 a month would be considered fair, but these figures are far above the standard wage rates paid, even by generous employers. Wages are almost always paid net, with the employer paying the employee's taxes.

Fringe benefits can add up to more than 100% of base wages. The only fringes stipulated by law are vacations (12 working days annually), national holidays, sick leave, maternity leave with one and a half months' pay, and severance pay. There is also a Workman's Compensation Act providing for compensation to the worker if he has an accident while on the job, and to his family if he should die. Retirement is generally at age 55, and an employee may ask for a pension after 30 years of service.

Other fringes are decided through collective bargaining. They normally include family and cost-of-living allowances, free medical (and sometimes dental) care for the worker and his family, extra rice allowances for the worker's family (in addition to the ration that the worker receives as a part of his base wage), housing and transportation (or allowances in lieu thereof), and work clothes. Some firms grant long leave of at least 45 to 60 days every few years, and firms usually pay annual bonuses ranging from one to three months' base wages. Top personnel are often provided with housing and company cars. Some firms have pension schemes, many of them contributory, but inflation seriously hinders an effective pension system. One US firm with a noncontributory scheme gives 40% of the employee's last wage as a pension.

The wage system, including the pattern of allowances and subsidies, used by one foreign company in Indonesia is shown in Table 3.

TABLE 3

Wage System Used by a Foreign Manufacturing Firm
September 1968

Allowances:

- wife — 5% of base wage (fixed by government)
- children — 2% of base wage, per child, up to six children (fixed by government)
- cost of living — 60% x (base wage + wife allowance + children allowance) (fixed by government)
- enterprise allowance — 40% of base wage
- housing allowance — 15% of base wage (only when company does not provide housing; otherwise the laborer stays in company without charge).

			Married with				
		Single/	1	2	3	4	5
Payments in kind (monthly):	**Unit**	**Married**	**child**	**children**	**children**	**children**	**children**
Rice	kg	35	50	60	70	80	90
Sugar	kg	2½	3	3½	4	4½	5
Cooking oil	kg	1	1	2	2	3	3
Flour	kg	1	1	2	2	3	3
Margarine	kg	2	2	2	2	4	4
Laundry soap	bars	10	10	10	10	10	10
Toilet soap	bars	3	3	3	3	3	3
Cigarettes	pkgs	10	10	10	10	10	10
Kerosene	ltrs	60	60	60	60	60	60
Milk powder	lbs	1	2	3	4	5	6
Textiles (quarterly)	mtrs	6/9	12	12	12	12	12

Wages in cash:

Salary group	A	B	C	D	E
Starting base pay	2,168	2,643	3,228	3,954	5,092
Base pay after 1st year	2,234	2,733	3,343	4,119	5,092
Base pay after 2nd year	2,300	2,800	3,435	4,283	5,596
Base pay after 3rd year	2,366	2,890	3,527	4,448	5,884
Base pay after 4th year	2,432	2,958	3,642	4,612	6,172

Under the system in use by another foreign company, free goods and services — rice, meals, transport, company products, etc. — add 90% to the base wages (including overtime) of its daily paid workers. The average before-tax income of these unskilled workers amounts to Rp4,000-5,000 monthly; their total pay, with fringes, is Rp9,000-9,500 a month. For weekly paid workers (semi-skilled and skilled — e.g., drivers, supervisors) whose incomes are higher, the relative value of free goods is lower. For monthly paid workers (mainly clerical staff) free goods and services add about 50% to the base wage. The company provides houses for 80 of its top staff, and 150 cars with 182 drivers.

A foreign firm with a smaller, mainly sales, operation has the following wage system: the chief clerk and office manager earns Rp30,000 monthly (net), a technician-salesman Rp20,000, a technican Rp30,000, an accountant Rp20,000, an experienced typist who has been with the company for many years Rp16,000, a fairly new junior salesman Rp14,000, a postal clerk Rp9,000, and a typist-secretary Rp35,000, plus 40 kilos of rice per month for each of them. Drivers earn Rp6,500 monthly, plus 300 grams of rice per person per day for each member of the family. The two key staff members also earn $3,000-4,000 (gross, on which the company pays the tax) per year, which is converted at the DP rate and remitted directly to a bank account abroad. Four staff members get free housing, including electricity and water, cars and drivers, and periodical trips abroad for training. In short, they are regarded as expatriates. For the other employees, the company provides transport and two weeks' leave per year and a long leave of three months every four or five years (plus passage if their home is elsewhere). Because of inflation, the firm does not accumulate pension funds, but on retirement an employee is paid one or one and a half months' pay for each year of service with the company.

Many foreign investors pay higher money wages to try to avoid payment in kind completely and to minimize major fringe benefits such as housing and transportation, in order to do away with the administrative time and trouble involved. Often the cost to the employer of providing these items is much greater than the amount that such items are considered (e.g., for tax purposes) to have added to the employee's wage. A car, for example, is considered to add only some Rp2,000-2,500 monthly to a salary. And one firm reported that the textiles and some other items used as payment in kind actually had to be imported; the workers would not accept some locally made goods, and the company could not find local producers who would guarantee quality control and contract to provide goods of high standard.

Under Indonesia's high inflation, wages have to be reviewed several times a year. Most foreign companies do not automatically increase wages with a rise in the cost-of-living index, but use the index as a trend indicator. One firm negotiates with its unions on wage increases whenever the cost-of-living has gone up by 15% or 20%. If there is a sudden price jump, the company pays workers an extra lump-sum bonus to allow time for negotiations. This company raised wages in mid-1967, and in January, April, and July 1968. Frequently the basic wage itself is left the same, but cost of living or other allowances are increased.

How fast rupiah wages rise in the future and how long payment in kind will continue to be widespread both depend on the Government's success in tackling inflation. But since rupiah wage increases lag behind price increases, real wages are unlikely to rise significantly for some time. For the forseeable future, Indonesian wage rates will remain considerably below those in most other Asian countries.

Dismissal

One of the most serious difficulties facing both government agencies and private businesses that have been operating in Indonesia over the past few years is overstaffing. Perhaps the most outstanding case of an outsized workforce is the government bureaucracy itself — where overstaffing has encouraged inefficiency and red tape, and where the necessarily low salaries have encouraged moonlighting and corruption. State enterprises, and the foreign companies that were nationalized or "controlled" by the Soekarno regime, also find themselves with vastly inflated labor forces. In order not to aggravate the unemployment problem, dismissals are being avoided or discouraged until such time as employment opportunities increase. The returned foreign investors generally had to agree not to dismiss any workers for the time being. Of course, a new foreign investor does not face the same overstaffing problem, but similarly strict rules apply to dismissals for disciplinary reasons. In some cases, dismissals for stealing have been brought to the arbitration board and were rejected.

There is some chance that as the economic situation improves, regulations on dismissals will be eased, but in late 1968 there were few indications of an early relaxation. In September 1968, PN Gaja Motors, a state company, dismissed 1,300 employees, and under a Presidential instruction on the reorganization of state enterprises, the company was to be liquidated. But several weeks later, after union objections, it was unclear whether the decision would stand. The same month, Garuda, the Indonesian national airline, dismissed several thousand workers, ostensibly because they had been involved in the attempted communist coup in 1965 — but probably also because rationalization of the labor force was essential for the company to operate effectively. Objections again resulted, and again, it appeared that some moves would be made to reinstate at least some of the dismissed workers.

To the returned foreign owners of plants, redundant labor is often the major problem. Several firms reported that a third or more of their work forces were unnecessary. By late 1968, some firms felt they would be able to absorb most of the excess labor within a reasonable time, as production climbed toward capacity, and as facilities were expanded. Others had been able (with considerable difficulty) to dismiss some workers. Stanvac came to an agreement with its unions on a termination package; each worker could opt to terminate his employment and take a lump-sum payment. Over 2,000 employees left, but each person who opted for the termination package had to appear before the Regional Labor Court and have his case approved individually. When Union Carbide's company was returned in May 1968, there were still 300 people on the payroll, even though the plant had run out of money and materials and had closed down in early 1966. Union Carbide made a separation agreement with the employees costing $50,000. Each employee received one month's salary for each of the first four years served with the company, and one month's salary for each additional five years. Union Carbide sold the company's automobiles to get cash for the payments. The settlement accomplished more than just stopping the pay-for-no-work, however; the company refused to pay until the occupants of the company-owned houses agreed to relinquish them. In ironic contrast to obstacles to dismissals are "forced" dismissals. Workers are still being screened regarding their political affiliations prior to the September 1965 coup attempt, and from time to time the Government arrests persons for alleged involvement in the coup. This is, of course, a political situation toward which foreign investors normally remain strictly neutral. But some foreign firms have strongly resented later being asked to re-employ "rehabilitated" workers to make good an official error.

Employing Expatriates

There are normally no difficulties in obtaining permission for employment of expatriate managers and technicians, since the Government is aware that qualified Indonesians are often not available for such positions. Law No. 3/1958 provides that the employers must obtain a written permit for each expatriate by submitting an application to the Department of Manpower's Office for Placement of Foreign Workers. In addition to the names, addresses, etc., of the employer and the expatriate for whom the application is filed, the application includes 1) a description of the occupation to be filled, 2) salary and other benefits to be paid to the expatriate, 3) the period of employment of the foreign worker (with copies of the work agreement attached), and 4) programs already under way or planned by the employer to train Indonesians for the job the expatriate would fill. Before the work permit can be granted, the expatriate must have at least a semipermanent visa.

Obtaining the work permit is the least of the problems, however. Once he is a resident, the expatriate must have a tax clearance to leave. More important, keeping him in Indonesia is costly. In addition to the 60% tax rate he is to pay on worldwide income (see Chapter 7), he must have transportation and housing. Automobiles priced at less than $2,000 may be imported, and a company car may qualify for duty-free treatment. But automobile taxes are high, and expatriates often encounter a great deal of red tape in bringing in the car.

Housing is the biggest problem for expatriates. A house suitable for an expatriate manager and his family rents for $500 to $1,000 a month — and often more — and rent is payable in dollars, usually for two or three years in advance. In addition, many houses available in Djakarta require substantial remodeling. Houses can be purchased for around $50,000 and up to whatever the market will bear.

VII—Taxation

INDONESIA'S TAX SYSTEM presents serious difficulties to the investor. Tax rates are among the highest in the world for a developing country, and because of inflation, are often higher than the rates indicate. In addition, the tax system is very confusing. It is based on old tax laws, many of them amended several times, to which new regulations covering means of collection or adjusting the tax burden to inflation have been added. On top of this there is a wide range of other taxes levied by regional and local authorities as well as by the national government.

The most serious problem is poor tax administration and extremely low tax morality. In 1967, there were only about 210,000 individual taxpayers registered out of a population of 110-120 million. Even allowing for low income levels, this is an amazingly low figure. Of these 210,000 persons, only 50,000-60,000 actually paid taxes; out of a total assessment of Rp4.5 billion, only Rp600 million, or 13% was paid.

There were some 22,000 corporate taxpayers registered, and although no figures are available, it is clear that many paid no taxes, or much lower levels of tax than they were legally required to pay. The situation has forced the Government to rely on indirect taxes rather than direct (but less collectable) taxes, and in many cases (e.g., taxes on exports) these tax production rather than con-sumption. The Government finds itself in the dilemma of recognizing that tax rates should be lower and that direct taxes should replace many of the indirect ones, but fears loss of revenue if the changeover is made before the tax administration is improved. But some steps have been taken already, and more substantial tax reform aimed at increasing revenue and encouraging production can be expected in the next year or two. The first moves will be aimed at producing greater reliance on direct taxation, and shifting the indirect tax burden from exports to imports. Direct taxes were expected to provide 33% of total tax revenues in 1968, but in 1969 the target is 41%. The collection system is being improved by a planned 10% annual increase in the number of tax collectors (there were only 8,500 in 1968), and by applying self-assessment and withholding tax systems to many sectors of the economy. By 1968, 120,000 persons were paying taxes monthly. This was double the 1967 number. For the present, new investors—foreign and domestic—may be granted tax holidays, and thus escape a major part of the tax burden for two to five years. Thereafter, a concessional tax rate may be granted for several additional years. There is a good chance that by the time the tax holidays run out, the present tax rates will have come down to more reasonable levels.

Corporate Taxes

The corporate tax rate is progressive, ranging from 20% to 60%, but under the schedule applicable for financial years ending after June 30, 1968, with the maximum rate on taxable profits of Rp1.5 million or more (converted at the BE rate in September 1968, $4,688). This effectively puts most of the income of most foreign investors in the 60% bracket. The specific tariffs are as follows:

Taxable profit in Rp	Tax payable in Rp
Up to 250,000	20%
250,000- 500,000	50,000 plus 30% on excess over 250,000
500,000- 750,000	125,000 plus 40% on excess over 500,000
750,000-1,000,000	225,000 plus 45% on excess over 750,000
1,000,000-1,250,000	337,500 plus 50% on excess over 1,000,000
1,250,000-1,500,000	462,500 plus 55% on excess over 1,250,000
1,500,000 and over	600,000 plus 60% on excess over 1,500,000

According to this schedule, on taxable income of Rp3.2 million (at the September 1968 BE rate, $10,000) a company would pay an effective rate of 50.6%. On Rp16 million ($50,000), the effective rate would be 58.125%. The income brackets to which the various rates apply (but not the rates themselves) are adjusted periodically by the Ministry of Finance to keep pace (partly, at least) with inflation, and this procedure will continue. Some foreign companies report that tax officials sometimes insist that "profits must have been higher," and charge additional tax — despite a firm's honest accounting, and despite already high taxes paid.

Taxable Income Defined

Taxable income is calculated by deducting normal business expenses. Reasonable royalties and fees paid to other companies are deductible. There are no special provisions for deduction of exchange losses. Taxes paid are normally neither deductible from taxable income nor creditable against tax payable. The tax authorities may, under the tax laws, calculate a company's taxable profit on the basis of gross turnover, but this is apparently not common. Losses may be carried forward for two years.

Indonesian companies are taxed only on Indonesian source income. Branches of foreign firms or nonresident firms with a permanent establishment in Indonesia are taxed in basically the same manner as Indonesian companies, but the capital gains rate on sales of the company's equipment does not apply.

Dividends received by a company from a domestic source are subject to 20% withholding as an advance payment of its corporation tax assessed over the financial year in which the proceeds are received. Tax is also withheld at source at a 20% rate on dividends paid to an individual, in which case it is treated as an advance payment of his personal income tax. The company paying the tax may deduct the amount due from the dividend paid, or, if it chooses to bear the tax, must calculate the dividend tax on 100/80 of the dividend paid. Dividends remitted abroad are also subject to 20% withholding at source.

There is no withholding tax, at present, on royalties, fees, or interest paid abroad.

Depreciation

With inflation on the scale Indonesia has had in recent years, depreciation is one of the most serious problems for companies. The Government recognizes the problem, but as of September 1968 had issued no overall regulations providing for revaluation of assets or other measures to protect the value of assets against future inflation. The Government has declared, however, that foreign firms may express their profit and loss accounts and balance sheets in dollars, which at least alleviates the problem somewhat. Some firms have been granted permission to use the last-in-first-out (LIFO) system for depreciation of stocks, and since no effective system for protecting the value of fixed assets had been devised, the INCO contract for nickel exploration and development provided for an eight-year tax credit. A ministerial decree regulating use of the LIFO (or some similar) system was expected by the end of 1968.

One company operating in Indonesia calculated the effects of the tax-system-plus-inflation, and some possible solutions, with striking results. If its profit in 1967, according to its own calculation methods, were taken as 100, the taxable profit under Indonesia's normal system would have been 400. Use of a dollar profit and loss account would have, in this case, reduced the taxable profit by nearly half, and if combined with a LIFO system, by more than half. The taxable profit would still have been considerably above the company's own calculation, however.

Under the present system of depreciation of fixed assets, the value of the asset is calculated on historical cost. Until the rules — expected fairly soon — come out, revaluation of assets is a matter of negotiation. (The Government is reportedly considering a system under which a premium would be added to the original acquisition value, but seems unlikely to opt for a system based on replacement value.) Fixed assets that have a life of more than one year are depreciated in equal amounts (straight-line method), in accordance with period-of-benefit schedules set out in a decree of the Ministry of Finance in 1965 (modifying a 1953 law).

Luxury automobiles may be depreciated in five to 10 years if they are used by top management personnel in connection with work. (See box.)

There is a scheme for accelerated depreciation, which allows firms engaged in agriculture, industry, mining, or transportation to depreciate assets over a four-year period, with an annual ceiling on the depreciation of 25% of the year's taxable profit. It is generally applicable only to new investments or expansions of capacity that directly increase production in one of the eligible economic sectors. Use of the scheme is at the option of the company.

There are no initial allowances or other schemes for accelerated depreciation, although the Foreign Investment Law mentions accelerated depreciation as an incentive that may be granted to new investors. Except by special negotiation — and there have apparently been no such cases — depreciation must begin the year the expenditures are made, and may not be delayed until after the tax holiday. This is partly compensated for, however, by an indefinite carryover of losses incurred during the tax holiday period. For purposes of valuing stocks, accounts kept in foreign currency can solve most of the problem, and application of the LIFO system can ease the burden. Under this system, materials consumed are considered to be the last goods purchased, while stocks are considered to be the first goods purchased. For example: a company has 100 tons of oil that cost Rp100 on January 1; it buys 100 tons of oil for Rp120 in

Normal Depreciation Schedules

	Years for depreciation
I. Expenses for equipment and exploitation:	
A. Buildings	
1. In agriculture, estates, fishery, animal husbandry, mining, industry, transportation, and other enterprises to be specified by the Ministry of Finance (excluding vacation bungalows)	
Permanent	15 - 40
Semi-permanent	10 - 15
Wooden and similar buildings	8 - 12
2. In enterprises not included in (1), excluding vacation bungalows	
Permanent	40 - 50
Semi-permanent	15 - 40
Wooden and similar buildings	10 - 15
3. Buildings for dwelling	
Permanent	50 - 75
Semi-permanent	20 - 40
Wooden and similar buildings	10 - 15
B. Nonluxury inventory, office machines.	5 - 10
C. Land transportation means, excluding luxury sedans and station wagons, including tractors, etc.	5 - 10
D. Water transportation means, including docks	10 - 15
E. Air transportation means	7 - 10
F. Luxury sedans and station wagons of taxi operators, used solely for public transportation	5 - 10
G. Exploitation over definite number of years	duration of exploitation
H. Exploitation over indefinite number of years	5 - 10
II. Expenses for equipment in (1) for:	
A. Agriculture, estates, fishery, animal husbandry	16 - 25
B. Industry, mining, and transportation	8 - 12

May, 100 tons of oil for Rp140 in September, and another 100 tons of oil at Rp160 in December. On December 31, it has 150 tons of oil in stock. In dollar terms, the value of its stock has increased by 50% (100 tons in January vs 150 tons in December). In rupiah terms, without a LIFO system, the value of its stock has increased by 130% (100 tons at Rp160, 50 tons at Rp140). But with the LIFO system, the stock value is calculated as if the December purchase had been used first, then the September purchase, and so on. The stocks remaining would therefore be worth Rp160 (100 tons at Rp100, 50 tons at Rp120), for an increase in value of 60%.

Excess Profits Tax

A "windfall" profits tax has been imposed at various intervals since 1949 to curb excess profits arising from inflation. It has mainly been applied to importers and manufacturers obtaining imported items at fixed prices, and its main purpose has been to control prices rather than obtain revenues. The end of price controls automatically canceled the tax. One type of import duty surcharges now levied have the same effect, but their purpose is to channel foreign exchange into essential imports and to raise revenue.

Capital Gains Taxes

The concept of taxing gains separately from ordinary income is recognized in Indonesia, but it is applied to corporations in only a few situations. Capital gains from the sale of a company's equipment, if the equipment has been held by the company for at least four years, is subject to a flat 10% tax. If the equipment has been in the company's possession for less than four years, it is taxed as ordinary income. There are also special rules relating to the sale of shares in a business after six months' holding. If the seller owns less than 25% of the shares, he is subject to no tax, but if he owns more than 25% the gain is taxed at 20% as liquidation tax. If the shares are sold less than six months after their acquisition, the gain is taxed as ordinary income. All other capital gains to a company are taxed at ordinary corporate tax rates, except gains on the sale of real estate under the land reform laws.

For individuals, capital gains on the sale of fixed assets held for more than 12 months are exempt from income tax if the sale price or the value of the compensation received is Rp600,000 or less. Gains from the sale of movable property are also exempt, provided the property has been held for at least six months and the sale price does not exceed Rp150,000. Property acquired through gifts or inheritance is completely exempted.

Turnover, Sales, and Excise Taxes

Excise taxes provide about 16% of government tax revenues. The main excise duties are levied on cigarettes (50%), beer (50%), alcoholic beverages (70%), petroleum products (10%), and sugar (10% — based on the cost price, and levied on sugar factories). They are levied ad valorem, but the prices used as the tax base often differ from the actual retail prices, and are subject to periodic review by the tax authorities.

Sales taxes are levied ad valorem on goods and services delivered by suppliers, and since early 1968, on imports. The producer of goods or services or the importer pays the tax. Large manufacturers pay through a self-assessment system. The taxes are based on the Sales Tax Law of 1951, but items exempted and rates applicable to various goods have been changed periodically. In April, August, and November 1967, sales taxes were abolished on some goods and lowered on others, to keep prices down on essential and semi-essential goods, encourage exports, and boost local production. Exempted items are mainly food products, some raw materials (e.g., tobacco leaves, stalks), export products, some processing materials for domestic industry (e.g., bleaching and dyeing materials), and domestically produced textiles and batik. The exemption on domestic textiles and batik was granted only in November 1967, as a measure to help bring the local textile industry out of recession. Sales taxes on imports, abolished since 1960, were finally reimposed in 1967 to remove the unfair advantage that imports previously had; factory prices of Indonesian-made goods often had to be kept lower than the landed cost (including customs duties) of competitive imports, in order to offset the local sales tax. Since the reimposition of sales tax on imports, it has been used (as in the case of textiles) to give some protection to domestic industry. When the local tire industry was faced with severe competition from low-priced imports in mid-1968, the sales tax on locally made tires was reduced from 10% to 5%, while the sales tax on imported tires was raised from 5% to 10%.

The sales tax rates range from 5-10% on essential and semi-essential goods, to 20% on less essential items, and 50% on luxuries. Under the 1967 regulations, sales taxes on such items as batteries, packing materials, construction materials, soft drinks, bicycles, agricultural tools, spare parts for transportation equipment, raw materials for the ceramics industry, and products of the rubber, paper, glass, motorized machinery, electrical equipment, and light food industries were reduced to 10%, provided the goods were domestically produced.

There is a 10% tax on certain services, including those of lawyers, notaries, accountants, brokers, contractors, architects, insurance firms, rental services, advertising agents and travel agents.

There is also a 20-30% Luxury Goods Contribution levied on goods delivered by manufacturers or importers on certain items.

Property Taxes

There is a tax on net wealth in excess of Rp2 million covering real estate, financial assets, equity in business, and such personal property as automobiles and household furnishings. The rate is 0.5% of the market value, and deductions are allowed for the cash value of all debts payable by the taxpayer. Payment is based on self-assessment, but the yield from the tax has been negligible, though efforts are being made to rectify this situation. This tax is not levied on corporations.

There is a 5% tax on net income from land. This is paid by the user, rather than the owner. As a result foreign companies (and individuals) pay this tax even though they cannot own land. For purposes of arriving at net income, the yield of the land is valued at market prices and deductions are allowed for inputs. In the case of urban land, assessment is made in the light of the location and use of the land. A recent survey in Djakarta suggested that a high-priced house on the average paid only Rp800 annually, and that the tax on business premises in active commercial areas does not exceed, on average, Rp2,500.

Revenue Stamp Tax

This tax applies to rental contracts, bond and stock sales, receipts, and other transactions. For receipts involving Rp1,000 or more there is a flat Rp1 tax, while a house rental contract requires stamps worth one mil per rupiah of the contract value, and stock and bond sales 1% of the sale value. The stamps are supposed to be provided by the buyer, but commonly the seller attaches them and counts them as a cost of the goods. However, from time to time there are shortages of the stamps, and speculators sell them on the black market at several times their face value. Without the duty stamps, the documents con-

cerned are not legal. Taxes are also levied on transfers of immovable property (e.g., real estate and houses) at the rate of 10%. A similar tax, but levied by local authorities, applies to transfers of titles to vehicles — 20% on cars less than five years old, 10% on cars more than five years old, and 10% on motorcycles. The tax reportedly applies to registration of a car in Djakarta by a person in whose name the car was already registered abroad.

Local Taxes

There is no authority for an income tax below the national level, except in Jogjakarta, but a variety of local and regional taxes are imposed. In outlying areas, illegal taxes can be a problem. One businessman recently counted 12 illegal tax collection posts on a 120 km road in Sumatra. But the central Government is trying to eliminate such taxes, and has had substantial success.

In Djakarta, in addition to the motor vehicle transfer tax mentioned above, there are entertainment taxes, a development tax of 10% on all payments in restaurants and hotels, and assorted fees for dog and liquor licenses, radios, television sets, and nonmotorized vehicles. There is an annual tax on motor vehicles levied at 1% and 2% on motorcycles and automobiles owned by Indonesian nationals, but at 3% and 7.5% for foreigners. The tax is on the value of the vehicle, which is revalued annually. In addition, there is a tax on foreigners, levied annually, of Rp1,500 for the head of the family, Rp750 for adult dependents, and Rp350 for children. An important local tax is the IREDA, or regional development contribution (called IPEDA outside urban areas). It is levied on the value of land and buildings, with the rates, ranging from 0.25-4%, depending on the acreage and location. The user of the land and buildings pays the tax.

Tax Incentives

The Foreign Investment Law exempts certain new foreign investors from the corporation tax and the dividend tax on profits paid to shareholders for a period of two to five years. The period of exemption depends on the degree of priority, the location and the size of the investment, and the rapidity with which the enterprise commences operations.

Under the Law, investors qualify for tax exemption either by investing at least $2.5 million during the first two years of the project's life or by entering into a joint venture with a local firm. The exemption is for two years from the start of production. If the enterprise either increases foreign exchange earnings for Indonesia or saves foreign exchange through import substitution, the tax holiday is for three years. In Decree No. 6 of January 27, 1967, the Government specified certain types of investment that may be granted additional years of tax holiday. One additional year of exemption is added for each of the following conditions the firm meets (with an overall limitation of five years' exemption):

• if the investment is outside Java;
• if the investment is in Java, but requires large capital or faces unusually great risks (e.g., infrastructure);
• if the investment was made in 1967 or 1968 and thus qualifies as "pioneer;"
• if the investment is in a joint venture with an Indonesian firm.

Qualifying for incentives is to some degree a matter of negotiation. Many foreign investors, or potential foreign investors, who cannot find a suitable local partner or do not want a joint venture partner, find the $2.5 million minimum for a wholly foreign-owned venture too high. When the reasons have seemed adequate, the Foreign Investment Board has made exemptions. For example, Australian-based Kiwi International, which is investing $200,000 for a boot polish plant in Djakarta, was granted a tax holiday with the stipulation that it should find a joint venture partner within two years. In addition, the Government recognizes that most local firms are not in a position to contribute substantial equity capital to a joint venture, and makes no demands regarding the equity split; in many joint ventures, the Indonesian partner's share is only 10% or 15%. Nevertheless, while the Government will continue to make some administrative exceptions to the $2.5 million minimum for wholly foreign-owned investments, no overall reduction in the minimum requirement is likely.

The tax holiday is also available on profits reinvested in the Indonesian enterprise for a period of up to five years from the time of reinvestment, or on expansions. There is some concern, however, that exempting from tax a part of a company's profits could prove extremely complicated,

and until some method of administering such exemptions is devised, the Government may well hesitate to grant this concession.

The Foreign Investment Law also provides the possibility of a reduction in the corporate tax rate for up to five years after the tax holiday. It allows indefinite carryover of losses incurred during the tax holiday, and particularly for major investments, provides a possibility of accelerated depreciation. Approved foreign investments are exempted from the capital stamp tax on the introduction of foreign investment capital.

Returned foreign investors — those whose enterprises had been put under government control — are granted three-year tax holidays on new capital brought in for rehabilitation or expansion. Banks are not eligible for tax holidays, nor are investments in certain services (e.g., airlines).

A Domestic Investment Law passed in 1968 provides tax holidays and other concessions similar to those in the Foreign Investment Law for rupiah investments.

Tax Incentives for Mining

Investments in mining — because they require high capital and technological inputs, and involve substantial risk — have been granted special tax concessions.

When Freeport Sulphur negotiated its contract for a $76.5 million investment in copper mining in West Irian, it negotiated special tax treatment. The contract provides for a three-year tax holiday, 35% tax during the following seven years, and 41.75% tax thereafter, with a proviso that in case of loss, taxes should not be less than 5% of net sales. Normally, however, mining ventures are not eligible for tax holidays. Consequently, in June 1968 the Government issued regulations granting special tax concessions to mining companies.

The basic corporate tax rates for mining depend on the nature of the mineral exploited. For the first ten years of the mining contract, tin mining firms are taxed at 40%, and firms mining nickel, cobalt, or bauxite at 37.5%. A 35% rate applies to companies mining copper, lead, zinc, iron, titanium, manganese, mercury, molybdenum, antimony, asbestos, chromite, iodine, natural asphalt, diamonds, sulphur, kaolin, and jarosite. From the eleventh year through the thirtieth year (since contracts are for 30 years' duration), the rates are 20% higher, i.e., 48%, 45% or 42%.

Depreciation schedules vary with the type of mining involved, with a maximum of 12.5% per year.

Additional tax benefits available to mining companies include:

• Exemption from dividend tax on dividends paid by mining enterprises domiciled in Indonesia.

• Exemption from corporation tax for interest and dividends received by or from bodies affiliated to mining enterprises.

• Indefinite carryover of losses incurred during the first five years of the operating period; losses incurred in later years are eligible for the normal two-year carryover provided for in the 1925 Corporation Tax Ordinance; these losses may be taken into account before losses with an indefinite carryover period.

• Deduction of certain taxes from corporate tax payable and from levies related to the authority to mine (royalties). The taxes for which such credits are given are the Regional Development Contribution (IPEDA), the foreign exchange allocation to regional authorities from export proceeds (ADO — see Chapter 9), and taxes levied by the local government.

• Classification of reasonable reserves against uninsured losses is as expenses, when used; but as long as they are not used, they constitute part of taxable profit.

• Limit on income tax paid by foreign personnel of mining enterprises: through the tenth year of the operating period, such personnel are subject to Indonesian income tax only up to the amount of tax they would pay in their country of origin.

• Additional incentives to mining enterprises that are extremely large and have an influence on regional growth and development.

The MPO and MPS Systems of Collection

Indonesia has introduced two new methods of tax collection, the MPO (calculating tax for others) and the MPS (calculating tax by oneself), and is in the process of widening their application. Both are essentially withholding systems aimed at increasing the number of taxpayers and increasing monthly payments of income, corporation, and property (wealth) taxes.

Under the MPO system, companies (or individuals) become tax collectors. It has long been customary in Indonesia for companies to calculate and pay income taxes for their employees, but under the MPO system, taxes are withheld from earnings of unaffiliated persons or companies as well. For example, a manufacturer selling to a wholesaler withholds 2% of the value of the transaction as an advance payment of the wholesaler's earnings. Banks withhold a specified percentage of an importer's letter of credit, as an advance payment on the importer's earnings. In general, the MPO system covers wholesalers, retailers, importers, exporters, and employees of companies. The MPO collector deposits taxes collected between the first and the 15th of the month by the 25th, and those collected between the 16th and the end of the month by the 10th of the following month. In theory, at least, at the end of the year, the taxpayer (or for employees, the company) calculates the actual tax due, compares this to the amount withheld during the year, and the adjustment is made.

The MPO system has so far proved fairly effective, but has drawbacks. For example, with an MPO rate of 2% (raised from 1% in September 1968) and a gross margin of 5% on sales, a wholesaler is paying 40% on his gross income. More serious is that since tax evasion has almost become a way of life (encouraged by a system of extremely high rates), wholesalers object to having the size of their business revealed by the manufacturer paying the MPO to the Government. The situation dampens good relations between manufacturer and wholesaler, and has caused some firms to obstruct the regulations. The MPS system is simply a self-assessment scheme under which individuals and companies pay taxes monthly to apply to income, property, or corporate tax. The MPO and MPS schemes replace an unwieldy system of temporary and final assessments by tax officials.

Personal Taxes

Indonesia's personal tax system can be both costly and complicated. Tax rates are extremely high at expatriate salary levels. In addition, companies normally pay net wages or salaries to employees, and are consequently faced with the administrative task of calculating the tax liability of each employee, and paying his taxes monthly. A few companies set wage scales on a gross wage basis, but in any case withholding tax on employees' income is mandatory.

Personal income tax rates are progressive, ranging from 21-60%. As in the case of corporate tax, the levels of taxable income to which the rates apply are redefined periodically to adjust for inflation, but the rates remain basically the same. In 1966 and 1967, separate rate schedules applied to laborers and managerial staff, but this distinction has been abolished. Under the regulations applicable in 1968, the income tax schedule was as follows:

Taxable Income in Rp	Tax Payable in Rp
Up to 90,000	21%
90,000 - 150,000	18,900 plus 27% of the amount in excess of 90,000
150,000 - 210,000	35,100 plus 36% of the amount in excess of 150,000
210,000 - 300,000	56,700 plus 45% of the amount in excess of 210,000
300,000 - 480,000	97,200 plus 54% of the amount in excess of 300,000
480,000 and over	194,000 plus 60% of the amount in excess of 480,000

The effect of the system is to make taxable income over Rp480,000 — about $1,500 at the BE exchange rate in September 1968 — taxable at 60%. Taxable income is calculated by deducting from gross income Rp12,600 for the taxpayer, Rp7,200 for each legal wife, and Rp3,600 for each other dependent (up to ten). The amounts of the deductions are altered periodically to compensate for inflation. Nonemployment income is supposed to be taxed as well, but since companies calculate and pay their employees' taxes monthly and calculate (and pay) any year-end adjustments, most company employees file no tax returns themselves. In addition, the system allows a person with two or more employers to escape a higher tax bracket than he would be in if his earnings were accumulated. In theory, the individual should calculate his total tax due at the end of the year and pay the difference, but this apparently happens infrequently.

Taxation of Expatriates

Foreign individuals who work in Indonesia for three months or more are considered taxable nonresidents. An absence of one month would normally break the continuity of the stay, but a shorter absence does not. A taxable nonresident is subject to tax on his Indonesian-source income.

An expatriate who intends to reside permanently in Indonesia, or who resides in Indonesia for 12 months (regardless of his intentions to remain there permanently or not) is considered a resident taxpayer, and is subject to tax on his total worldwide income. Dividends from firms domiciled outside Indonesia are exempted, however. The expatriate is eligible for a tax credit against taxes paid to a foreign government, but only at the rates at which the same income would have been taxed if earned and taxed in Indonesia.

If the salary is paid in foreign currency, the tax must be paid in foreign currency. For earnings after June 1967, the conversion rate used has been Rp94.5:$1, but this rate is adjusted periodicially to keep pace with inflation. The system works this way: for an expatriate with a wife and two children earning $10,000 per year, the $10,000 is first converted to rupiahs at the Rp94.5:$1 rate (=Rp945,000); the personal and family deductions (totaling Rp27,000); are subtracted, to get taxable income of Rp918,000. The tax totals Rp457,200 (Rp480,000 plus 60% of Rp438,000). This figure is then reconverted to dollars at the Rp94.5:$1 rate to arrive at the tax payable of $4,838, or 48.38%. A married man with two children who earned $20,000 would pay tax of $10,831, or 54.16%. One company calculated that to keep a man in Djakarta earning the equivalent of $25,000 would cost the company over $84,000. Taxes, both the basic income tax and the system of taxing fringe benefits and payment in kind, were no small part of the total.

Taxation of Fringe Benefits and Payment in Kind

Payment in kind (e.g., rice) and fringe benefits such as housing or provision of a car must be included in an employee's income and are taxed. There are complicated rules to determine the value of each item. In several cases, payment in kind or fringe benefits granted to managerial personnel are valued differently from payments or benefits for nonmanagerial employees. For managers, payment in kind is valued at the market prices of the goods. For nonmanagerial personnel, payment of rice is valued according to the market price up to a ceiling of Rp15 per kg; for the other eight basic commodities (sugar, salt, etc.) the value is calculated on the market price but must not be higher than official prices if they exist; payment

Wage Equivalents of Meals Provided						
	3 meals/day		2 meals/day		1 meal/day	
	per day	per month	per day	per month	per day	per month
employee	Rp90	Rp2,900	Rp60	Rp1,800	Rp30	Rp900
each wife	Rp45	Rp1,350	Rp30	Rp 900	Rp15	Rp450
each child	Rp30	Rp 900	Rp20	Rp 600	Rp10	Rp300

in kind of other than the nine basic commodities is based on market prices.

Meals provided by the company are valued according to the price paid, for managers; for nonmanagers, the first Rp25 per meal is not considered an addition to income. If meals exceed normal Indonesian standards, the value is fixed by local tax authorities. If meals are provided for the worker and his family, additions to his wages are calculated as shown in the box.

If the company provides housing, and the individual has the right to choose his house, the addition to his salary is calculated at 20% of his salary. For a manager, the minimum addition to salary is Rp2,000 per month; for nonmanagers Rp2,000 is the maximum that may be added to his monthly wage.

If the employee does not have the right to choose his house, the addition to salary is 10%, with a minimum addition of Rp1,000 per month for managers and a maximum of Rp500 per month for nonmanagers. If the employee is housed in a hotel, the full paid price of his lodging and

meals is added to his salary for tax purposes; if he is not a manager, the addition must not exceed the total amount that would be added for lodging and meals according to the formulas above.

The value of uniforms is not added to wages if no more than three sets are provided and if they are not usable outside working hours. Otherwise, the full price of the uniforms is considered as additional salary.

No addition for tax purposes is made to an employee's income for transportation if it is to and from work only (e.g., in company buses). Additions are calculated, however, if the company provides the employee a vehicle for his own use. Sedans of vintage 1965 or newer represent an additional salary of Rp5,000 per month (manager) or Rp2,500 per month (nonmanager). Cars dated 1960 through 1964 add Rp4,000 or Rp2,000, and cars from 1959 or older Rp3,000 and Rp1,500 (all monthly). Other four-wheeled vehicles add Rp2,000 and Rp1,000 per month, and other motor vehicles (e.g., motorcycles) add Rp1,000 and Rp500 per month.

VIII—Marketing and Distribution

DETERMINING WHAT the Indonesian market for a particular product is and what it will be—and how soon—is a challenging task. Probably no company selling in Indonesia, whether manufacturing locally or not, has a very accurate idea of the present and potential market for its products there. But a good many firms, mainly European and Japanese, have made some educated guesses and are doing profitable business. Ironically, US firms, which have the initial advantage that the brand-conscious Indonesians would probably prefer many US products if they were available, have in general made few effective efforts to get a start in the Indonesian market. The result is likely to be that when the market is clearly more important than it is now, companies that have waited will have an uphill fight to get their products accepted.

Most of the standard statistical tools for estimating a market are either nonexistent, out-of-date, or unreliable in Indonesia. The Government is placing considerable importance on improved statistics for its own planning, and the Central Bureau of Statistics is working hard to provide them. Between 1964 and 1967, practically no statistics were published. In some cases, at least, this was to avoid putting the economic decline on paper. They are now becoming available, but they must be used with great care. One generally accepted estimate is that per capita income in Indonesia is around $80 per year. Low enough to discourage many companies from making an effort to sell in Indonesia, the estimate really says very little about the market. For one thing, something closer to $50 or $60 per capita per year is probably a more realistic figure for the majority of the population, while several million people, mainly in the cities, would account for the rest, and would represent a small, but comparatively wealthy, market.

On the other hand, whether the average figure is $50 or $60 or $80 or $100, it does not realistically reflect the standard of living. Due to the fertile soil and the tropical climate, neither food nor housing are the problems one might imagine. There is some hunger, mainly in parts of Central Java, but very little starvation, and much less of both than one would find in another country with similar statistics. One of the most striking features of the market is the youthfulness of the population (see Table 1 and Appendix XI).

One can get some picture of the distribution of what wealth there is from Appendices XII and XIII, which show a percentage breakdown of the population in various regions according to their monthly expenditures, and monthly expenditure on various items by urban and rural populations in Java and outside Java. But a note of caution: these appendices, and any data similar to them, are useful only as general indications of

TABLE 1.

Population Projection of Indonesia 1961 — 1976

According to age groups
(thousands)

Age	1961	1966	1971	1976
0- 4	18,473	20,643	20,991	23,569
5- 9	8,966	17,725	19,937	20,402
10-14	15,323	15,132	17,537	19,760
15-19	6,921	8,846	14,958	17,367
20-24	8,136	6,785	8,697	14,743
25-29	7,870	7,944	6,648	8,548
30-34	7,662	7,675	7,775	6,581
35-39	6,094	7,457	7,498	7,622
40-44	4,989	5,905	7,257	7,323
45-49	3,979	4,794	5,700	7,036
50-54	3,063	3,772	4,497	5,457
55-59	2,212	2,843	3,523	4,289
60-64	1,535	1,985	2,572	3,211
65-69	998	1,297	1,704	2,229
70-74	629	776	775	1,360
75 —	117	426	394	548

Source: Population workshop, Univ. of Indonesia, May 1964, Drs. Tan Goan Tiang

relative levels of expenditure from area to area or item to item. The absolute amounts are hopelessly distorted and out of date.

A company that tries to calculate the apparent consumption of an item over the last few years (i.e., production plus imports minus exports) runs into equally bad, or even worse, statistical problems. The production figures from 1964 to 1967 are questionable, and in any case, production declines have occurred due to many factors other than declining demand (e.g., worn-out machinery, lack of spare parts, poor management). For many products, the demand clearly was not met. Neither have imports reflected demand; they were determined by licensing, foreign exchange allocations, and political favoritism. One company considering a major investment thought that the best way to estimate demand would be to assume that the situation is vaguely as it was in 1962 and project some growth rates from the 1962 data.

Several companies operating in consumer and durable goods fields have put together a picture of their market through basic field work — by talking to hundreds of small manufacturers or likely customers for the product. One US pharmaceutical company sends half a dozen salesmen out monthly with a questionnaire to ask local druggists what items are moving best. This enables the firm to pinpoint the top ten products competitive with its own. For companies producing such products as industrial chemicals or machinery, the process is simpler; the market is based largely on the scale and timetable of new investment, and the priorities and possible policy changes of the government.

Limitations on Foreign Firms

There are two major restrictions on sales and distribution operations of foreign firms. One is the rule that all importers must be Indonesian nationals. Foreign-owned companies manufacturing in Indonesia have rights to import directly, but if local manufacture is not involved, the importer must be Indonesian. The result is that a sales office's costs are slightly higher — by the amount of the indentor's fee (say 3% of the f.o.b. value of the imports) — but otherwise the company's marketing operations are not affected.

The other restriction, in a Presidential Regulation of 1959 known as PP10, bars aliens from participating in retail trade below the level of provincial towns. (The restriction is on retail trade outside the major cities of the Kabupaten, or second-level provinces, of which there are 225 in the country.) The regulation was intended to restrict alien Chinese from retail trade in rural areas, but applies to any foreign firm. The restriction does not hamper most normal marketing operations, since few if any foreign firms would extend their distribution networks beyond the wholesaler level. But as it has been interpreted it does hinder some advertising and promotion that may be important to market development. Unilever, for example, has used a travelling van that provided film showings and demonstrations in rural areas, and sold products to the public after the film showings. But PP10 was invoked to prohibit the post-demonstration selling, and Unilever found that the film van operation lost much of its effectiveness. There is a chance that objections to Unilever's demonstration-plus-selling techniques will be lifted under a nondiscrimination clause of a recent Netherlands-Indonesia agreement. But until the regulation, or at least its interpretation, is changed, companies' rights to apply their best marketing methods will be in question. (In purely economic terms, the more serious disadvantage of PP10 is that it effectively bars from rural retail trade the ethnic Chinese — many of them Indonesian citizens — who had developed the greatest expertise in the field.)

Other marketing problems emerge on a practical rather than policy level. Distribution efforts are often hindered by poor internal communications, and the lack of transport facilities slows deliveries. In addition, distribution throughout the country means that the company must cope with attitudes and actions of regional and local officials and military units, which sometimes differ considerably from policy made in Djakarta; this may involve paying illegal taxes, or taking extra precautions against equipment damage, for example. One US company, which distributes spare parts in some outlying areas, decided to discourage anyone from comandeering their new delivery trucks by denting and scraping them until they look old, but this kind of extreme solution is probably unnecessary for most firms.

Some companies that produce in Indonesia find that packaging is a problem, and have to import some of their packaging materials. Good printing and paper packaging (often with imported paper) are available in Indonesia, however, but finding the right printer and getting the arrangement going may take some time. For companies that do not manufacture in Indonesia, samples are often important to the marketing effort; but the massive red tape often causes long delays in clearing samples through customs, especially if they are to be brought in duty-free.

Distribution Patterns

Until World War II, marketing in both domestic and foreign trade was dominated by large Dutch trading enterprises. Chinese and some Arabs and Indians were the middlemen in internal distribution, and as all of them were dependent on the Dutch trading houses for credit, the major trading firms exercised considerable control of distribution. Many of the Government's regulations concerning trade since that time have been aimed at reducing the role of first the Dutch, and then the Chinese, to give Indonesian nationals the dominant place in distribution.

During the colonial period, the "big ten" Dutch commercial houses integrated into their activities estates, manufacturing, and marketing outlets, plus auxiliary services such as banks and shipping companies, and acted as sole representatives of overseas firms. They were financed through banks in the Netherlands, and had access to the international money market. Their main purpose was to collect primary products from the peasants to be marketed through the Netherlands; to do this effectively, the Dutch houses provided consumer goods, raw materials and equipment, and sometimes cash. These goods were funneled through the network of Chinese wholesale distributors and middlemen to the peasants, and exchanged, on regular collection days, for the peasants' produce. Each level of the network extended credit to the level below. The system was effective because it was well financed and well organized, and because ties of kinship strengthened the commercial relationships of the Chinese.

After independence, the Government gave special credit facilities to Indonesian nationals to help them establish themselves in the import and manufacturing sectors, and gave some national companies exclusive rights to some geographical (Hong Kong, Singapore, Japan) and industrial (textiles, flour) sectors of the import business. These national firms were called *benteng* (fortress) groups. But although some national firms that are important today got their start then, many of them suffered from lack of bank credit and experience. Foreign firms still dominated the plantation sector. Chinese middlemen were still important, and their links with Hong Kong and Singapore helped them in trade and finance. It was then that the "Ali Baba" system — where national firms act as a cover for Chinese firms — began to develop, as faltering national firms with licenses sold them to the Chinese. The Ali Baba system is still important. Recently, with Indonesian traders much weaker in relation to the strong financial and commercial links of the Chinese, its reverse has appeared; under the "Baba Ali" system, Indonesian traders do the bidding of the Chinese.

In 1957, the Dutch trading companies were taken over by the Government, and at the end of 1958, they were nationalized. The Government had already established two trading companies — Central Trading Company (CTC) in 1948, and PT Usindo in 1956 — which the Government controlled only as a shareholder. In 1959, the Government converted six of the Dutch "big ten" into state trading companies, and gave the eight state enterprises a monopoly on essential imports. In subsequent years, the Government abolished the system of vertical integration — the links with production, shipping, etc. — that had been important to the Dutch trading houses. The state trading companies were in competition with one another, handling the same goods. They were financed by Government credits, and their management became bureaucratic, rather than business-oriented.

The process of nationalization backfired in two ways. One result was a decline in the effectiveness of the state trading companies. These companies had by far the most thorough distribution networks in Indonesia when they were taken over, and probably still do. They were the agents for most overseas firms, many of which had used the Dutch trading houses before. Some companies still use the state trading firms to some degree, particularly in the outer islands, but many are switching to private distributor networks. One firm is gradually reducing the area each state company covers, and is adding private distributors to take their place (with good results, so far). Another firm refuses to sell to the state trading companies, because the buyers for these organizations frequently demand bribes; so the company sells to wholesalers who take their cut, pay the bribes, and sell to the state trading companies. This keeps everyone happy except the consumer, who pays a higher price.

The state trading companies, after several reorganizations, operate as Aneka Niaga, Aduma Niaga, Tjipta Niaga, Satya Niaga, Dirga Niaga, Kerta Niaga, Dharma Niaga, Pantja Niaga, and Pembangunan Niaga. The Soeharto Government, determined that they should operate as businesses, cut out their subsidies, and in some cases, the management has changed somewhat. Now they are to be turned into limited liability companies. The end of subsidies left several of the companies in dire financial straits, and some of them are bankrupt or nearly so. They are not all equally bad, however. A couple have managed to remain fairly effective, and with improved management, several could be viable organizations in a few years, still with the best distribution facilities in the country.

When the Dutch left, the state trading companies and privately owned national companies could not fill the gap: the result was a larger role in distribution for the Chinese minority, which today controls by far the greatest part of distribution in Indonesia. About 99% of Philips NV's 200 dealers are ethnically Chinese, and this is true of most other companies. Many companies prefer Chinese distributors, both because they have a reputation for effectiveness, and because, for many companies, the majority of their customers are Chinese as well.

Many of the Chinese traders and distributors are Indonesian citizens, and legally have the same rights as any other Indonesian national. The new Domestic Investment Law has legitimized trading and other activities by alien Chinese and other resident foreigners, but with some limitations. The Law, referring to rupiah investment, defines a national enterprise as one with at least 51% of the invested capital owned by the state or private Indonesian nationals, with a provision that the percentage should reach 75% by January 1, 1974. "Foreign" undertakings — those not complying with the 51% and 75% equity provisions, are granted limited operating permits. In the field of trade, the permits expire on December 31, 1977, and in industry on December 31, 1997.

How Companies Sell in Indonesia

For firms that do not produce in Indonesia, there are basically three methods of effective selling, in all of which the company must be willing to spend some time and money, and to adapt its methods and its products, if necessary, to the Indonesian market.

The Hotel Indonesia in Djakarta is full of company executives who squeeze in two or three days in a tightly scheduled Asian trip for a quick look at prospects for sales in Indonesia (probably with sales literature in hand, and a firm intention to see several ministers and some potential customers). Meanwhile, executives are sitting in corporate offices in many countries thinking that there must be sales opportunities in Indonesia, and wondering why, especially since their governments have granted tied-import credits to Indonesia, the orders aren't coming in. For most companies, neither approach is likely to bring much success. The more effective methods are to have a manufacturer's representative (either by sending a man to Indonesia or by contracting with someone already in Indonesia acting as representative for other firms), sign up a local distributor, or establish a sales company or distribution network.

One foreign manufacturing company has had experience with both of the first two methods. Its experience in Indonesia began early in World War II, when it sent a technical team to the country and appointed a Dutch agent to import its products. It was out of Indonesia during the Japanese occupation, but returned after the war as general merchants. In 1952, it put its sales set-up in charge of a manufacturer's representative. Until 1957, the company had 15 expatriates representing it in Djakarta, Semarang, Bandung, and Surabaja, but after 1957 only one remained. The office does no importing, but simply convinces local customers to import its products from Europe. The tools of its trade are basically a price book and a technical library, plus thorough knowledge of products (by trained local employees as well as the one expatriate) and by now, a good understanding of Indonesia. Most of its business is done in Djakarta, but it has two liaison and marketing people in Bandung, and one in Surabaja. Under this system, the office has no source of rupiah income at all, and must actually remit money from Europe to pay salaries and taxes on employees' incomes.

Several other chemical and pharmaceutical companies and equipment suppliers — mainly European — have set up similar arrangements, many of them with companies or individuals already established as representatives in Indonesia. This system is, of course, considerably less costly than that of a firm putting its own man in Indonesia, and allows a company to test the market by providing little more than the representative's fee and samples of its products.

Some persons with considerable experience in Indonesia think the day of the manufacturer's representative may be coming to an end. They feel that within a few years a regular distributor with stocks will be necessary, because now that imports are free from licensing and foreign exchange allocations, importers will be unwilling to wait the several months between the time the order is placed and when the goods arrive, and factories (which import through the importers) will want continuity of supplies. A company could export goods on consignment to Indonesia, but since these must be paid for at the DP rate, the high price can make the goods too expensive.

The possibility of a sharp rise in the DP rate makes even six-month supplier credits impractical in many cases. There are two possible solutions, though, that can ease the problems of a manufacturer's representative. The bonded warehouses now under discussion in the Government would be the best answer. In the meantime, importers sometimes ask the foreign supplier company to consign the goods to an agent in Singapore. This means that if the goods come from, say, the US, the Indonesian importer's money is tied up only for the period of shipment from Singapore to Indonesia.

How IBM Operates

Halfway between the manufacturer's representative system and the local distributor method is the establishment of a sales and service company in Indonesia, but this is, at least legally, more involved. IBM, which has operated in Indonesia since 1937, has established a limited liability company (PT) under Indonesian law. The company works as the sole agent of IBM World Trade Corporation, which maintains ownership of computers placed in Indonesia. The local company collects the monthly rentals from Indonesian customers (such as oil companies and Garuda) and remits them abroad in dollars to IBM World Trade Corp. IBM World Trade Corp pays a commission to PT IBM as an agent fee, which covers the sales company's operating expenses. PT IBM is, of course, taxed on the amount of the commissions. The agreement between IBM World Trade and its Indonesian subsidiary was approved by the Government. IBM's headquarters is in Djakarta, and all its sales and service personnel work out of Djakarta, travelling as necessary around the country. But IBM plans to open branches elsewhere. As a part of its marketing effort, in April 1968 IBM opened an education center in Djakarta, and invited its customers and prospects to attend courses (in Indonesian).

Setting up a Marketing Network

Upjohn of the US has stationed one expatriate in Indonesia to organize and supervise six local salesmen. Upjohn uses Connell Bros. of the US as an importing agent; because of the prohibition on foreign importers, Connell Bros. actually brings in the goods from Hong Kong or Singapore through an Indonesian importer, who is paid an indenture fee of 3-5% of their f.o.b. value. Upjohn finds that it is important to have an expatriate in Indonesia to teach distribution and service to the local salesmen, and to stay on top of the changes in regulations. The company has provided each salesman with a motorcycle, and finds that because this eliminates problems of traffic jams and parking, the salesmen make 30% more calls than if they used cars. In addition, of course, it saves money, and avoids the problem of items on cars being stolen.

The Unilever Network

Firms that manufacture in Indonesia, such as Unilever and Philips NV, naturally have more elaborate distribution networks. Unilever has set up ten area offices (two were added in late 1967) throughout the country. There are four in Java, three in Sumatra, two in Kalimantan, and one in Sulawesi. The area office manager orders goods from Unilever's factories, warehouses them, and sells them to a wholesaler. In some more remote areas, there are "stockists" — middlemen between the area office and the wholesaler, involved in about 5% of Unilever's trade.

Philips now has five major distribution points where goods are stocked — in Djakarta, Semarang, Medan, Bandung, and Surabaja — but plans to expand into the outer islands. Two hundred dealers are served from the five distribution centers.

Many firms selling in Indonesia use single local distributors, who have facilities for distribution at least throughout Java and Sumatra. Other companies use a number of local distributors in various areas. The arrangement is generally that the distributor earns a commission of say, 10% of the f.o.b. price of the goods sold, and often the distributor can collect his commission where he wants, in whatever currency he chooses. Many companies selling in Indonesia are convinced that companies should keep expatriate representatives in the country to work with the distributors, and to train them in marketing and service.

There are no unusual regulations governing distributor contracts. The regulations that do exist are based generally on the Commercial Code of the Netherlands, but custom is the more important guide. If a distributor contract does not specify a duration, or if the life of the contract has run out and the contract has been indefinitely extended, either party may unilaterally terminate the contract with reasonable prior notice; the notice required is generally stipulated in the original contract. If the contract is unilaterally canceled without prior notice, there may be liability for damages.

Pricing and Credit

Price setting is free, and often quite competitive. Because of inflation, prices of consumer goods have had to be raised every month or two, on average, for the last couple of years. But prices have been known to go down, as well — generally because raw material prices fell. A bar of Unilever's Sunlight soap, for example, was priced at Rp30 in January 1968, and Rp43 in July, an increase of about 43%. In April the price had gone up to Rp35, then Rp37.50, in June to Rp45, then Rp40, and in July was up to Rp43.

There is no actual resale price maintenance (RPM), but Unilever prices its products as if there were: for example, if the retail price of an item should be Rp45, the company calculates its ex-factory price by subtracting an assumed retailer's margin of 10%, a wholesaler's margin of 5%, and, where necessary, a stockist's margin of about 10%.

Indonesia has traditionally been a cash economy; only very short-term credit is extended by local manufacturers to their distributors. Unilever's area managers are responsible for collecting from the wholesalers, and the company generally has its cash back within two and a half weeks. Companies such as BAT, Faroka, and Heineken generally operate on a cash basis or grant one-week credit. Philips grants one-week credit to some of its dealers, and three-week credit to others, keeping the average at two-week credit.

IX—Foreign Trade

INDONESIA IS ONCE again becoming an important Asian market, and present indications are that both imports and exports will rise substantially over the next few years. From a peak of $1,056 million in 1961, imports were reduced by strict licensing to a low of $562 million in 1963. By 1965 imports had risen again to $718.2 million, only to dive again in 1966 to $572 million. By 1967 and 1968, however, the trend was sharply up, as the end of import licensing and the new reliance on market forces took effect. Exports peaked at $881 million in 1960, and since have followed somewhat the same pattern as imports.* By 1967 they were lagging behind imports by $76.9 million, but expected increases in oil and forestry exports in the next few years should boost them dramatically and improve the balance of trade. (See Table 1.)

About 65% of Indonesia's total trade (imports and exports) is with the Atlantic basin countries — Western Europe, the US, and Canada. Something less than 35% is with the Pacific basin (but there is some double counting of North America), and

4-5% with the socialist countries of Eastern Europe. (See Appendices XIV and XV.)

Japan is by far the most important trading partner in Asia. Indonesia's overall trade policy is aimed at increasing trade with the Pacific area. Japan has already signed some long-term contracts to import Indonesian minerals, and will be the major market for Indonesian oil; and Japanese companies, already important suppliers to Indonesia, are boosting their sales efforts. Clearly, Japan's position in the Indonesian market will become more and more significant.

An important factor in Indonesia's pattern of trade could eventually be ASEAN — the Association of Southeast Asian Nations, comprising Indonesia, Malaysia, Singapore, Thailand, and the Philippines. The ASEAN nations are already cooperating in such fields as transport and tourism, and have begun to discuss the possibility of integrating in certain industries and eliminating tariff barriers among the five countries. Concrete results may be a long way off, but the organization is heading toward integrating the Southeast Asian market.

The Bonus Export (BE) System

The basis of Indonesia's foreign exchange transactions is the Bonus Export (BE) System, introduced in October 1966 and since modified and simplified several times in 1967 and 1968. The

*All figures in this paragraph are from balance of trade statistics of the Central Bureau of Statistics. 1967 data are preliminary. All figures include oil, but exclude West Irian. Trade data are also compiled by the Central Bank, the Ministry of Finance (Customs), and the Ministry of Trade. They are often calculated on different bases, and consequently not all trade data in this chapter and the appendices will match.

TABLE 1.

Indonesia's Balance of Trade [1]

($ Million)

	Including Oil			Excluding Oil		
	Exports	Imports	Balance	Exports	Imports	Balance
1964 [2]	724.2	690.7	+ 33.5	456.8	682.4	− 225.6
1965 [2]	707.7	718.2	− 10.5	435.8	705.6	− 269.8
1966 [2]	678.7	572.6	+ 106.1	475.1	571.0	− 95.9
1967 [3]	657.8	734.7	− 76.9	420.0	722.6	− 302.6
Jan/Apr '66 [3]	221.3	157.3	+ 64.0	167.5	153.8	+ 13.7
Jan/Apr '67 [3]	202.2	214.7	− 12.5	125.4	209.1	− 83.7
Jan/Apr '68 [3]	204.7	195.0	+ 9.7	129.0	193.8	− 64.8
1968						
Jan	48.5	47.8	+ 0.7	29.0	47.3	− 18.3
Feb	50.1	45.6	+ 4.5	30.3	45.3	− 15.0
Mar	55.6	46.9	+ 8.7	35.0	46.7	− 11.7
Apr	50.5	54.7	− 4.2	34.7	54.5	− 19.8

(1) Excludes West Irian
(2) Revised data.
(3) Preliminary data.

Source: Central Bureau of Statistics

basic aim of the BE system is to put greater reliance on the market mechanism and reduce government control over the economy, and simultaneously to direct foreign exchange resources into goods needed for stabilization, rehabilitation, and development of the economy. But by mid-1968 the Government was playing a larger role in influencing the market forces. This is, however, less a change of policy than a means of dealing with the extreme scarcity of foreign exchange. (For a more detailed discussion of the BE system, see Chapter 5.)

Under the BE system, an exporter selling Indonesian goods to any foreign currency market receives his export proceeds in the form of certificates known as "BE," rather than the actual foreign exchange proceeds of the sales. The BE certificates are expressed in the foreign currency in which the export is being financed. Under the May 1968 regulations designed to reduce speculation, the exporter must sell the BE certificates to a foreign exchange bank at the rate prevailing on the day the export draft is negotiated and is guaranteed payment in cash the same day. Formerly, the exporter who earned BE's was entitled to utilize the certificates for the import of certain essential or semi-essential goods (those appearing on the BE List of Imports), or to sell the BE certificates to others to be used for such imports, or other foreign exchange transactions. A BE Exchange, or Bourse, was established by the Government in May 1967. All trade in BE is now conducted through Exchange, to which all foreign exchange banks and a few brokers belong.

There are three "BE calls" each week, when the BE rate is announced by the central bank (basing the rate on estimated supply and demand). This "BE rate" is, in effect, the major exchange rate for the Indonesian rupiah. The rate fluctuated around Rp260:US$1 from January until the end of March, when the after-effects of the run on gold in Europe sent the rate up to around Rp280:US$1. By early April, however, the rate was back to around Rp265:US$1. It rose by May to Rp300:-

Foreign Exchange Rates Related to Trade

Type	Rate September 1968	Use
General BE (fluctuating)	Rp317	Indonesia's major exchange rate, used for most of the country's imports.
Credit BE, or "special" BE Rate (adjusted periodically)	Rp265	Formerly, the rate the importer paid if he imported goods under foreign aid credits, but now used as the rate at which the Central Bank repurchases expired BE.
DP (fluctuating)	Rp430	Free foreign exchange good for all but prohibited imports, used mainly for luxuries and invisibles.
ADO (fluctuating)	Rp317	Arises from export taxes, and is paid to provincial governments to be used to import BE-List goods or sold to a foreign exchange bank; it is the same as General BE except for its ownership.
Customs rate (adjusted periodically)	Rp305	Rate on which import duties are calculated.

US$1, and with the help of Central Bank influence, stayed at this rate through midsummer. By September 1968, the rate was up to Rp317:US$1.

Under the BE system, there are four types of foreign exchange that may be used to import (General BE, Credit BE, DP, and ADO), and special exchange rates apply to certain aspects of trade (see box).

"Credit BE" arises from foreign loans earmarked for financing imports. The exchange rate for Credit BE at first was not a free rate like the General BE rate, but rather was administered by the central bank (Bank Indonesia). It was raised in January 1968 to Rp240:US$1, but was later lowered to Rp235:US$1. The central bank altered the Credit BE rate so that the difference between it and the General BE rate was always about the same. It was deliberately set lower than the General BE rate for several reasons, including 1) encouragement of importers to utilize the foreign exchange provided through foreign loans; and 2) compensation of the importer for several disadvantages of importing under Credit BE rather

than General BE. These disadvantages include longer shipping periods involved in importing goods from say, the US, rather than from Singapore, and the restrictions that countries may place on the lists of goods that may be imported with their credits.

Since May 1968, however, the two kinds of BE's have been "integrated" in the sense that Credit BE is now sold at the same rate as General BE. A lower rate for Credit BE exists only for the central bank; to the importer, Credit BE and General BE are the same. This step was taken to reduce the number of prevailing official foreign exchange rates.

Under the system now in effect, the exporter is ensured of getting rupiah payment for his BE on the same day the export draft is negotiated at the rate of the last "call." The foreign exchange bank on the same day must report to the central bank the amount of BE bought from exporters, receiving payment from the central bank immediately. It is then the central bank which offers BE at the "call" as the sole supplier.

Because the central bank now commands the whole supply of General BE available on one day, with no possibility for exporters to withhold their supplies, the Bank Indonesia now has far better control over rates. With the General BE it offers, and any Credit BE available on a given day, the central bank hopes to be able to meet demand and to drain rupiahs from speculators.

Under this system the importer does not know whether he buys General BE or Credit BE for his imports (although his application for BE must state whether the goods he wants to import are eligible to be imported under foreign government credits). Whether a certain import is actually charged against a credit account with some creditor country or against other reserves of foreign exchange is no longer a problem for the importer.

Complementary Foreign Exchange

Another type of foreign exchange is known as DP (*Devisa Pelengkap*), or Complementary Foreign Exchange. This arises from the proceeds of invisible transactions, and from the excess between realized export proceeds and the government-set "check prices," or posted prices, for certain export commodities. Exports are divided into two categories, A ("hard" products) and B ("soft" products).

For category A goods — rubber, coffee, copra, pepper, tobacco, palm oil, palm kernels, and tin — the Government periodically establishes a "check price" as the basis for calculating the amount of foreign exchange to be yielded to the Government and the share the exporter acquires as DP. The check price is based on net f.o.b. prices, and is normally placed at slightly below world market prices. If the exporter sells above the check price, he earns the difference, or "overprice" in DP.

DP may be used for invisible transactions, for imports of all goods except the few completely prohibited items (i.e., its use is not restricted to the "BE list" of essential and semi-essential imports), or for trading in the DP market. DP is actual free foreign exchange and is transferable through foreign currency accounts at authorized exchange banks. DP has a free exchange rate that fluctuates with supply and demand. There are daily quotations at the Bourse, but turnover is sharply limited. In mid-1968 the DP rate was Rp380:US$1, after being Rp440:US$1 earlier in the

year when the Government temporarily halted the sale of General BE. By September the DP rate had climbed back up to Rp430:US$1. Because the use of DP is not restricted, its exchange rate is always higher than the BE rate.

Automatic Foreign Exchange Allocation

Finally, there is ADO (*Alokasi Devisa Otomatis*), or automatic Foreign Exchange Allocation. This is the portion of an exporter's foreign exchange earnings (after deducting the overprice he may have earned in DP) that is allocated to the government of the regions where the exports originated. The regional governments may use ADO to finance their own imports. If they do not use their ADO for imports, they are obliged to sell it to a foreign exchange bank at the prevailing BE-rate.

ADO in general has always been treated along the same lines as BE, and goods importable with ADO are the same as those on the BE list. Imports with ADO by regional governments are supposedly always meant for the development of the region; this is the reason why regional governments, even after May 1968, need not submit the ADO to a foreign exchange bank as does an exporter with his BE.

Types of Trading

Barter deals and government-to-government trading are no longer very important in trading with Indonesia. Any Indonesian importer who has the necessary rupiahs can obtain foreign exchange for imports.

The most usual terms of trading at present are based on Indonesian sight draft letters of credit allowing sight drawings (i.e., "cash"). Such letters of credit are unconfirmed. Indonesia, as a policy matter of long standing generally refuses to confirm letters of credit, but apart from administrative delays, these L/C's can be considered sound. Present Indonesian financial regulations are such that a letter of credit cannot be opened unless the full amount of the foreign exchange required to meet it is already held by an Indonesian foreign exchange bank.

Letter of Credit Delays

Problems related to present Indonesian letters of credit for sight drawings arise from communication and administrative delays in getting the money into the right bank account abroad. Although the letter of credit cannot be opened until the relevant foreign exchange has been earned and received by Indonesian exporters and is held by a foreign exchange bank on behalf of the importer, Indonesia suffers from serious communication and administration problems. The letter of credit documents often reach the foreign bank some time before the transfer of the necessary funds has been completed. There have therefore been a number of cases where, on presentation of shipping documents, the overseas exporter has been told that funds have not been received to meet the letter of credit. The delays are sometimes only two or three days, but have been known to be as long as a month or more.

There is a large number of Indonesian firms whose credit records and financial standing are beyond question, but selling to such firms on credit, i.e., "without cover," must be entirely a matter of personal trader-to-trader trust. Deals on this basis, while in some cases acceptable to Chinese and European traders, are very difficult for some US firms to undertake in view of their limited knowledge of the market. This type of trader-to-trader credit without cover is considered by most export payment insurance organizations to be fraught with too many risks (especially in relation to fluctuations in the exchange rate) to be insurable.

Imports under "BE without cover" took on enormous proportions in the first half of 1967 when the emphasis of the economic policy of the Government was on checking inflation and stabilizing prices. The Government, in an effort to flood the market with goods, opened the possibility for importers to import first and pay later (normally after six months) with BE's. These "imports with BE without cover" were banned in the latter part of 1967.

By then the volume of these imports was estimated at over $100 million, of which some $40 million still had to be paid for. The strong and frantic demand that resulted meant that buyers were willing to pay any price for BE. This was one of the forces behind the steep rise in BE rates in the last quarter of 1967. In early 1968, imports with BE without cover were opened again but only for rice imports needed to meet the seasonal shortage.

Domestic credits for imports are prohibited. With the high propensity to import prevailing in the economy, however, the lack of credits from the banking system has not resulted in imports becoming unattractive to business. The Government, through a system of prepayments, requirements to produce a tax certificate, and surveyor's reports, has discouraged imports to keep them within the limits of available foreign exchange.

Exports

Indonesia's total exports in 1966 amounted to $679 million, with oil accounting for $204 million. Commodities such as rubber were affected by lower world market prices in 1967, and total exports dropped by about 3% to $658 million. (But petroleum exports were up by 17%.) See Appendix XVI. The major markets for Indonesian exports in 1967 were Japan, the US, the Netherlands, Singapore, Australia, and West Germany (see Appendix XIV).

The $658 million total for 1967 includes oil as well as the "overprice" received by exporters (estimated at around $65 million). The question of "overprice" has been a controversial issue among trade policy makers for the last two years. One side is of the opinion that the "overprice," which makes possible luxury imports with DP, is a social loss, and opens possibilities for capital flight. On the other side, exporters and some policy makers feel that without an overprice, the export sector is not attractive for business. The latter school advocates a more lenient attitude on the matter, as long as the volume of conspicuous imports is still "within reason" and so long as the bulk of the foreign exchange comes back into the country as imports rather than fleeing the country. Since exports are one of the prime movers in the economy, this group insists that the most urgent problem is to get exports moving, even at the cost of some loss of foreign exchange for the Government.

The official policy at present is between the two extremes. Check prices are now announced once a month in principle so that exporters can benefit from rising prices in the world market. On the other hand, if prices are falling, check prices will be lowered accordingly. While it is government policy to prevent violent fluctuations in the BE rate in this way, the exporter can get some "overprice" for which the rate is not so controlled.

According to preliminary figures from the Department of Trade, the "overprice" in exports over the first six months of 1968 is estimated at around $48 million on top of the registered export revenue (excluding oil) of $201 million, making a total of $249 million.

Petroleum production is expected to increase by 21% in 1968 and petroleum exports by 24%, to nearly $300 million. Non-oil exports are expected to increase by 6% in 1968, with rubber (which accounts for 40% of these exports) lagging due to declining world prices, but with other exports increasing by 10%.

Export Taxes and Incentives

For category A exports, the exporter is granted 85% of his export proceeds (up to the check price) in the form of BE; an export tax of 5% is allocated to the Foreign Exchange Fund of the central Government, and the remaining 10% is allocated to the regional governments in the form of ADO certificates expressed in foreign currency. Until September 1968 the tax had amounted to 25% instead of 15%, and in 1967 it had been 40%. The Government intends eventually to abolish the export tax completely, replacing it with revenues from import duties.

For category B exports — all those goods not in Category A — the exporter is granted 90% of the foreign exchange proceeds in the form of BE certificates, and the regional governments get 10% as ADO.

The table below summarizes the division of export proceeds:

Commodities	Foreign Exchange Proceeds		
	Exporter	Govt.	Prov. Govt.
GROUP A —major export commodities yielding collectively about 90% of export income	85%	5%	10%
GROUP B —other export commodities (including manufactures) yielding about 10% of export income	90%	0%	10%

While the Government taxes exports, it also encourages them. Exports have the highest priority — and therefore the lowest interest rates — in the government's selective credit policy. (See Chapter 5.) In addition, the length of the tax holiday available under the Foreign Capital Investment Law is increased for export industries, and the application of the ownership requirements of the Law and subsequent regulations on foreign investment would probably be more lenient for a firm manufacturing for export. The Government is also thinking of establishing a system of rebates on import duties paid on raw materials and components for products subsequently exported.

Imports

Imports for 1967 were $735 million (preliminary), compared with $573 million in 1966. Non-oil imports increased by some 27% to $723 million. All but a small portion of non-oil imports consisted of general imports not related to projects. Of the total BE and ADO imports of $366.1 million during January-September 1967, textiles accounted for 34%, rice 13%, wheat flour 3%, and various regional government imports 6%.

Imports financed by foreign aid totaled $82 million during the first nine months of 1967. Raw cotton accounted for 11%, chemical products 10%, rice 9%, textiles 8%, and spares for road transport equipment 7%. Imports of capital goods were limited by the fact that they were not placed on the BE list until July 29, 1967, as well as by the shortage of domestic capital.

Imports under foreign aid credits in 1967 totaled $101.5 million, including $19.5 million under the US PL-480 for the importation of rice. Of the total, $35.4 million (35%) was used to import consumer goods, $32.4 million (32%) for raw ancillary materials, $6.7 million (6%) for spare parts, $21.4 million (21%) for capital goods, and $5.4 million (5%) for other commodities.

Imports for 1968 are estimated at $888 million. Of this amount, 92% is for the non-oil sector. The 1968 import projection takes into account the shift from DP to BE imports, a substantial increase in rice imports to 600,000 tons, larger imports of capital goods, and an improvement in domestic production, especially with respect to textiles.

Imports through July 1968 reflect these trends as far as the proportions are concerned, but total imports were lagging since foreign credits were slow to materialize. Of the total of $379.2 million, $203.1 million (54%) was for very essential "group A" imports, $113.6 million (30%) for essential "group B" commodities, $55.7 million (15%) for less essential "group C" goods, and $6.9 million (2%) for nonessential items. (See Appendix XVII and Table 2.)

Import Controls

The Indonesian Government periodically issues lists of items that may be imported with the various types of foreign exchange (General BE, Credit BE, DP, ADO). Under the import policy for 1968, imports are divided into three lists.

List 1 consists of three groups of goods: *Group A* includes the most essential items, such as rice, flour, powdered milk, cotton, medicine, some fertilizers and insecticides, agricultural and industrial machinery and equipment, and some raw materials; *Group B* includes essential goods such as raw materials and spare parts for industry; and *Group C* covers less essential items, and locally produced goods that need protection against imports.

List 2 covers four prohibited items: sedan automobiles costing over $2,000, large-screen TV sets, console radios, and batik.

List 3 includes some consumer goods and manufactures, luxuries, and some goods produced locally.

All goods on List 1 may be imported with General BE. Credit BE may be used to import only Group A and Group B commodities. Goods included in List 3 may not be imported with BE, but only with DP.

While this is the official framework for all imports, some further restrictions apply in practice. For example, although DP may be used to import any items on Lists 1 and 3, it is little used except for goods on List 3. This is because DP is relatively scarce, and is naturally used to best advantage where other forms of foreign exchange may not be used. Similarly, all goods in Groups A and B of List 1 may sometimes not be importable with Credit BE. When foreign governments grant credits to Indonesia, they generally stipulate that certain items in Groups A and B (i.e., those goods that the Indonesian Government will allow to be imported under credits) may not be imported under their specific credits. Such lists are called "negative lists." In addition, since nearly all foreign credits are tied to imports from the credit-granting country, some items in Group A and B may simply not be available from that source.

Tariffs

Duties range from 0-100%, depending on whether the imports are essential or luxury goods. Tariffs are calculated on the US dollar landed value of the item at the "customs rate" of exchange, a rate adjusted monthly by the Ministry of Finance. In January 1968 it was raised from Rp130 to Rp240:$1; by midsummer it was at Rp275, and by September Rp305. In general, duties follow this pattern:

Import List 1: Group A — duties range from 0-10%
             Group B — duties range from 20-40%
             Group C — duties range from 50-70%
       List 3: Import duties range up to 100%.

Indonesia's tariff schedule is a double-column one, providing most-favored-nation treatment according to GATT rules. But the MFN treatment is only theoretical; on goods imported from GATT countries, a special tax is imposed to bring the total tariff-plus-tax up to the higher duty applicable under Indonesia's tariff regulations.

While Indonesia intends to switch to the Brussels Tariff Nomenclature, at present its tariff code is very general (only 943 items) for some types of products. This, plus a lack of technical know-how on the part of customs officials, sometimes means that a higher tariff is applied than should be. For example, the tariff on tape for computers is the same as the tariff on sound-recording tape, which is very high.

Import Surcharges

In addition to tariffs, import surcharges ranging from 50% to 400% (but usually 100%) are imposed on most imports. Luxury goods and goods competing with locally produced ones generally face the highest surcharges. For some items, there is also a levy for "excess profits" ranging from Rp25 to Rp190 per US dollar. This levy generally applies to items on which no duties or surcharges are imposed. A regulation of June 1968 designed to ease the pressure on the BE market stipulated that customs levies (tariffs, surcharges, and excess profit tax) must be prepaid at the time the letter of credit is opened for goods in Groups B and C of the BE Import List (List 1), if they are imported with BE. Several months later, the requirement was lifted for goods imported under foreign credits, but otherwise it remains in force.

Since March 1968, imports have been subject to sales tax as well. The tax base is the c.i.f. price in foreign currency plus customs duty and surcharges, plus port entry and exit charges, plus a 5% profit margin. On goods that pay no import duty, the tax is zero; on goods in the 5%, 10%, and 20% import-duty categories, the sales tax is 5%; with import duties of 30-40%, the sales tax

is 10%; and goods that pay duty of 50% or more pay 20%. Some luxury items are taxed at 50%. There are some variations, however, because the sales tax on imports has been used in a few cases to protect local producers. The sales tax on imported tires, for example, was raised from 5% to 10% (while the sales tax on domestically produced tires was lowered from 10% to 5%), when competition from cheaper imports (and smuggled tires) forced Goodyear and Dunlop to close their factories in mid-1968.

In general the Government believes in tariff protection for local industry, and the 1968 import policy added some domestically made items to higher-tariff categories. Many foreign investors operating in Indonesia find that protection against imports has been reasonably good. In contrast, the Government will not guarantee a foreign investor that he will be able to continue importing necessary raw materials and components if the investment is in manufacturing (but such a guarantee is available to mining enterprises). Nevertheless, while the Government makes no pledge not to ban or impose prohibitive tariffs on goods needed by local producers, to do so would completely contradict its policy of protecting domestic industry. Except in the most extreme circumstances, therefore, such action seems unlikely.

Exemption From Import Duties

Under a Finance Ministry decree of August 1967, approved foreign investors are granted exemption from import duties on:
- machines, tools, and spare parts that form part of the plant or equipment of the enterprise;
- raw materials, semi-finished and finished goods (presumably components) to be processed by the enterprise (the exemption is for two years, but may be extended);
- vehicles and other transportation equipment to be used for transport of goods;
- used personal effects belonging to expatriate employees of the enterprise;
- consumer nondurables (food, clothing, etc.) up to a value of $50 per person or $100 per family per month for expatriate employees of the enterprise;
- office equipment, furniture, and motor vehicles (but not sedans) for the use of personnel, if

approval of the Ministry of Finance is obtained; and

• construction and building materials for factories, offices, housing for personnel, and schools, hospitals, etc., connected with the enterprise, if Ministry of Finance approval is obtained. Exemptions from sales taxes on imports follow the same pattern.

In practice, however, exemptions from import duties have sometimes been difficult to obtain, and recent regulations of the Ministry of Finance have considerably narrowed the possibilities. A decree of September 1968 specifies, for example, that raw materials and semifinished or other goods are eligible for the two-year exemption only if the enterprise uses a chemical or mechanical process that actually alters the original nature or shape of the imported commodity; if the enterprise is "pioneer" in character; and if the materials to be imported are essential to production and cannot be secured in Indonesia in sufficient quantity or suitable quality. A still more limiting provision of the same decree allows exemptions from duties and sales taxes on imports only if the imports are financed by DP foreign exchange (not BE or credit BE). In addition, the foreign exchange used must be included in the initial budget of the planned investment. Finally, the company seeking exemptions must prove that it has not made capital transfers abroad except through the BE system before the capital investment is made. It would appear that unless these rules are relaxed, duty exemptions will only rarely be available to manufacturing firms. Separate and more lenient rules may apply, however, to investments in mining and forestry.

Exemptions from duties and sales taxes on imports, if available, are granted by the Director General for Customs and Excises and the Tax Director General, both of the Ministry of Finance. The investor must submit an application that includes specifications of the goods for which exemptions are sought, and the Department concerned with the particular investment must give a technical recommendation to the Ministry of Finance before exemptions are granted.

Importing Procedures

By law, only Indonesian nationals may normally be importers, but a 1968 regulation allows foreign investors in manufacturing or other productive ventures to directly import their needs and directly export their products. In order to open a letter of credit, an importer must provide evidence that he is a bona fide registered importer. A reregistration was carried out in mid-1968, during which over 1,200 importers registered, over 1,000 of them in Djakarta. To be approved by the Department of Trade, however, an importer must have the recommendation of the importers' association, OPS Impor. The other major requirement for an importer is that he have a fiscal declaration every three months to prove that his taxes are paid.

An importer, having accepted an offer of goods, obtains foreign exchange in one of two ways: 1) by buying BE exchange at the BE bourse through a bourse member (foreign exchange bank or broker), or 2) by buying private overseas funds or purchasing DP exchange on the open market or at the DP "call" at the Foreign Exchange Bourse. To obtain a letter of credit, he presents the BE exchange certificate or foreign exchange to the Bank Indonesia or to an approved foreign exchange bank (and in the case of List 1 B and C goods imported with General BE, he prepays the import levies).

One importing procedure which has become more and more popular, especially for the import of luxury non-BE items, is importing without letter credit as "gifts" (see the section on Singapore and Hong Kong, below). This method became even more attractive when prepayment of duties and surcharges was required for certain kinds of BE imports (groups B and C). If no letter of credit is opened, there is naturally no way to impose prepayments, even though such payments logically would have been more justified, considering the more luxurious and nonessential character of the goods.

Credits from Abroad

From time to time, the Bank Indonesia announces the availability of Credit BE from a particular country. Depending on the country, the size of its foreign credit, the arrangements made between that country and the central bank, and the demand for the goods importable under credits from that country, the Credit BE for imports from a certain country may be available for only a few days or weeks at a time. In addition to tied purchases and negative lists, conditions or restrictions on imports under its credits may be stipulated by the credit-granting country.

For example, thé Bank Indonesia announced in mid-March that Credit BE for import of US merchandise (based on the balance of US credits in 1967 and on new US loans) was available. The announcement said that previously announced provisions for imports under US credits would be in effect. It also stipulated that a letter of credit opened for import of goods under these credits could not amount to less than $5,000, and its validity period could not exceed the end of September 1968.

For a three-week period in July 1968, the Government halted sales of General BE completely and announced that imports with BE could be conducted only under the foreign credits then available — from the US, Japan, West Germany, France, and the UK. (The move, made to allow some time to build up ordinary exchange reserves, and to encourage use of the credits, created havoc with most importers and manufacturers. Suddenly, imports from Singapore, Hong Kong, and elsewhere could be purchased only at the far more expensive DP rate.) These five were not, of course, the only creditor countries, but they were the only countries whose credits were available at that time.

Altogether, Indonesia had used foreign credits amounting to $59.4 million in the first eight months of 1968, out of a total of credits available of $124.3 million. A Dutch credit was entirely used, French and West German credits were mostly used, and about half of Japan's $67 million had been used. Some funds from Belgium, Australia, the UK, and India had been used as well, and Italy, Canada, and South Korea had promised credits. Total US credits for 1968, including PL-480, were expected to amount to over $100 million. Japan committed $110 million, of which $65 million is for BE imports, $5 million for food, and $40 million ($10 million for 1968) for projects. Australia doubled its 1967 credits to $14 million in 1968. The total available from all sources to finance imports was expected to be in excess of the $250 million Indonesia originally requested.

Use of foreign credit — particularly European and US credits — poses severe problems for the importer, however. The initial difficulty is that since Indonesian importers must make a prior deposit of 100% of the value of the letter of credit, long shipping distances tie up the importer's money for a long time. At interest rates of 8% or so per month, importers often simply cannot afford to wait the six months or more it frequently takes for a shipment under a credit to go from the US or Europe to Indonesia. In the case of the US, the problem of long shipping distances is aggravated by AID requirements that US-flag carriers must normally be used; often a US-flag carrier is not available, or else it refuses cargo with a low freight rate. In addition, extensive documentation is required by AID, sometimes involving sending documents for approval to Washington D.C. — a process that can add several weeks to the shipping time. The upshot of all this in 1968 was that by September, only a few hundred thousand dollars of a $25-million US credit had been used.

The eventual solution to the problem will probably be a bonded warehouse system, which the Government is interested in establishing. In the meantime, though, a way had to be found to use the $25 million. As of September 1968, the plan, worked out by AID and the Government of Indonesia, but not yet officially announced, was something like this: The US would offer a $6.5-million credit for the Djakarta area and $3.5 million for the rest of Indonesia. (The other $15 million would presumably be used in a similar way if the plan works.) These amounts would be allocated to bona fide importers through the importers' association. The importers (mainly indentors) would be required to make a down payment of only 20% of the value of the letter of credit. The banks would cover the full amounts of the letters of credit upon obtaining suitable guarantees from the importers; and the importers would pay 1% per month on the total value of the letter of credit. The proposal had aroused the interest of a great many importers, but at least one question remained before the scheme could be put into effect. This was whether the importer would pay up the letter of credit (i.e., the remaining 80%) at the BE rate of the day it was opened, the day the documents arrived, or the day the goods were cleared.

Smuggling

Actual Indonesian exports are considerably higher than those recorded. The value of smuggled exports has been estimated at $100 million annually, and has by all accounts increased dramatically since the ending of confrontation with Malaysia and Singapore. Still greater incentives for legal exports appear to be the only means of curtailing smuggling. However, a considerable portion of the proceeds of smuggling returns as lower-priority imports. Smuggled imports are abundant as well, but the Government has made some progress in curtailing the inflow. Some of it was probably stopped when Minister of Trade Dr. Soemitro, in June 1968, abolished the armed forces' privilege of importing goods duty-free. Philips NV found some improvement in competitive conditions after the police in Medan one day picked up all the smuggled radio sets; shopowners have since been reluctant to stock them.

Singapore and Hong Kong

The geographical proximity of Singapore and Hong Kong has placed these two countries in a special position in Indonesia's international trade relations. Because an Indonesian importer must deposit the full amount of letter of credit when it is opened, and because of Indonesia's extremely high interest rates, importers naturally prefer to trade through Singapore and Hong Kong, to take advantage of fast turnover in imports and exports and thus reduce costs. For these reasons, Singapore and Hong Kong have become favorite clients for Indonesian exports and favorite suppliers for imports, while more distant suppliers — even countries that have granted aid credits to Indonesia — have trouble selling to Indonesia. But the popularity of trade with Singapore and Hong Kong has led to imbalances and manipulations that culminated in the blacklisting of 39 Hong Kong and Singapore suppliers and six Hong Kong and Singapore shipping companies, and the suspension of 35 importers in Indonesia in late August 1968 for involvement in manipulations of BE. To put order into imports from these two countries, payment for imports may now be made only after the goods arrive in Indonesia and a surveyor's report has been submitted to verify the goods.

These developments were the culmination of progressively tighter sets of measures aimed at reducing Indonesia's dependence on these two suppliers. Especially after the "integration" of the BE system and the abolition of the prefer-

ential lower rates of Credit BE's, imports from Singapore and Hong Kong became more attractive than ever. Their appeal increased still more when prepayments of import duties and surcharges were required on BE-imports for the less essential groups B and C, since interest has to be paid on these prepayments.

The result was that more and more imports had to be charged on the foreign exchange reserves originating from exports, rather than on credit accounts from creditor nations. One effort to reverse this was the Government's ban on all BE imports for three weeks in July except those that could be paid with foreign credits, in order to gain time to increase the foreign exchange reserves. The effect, however, was a steep jump in the free foreign exchange (DP) market, and pressure from creditor nations whose credits had almost been used up.

The new requirement of a surveyor's report was added after it was discovered that some goods supplied from Singapore and Hong Kong did not coincide with the specifications in the letters of credit; in some cases no goods at all were shipped, and in others worthless trash was unloaded instead of the essential "BE commodities." All these manipulations — mainly designed to get foreign exchange out of the country at the low BE rate — were possible only through cooperation between importer, supplier, and shipper, and most likely with the help of officials.

Apart from these illegal schemes, however, Indonesia faces a dilemma in its trade relations with Singapore and Hong Kong. On the one hand, increased trade volume with the two countries is natural, given Indonesia's high interest rates and the geographical factors. On the other hand, structural, political, and economic factors require a limitation of this trade. For example, Indonesia prefers to have direct trade relations with countries consuming its exports and countries producing its imports. It also wants to absorb whatever credits it has acquired from creditor nations, and cannot afford the heavy burden of paying for imports from Singapore and Hong Kong from its own foreign exchange reserves. Only with a substantial increase in Indonesia's total trade, so that increases in trade with Singapore and Hong Kong are less significant, is the dilemma likely to disappear.

The measures taken in relation to Hong Kong

and Singapore, and the regulations issued to build up the foreign exchange reserves have been a part of one of the most serious difficulties facing companies in Indonesia: the constantly changing regulations — often effective immediately or retroactively — which make business planning nearly impossible. This problem should be alleviated, though, as the economy stabilizes.

Appendix I

Consumer Price Index for Djakarta

(1958 = 100)

End of Period	Food (63%)	Housing (11%)	Clothing (9%)	Miscellaneous (17%)	General Index (100%)	Quarterly Increase (%)	Monthly Increase (%)
1961	426	373	568	272	384		
1962	1,060	332	2,090	870	1,037		
1963	2,574	621	3,628	1,542	2,275		
1964	5,272	2,574	9,572	4,619	5,234		
1965	41,404	17,184	40,447	27,728	36,347		
1966							
Jan.	58,851	42,443	65,378	49,497	56,920		57
Feb.	66,996	40,630	82,354	77,676	67,312		18
Mar.	87,673	41,149	92,273	114,536	87,704	141	30
Apr.	97,901	41,149	108,093	117,388	96,030		9
May	100,809	42,400	146,114	124,697	102,509		7
June	138,944	107,922	173,123	135,376	137,894	57	35
July	145,762	115,876	235,641	138,931	149,009		8
Aug.	163,180	116,430	336,686	178,708	175,598		18
Sept.	180,963	134,469	390,884	220,243	200,615	45	14
Oct.	217,453	155,939	427,255	274,920	238,630		19
Nov.	247,779	141,042	354,936	329,547	259,556		9
Dec.	248,521	166,056	386,172	340,519	267,276	33	3
1967							
Jan.	271,348	216,084	387,984	366,245	291,748		9
Feb.	329,709	273,020	390,850	443,861	348,566		19
Mar.	344,809	290,894	372,150	462,148	361,640	35	4
Apr.	352,780	316,221	337,635	447,819	364,005		0.7
May	341,735	322,735	382,706	457,974	363,296		− 0.2
June	350,102	381,931	376,402	460,230	374,831	4	3
July	366,414	328,924	409,013	461,363	382,437		2
Aug.	394,390	328,728	441,858	461,363	402,950		5
Sept.	431,925	336,112	466,658	475,998	444,873	19	10
Oct.	493,111	351,395	471,781	497,877	476,858		7
Nov.	613,974	533,999	475,783	513,324	576,178		21
Dec.	611,908	413,329	535,595	514,054	567,088	27	− 1.6
1968							
Jan.	915,018	437,776	660,821	631,060	792,834		40
Feb.	1,011,229	416,495	698,945	696,159	866,062		9
Mar.	1,061,807	446,289	710,481	807,593	893,079	57	3

Source: Central Bureau of Statistics

Appendix II

Indonesia's Foreign Exchange Reserves

(in $ million)

**Foreign Exchange Fund and Issue
Department of Bank Indonesia**

Year-End	Gross Reserves	Foreign Exchange Liabilities	Net Reserves
1960	313	12	301
1961	133	11	122
1962	108	14	94
1963	58	74	— 16
1964	25	74	— 49
1965	21	94	— 73
1966			
Mar.	17	106	— 91
June	17	100	— 83
July	17	103	— 86
Aug.	18	102	— 84
Sept.	31	102	— 71
Oct.	23	102	— 79
Nov.	24	102	— 78
Dec.	23	100	— 77
1967			
Jan.	19	99	— 80
Feb.	17	97	— 80
Mar.	17	94	— 77

Appendix III

Indonesia's Agricultural Production

(in '000 metric tons)

	1960	1961	1962	1963	1964	1965[1]	1966[1]	1967[2]
Rice (milled)	8,430	7,950	8,556	7,628	8,420	8,840	9,137	9,324[1]
Corn (in kernels)	2,460	2,283	3,243	2,359	3,769	2,283	3,220	2,960[1]
Cassava (robbs)	11,376	11,190	11,386	11,575	12,223	10,274	13,351	12,920[1]
Sweet potatoes	2,669	2,464	3,680	3,015	3,931	2,724	2,274	2,160[1]
Copra (coconuts)	1,239	1,361	1,387	1,379	1,193	1,249	1,350	1,320
Sugar	927	956	769	826	1,087	1,188	1,045	1,106
Estate (centrifugal)	672	651	585	650	649	774	612	666
Other (noncentrifugal)	255	305	184	176	438	414	433	440
Tea	83	80	84	78	87	86	83	85
Estate	46	43	47	39	46	44	41	39
Smallholder	37	37	37	39	41	42	42	46
Coffee	96	108	111	145	87	112	119	138
Estate	18	19	12	18	7	20	12	21
Smallholder	78	89	99	127	80	92	107	117
Rubber	622	705	713	706	732	738	747	747
Estate	219	229	217	216	232	228	219	217
Smallholder	403	476	496	490	500	510	528	530
Oil-palm products	174	180	174	181	195	190	211	178
Peanuts (shelled)	256	252	261	231	261	279	263	242[1]
Soybeans	442	426	397	353	392	356	375	363[1]
Spices	22	24	62	66	65	60	68	74
Kapok	21	26	26	21	22	25	26	27
Tobacco	76	84	80	91	59	89	97	100

(1) Revised estimates.
(2) Projections.
Source: Data supplied by the Indonesian authorities.

Appendix IV

Indonesia's Foreign Debt

(As of December 31, 1965)
(in $ million)

Country	Medium/ Long Term	Short Term	Total [1]
Communist Countries			
USSR	980	10	990
Yugoslavia	108	7	115
Poland	98	2	100
Czechoslovakia	58	19	77
East Germany	70	2	72
Hungary	17	2	19
Rumania	15	1	16
China (Mainland)	13	—	13
Other	2	—	2
Total	1,361	43	1,404
Western Countries			
USA	172	7	179
West Germany	112	10	122
France	113	2	115
Italy	84	7	91
UK (incl. Hong Kong)	40	2	42
Netherlands	12	16	28
Switzerland	—	3	3
Other	6	1	7
Total	539	43	587
Asian Countries			
Japan	168	63	231
Pakistan	—	20	20
India	8	2	10
Total	176	85	261
African Countries			
United Arab Republic	3	1	4
International Agencies			
IMF	102	—	102
Grand Total	2,181	177	2,358

(1) The totals do not include compensation to foreign owners of
estates etc. then under negotiation, nor the $110 million due to
the Shell Oil Company in payment for its assets.

Source: **Bulletin of Indonesian Economic Studies**, no. 4, June 1966,
Dept. of Economics, Australian National University.

Appendix V

Indonesia's Debt Profile

(in $ million)

| | Participating and Other Countries | | | | | | |
| | Payments Subject to Rescheduling | | Payments Not Subject to Rescheduling | | | Other Eastern European Countries[3] and Mainland China[4] | |
	Maturities Prior to Rescheduling[1] (1)	Maturities after Rescheduling through 1968[1] (2)	Loans Contracted after June 30, 1966 (3)	Other Payments[2] (4)	USSR	(5)	Total (6)
Arrears	68.5						
1966	77.6	—	—	15.3	—	—	15.3
1967	165.2	—	4.5	36.4	—	—	40.9
1968	112.1	—	8.1	35.6	—	17.4	61.1
1969	100.3	100.3	9.9	20.7	—	17.4	148.3
1970	87.4	87.4	9.9	21.4	25.0	34.1	177.8
1971	71.7	105.7	15.5	5.2	45.0	30.0	201.4
1972	45.0	106.0	17.6	2.2	50.0	33.4	209.2
1973	26.6	91.7	17.1	2.2	55.0	36.3	202.3
1974	20.7	84.2	17.4	7.5	55.0	36.3	200.4
1975	16.2	93.6	24.0	7.6	55.0	37.3	217.5
1976	10.8	91.5	18.0	7.6	58.0	39.6	214.7
1977	7.7	85.9	15.0	7.7	63.0	43.0	214.6
1978	10.6	101.9	15.0	7.8	68.5	46.5	239.7
1979	4.0	29.6	14.4	5.5	68.5	46.5	164.5
1980	2.8	2.8	14.1	5.6	74.0	50.0	146.5
1981	0.7	0.7	13.6	5.6	78.0	53.0	150.9
1982 and after	0.7	0.7	114.6	139.2	172.6	99.4	526.5
Total	828.6	982.0	328.7	333.1	867.6	620.2	3,131.6

(1) Excludes maturities on loans guaranteed by Japanese War Reparation payments, and 50 per cent of maturities on non-government-guaranteed private loans; the latter are assumed by the Indonesian authorities to be converted by creditors into investments in Indonesia under the Debt/Investment Conversion Scheme. As part of an agreement reached in June 1967 maturities on loans guaranteed by Japanese War Reparations will be settled by offsetting them against War Reparations availabilities. Also excludes amounts shown in columns (3) and (4).

(2) Compensation payments to the Netherlands Government and to the Shell Company, payments on 180-day credits and payments to private companies with which separate agreements have been reached.

(3) It has been assumed that these European Countries will apply the same terms for the rescheduling of outstanding debt as the USSR.

(4) The outstanding debt to Mainland China has not been rescheduled.

Source: Data provided by the Indonesian authorities.

Appendix VI
Foreign Investment in Indonesia

A. Approved Foreign Investment Projects[1]
January 1967 — Sept. 30, 1968
By Country of Origin[2]

($ million)

SECTOR

Country	Industry	Mining	Fishery	Forestry	Communications	Pharmacy	Trade	Public Works	Estates	Total
US	7.00	1	—	—	1	—	1	2	1	12
	25.09	76.50			6.50		1.10	5.00	0.40	114.59
Netherlands	6	1	—	1	1	—	2	1	—	12
	10.80	7.00		1.50	0.13		1.00	0.13		19.43
Japan	3	—	4	3	—	—	—	—	—	10
	4.20		6.50	6.50						17.20
Australia	2	—	—	—	—	—	—	1	—	3
	1.55							0.10		1.65
West Germany	3	—	—	—	—	2	—	—	—	5
	2.75					2.90				5.65
Hong Kong	7	—	—	1	—	—	—	1	1	10
	3.85			6.00				0.30	1.00	11.15
Philippines	—	—	1	3	—	—	—	—	—	4
			1.50	11.00						12.50
United Kingdom	3	—	—	—	1	—	—	1	—	5
	3.97				0.03			0.01		4.01
Belgium	2	—	—	—	—	—	—	—	1	3
	0.55								5.00	5.55
Canada	2	1	—	—	—	—	—	—	—	3
	0.87	75.00								75.87
Denmark	—	—	—	—	—	1	—	—	—	1
						1.00				1.00
France	—	—	—	1[3]	1	—	—	—	—	2
				2.50	2.50					5.00
Panama	1	—	—	—	—	—	—	—	—	1
	9.00									9.00
Singapore	1	—	—	1	—	—	—	1	1	4
	0.30			1.00				2.60	0.50	4.40
Switzerland	—	—	—	—	—	1	—	—	—	1
						0.25				0.25
South Korea	—	—	—	1	—	—	—	—	—	1
				48.50						48.50
Norway	2	—	1	—	—	—	—	—	—	3
	2.11		1.00							3.11
Kuwait	—	—	1	—	—	—	—	—	—	1
			2.50							2.50
Malaysia	—	—	—	2	—	—	—	—	—	2
				2.00						2.00
Total No.	39	3	7	13	4	4	3	7	4	84
Capital	62.58	158.50	11.50	79.50	8.76	4.15	2.10	8.14	6.90	342.13

(1) First line of each country gives number of approved projects; second line shows total capital involved.

(2) Excludes oil ventures, but includes the capital of the Indonesian partner in joint ventures.

(3) Includes SCAC, SMGL and Cicofrance, which together are investing in one project.

Source: Foreign Investment Board.

Appendix VI (continued)

B. Approved Foreign Investment Projects
January 1967 — Sept. 30, 1968
By Stage of Approval[1]

	Final Approval by Government		Approval by Foreign Investment Board		Total	
	Number	Total in $ Million	Number	Total in $ Million	Number	Total in $ Million
1. Manufacturing	29	56.33	10	6.25	39	62.58
2. Mining	3	158.50	—	—	3	158.50
3. Fishery	7	11.50	—	—	7	11.50
4. Forestry	9 [2]	70.00 [3]	4	9.50	13	79.50
5. Communications	4	8.76	—	—	4	8.76
6. Pharmacy	4	4.15	—	—	4	4.15
7. Commerce	1	1.10	2	1.00	3	2.10
8. Public Works, Real Estate	4	5.40	3	2.74	7	8.14
9. Plantations	2	5.40	2	1.50	4	6.90
Total	63 [4]	321.14	21	20.99	84	342.13

(1) Includes capital of Indonesian partners in joint ventures.
(2) Includes SCAC, SMGL and Cicofrance, which together have one joint venture.
(3) This amount includes a South Korean forestry investment estimated at $48.5 million.
(4) This includes two projects for which final approval, expected in September 1968, was delayed.
    Thus by Sept. 30, 1968, approvals by the government totaled 61, and FIB approvals totaled 23.
Source: Foreign Investment Board

C. Approved Foreign Investment Projects
January 1967 — Sept. 30, 1968
By Type of Investment[1]

	Straight Investment		Joint Enterprise		Total	
	Number	Total in $ Million	Number	Total in $ Million	Number	Total in $ Million
1. Manufacturing	11	19.24	28	43.34	39	62.58
2. Mining	3	158.50	—	—	3	158.50
3. Fishery	2	4.00	5	7.50	13	79.50
4. Forestry	4	58.50	9	21.00	4	8.76
5. Communications	1	6.10	3	2.66	4	4.15
6. Pharmacy	1	1.00	3	3.15	3	2.10
7. Commerce	1	1.10	2	1.00	7	8.14
8. Public Works, Real Estate	3	3.14	4	5.00	4	6.90
9. Plantations	—	—	4	6.90		
Total	26	251.58	58	90.55	84	342.13

(1) Includes capital of Indonesian partners in joint ventures.
Source: Foreign Investment Board.

D. Approved Foreign Investment Projects
January 1967 — Sept. 30, 1968
By Size of Investment [1]

	$2.5 million or more		Between $1 million and $2.5 million		Smaller than $1 million		Total	
	Number	Total in $ Million	Number	Total in $ Million	Number	Total in $ Million	Number	Total in $ Million
1. Manufacturing	5	36.15	13	19.11	21	7.32	39	62.58
2. Mining	3	158.50	—	—	—	—	3	158.50
3. Fishery	2	5.00	5	6.50	—	—	7	11.50
4. Forestry	6	67.50	7	12.00	—	—	13	79.50
5. Communications	2	8.60	—	—	2	0.16	4	8.76
6. Pharmacy	—	—	3	3.90	1	0.25	4	4.15
7. Commerce	—	—	1	1.10	2	1.00	3	2.10
8. Public Works, Real Estate	2	5.60	1	2.00	4	0.54	7	8.14
9. Plantations	1	5.00	1	1.00	2	0.90	4	6.90
Total	21	286.35	31	45.61	32	10.17	84	342.13

(1) Includes capital of Indonesian partners in joint ventures.
(2) Previous lists mentioned $13.5 million, which included all assets. New capital investment is $5 million.
Source: Foreign Investment Board.

E. Approved Foreign Investment Projects
January 1967 — Sept. 30, 1968
By Location [1]

	Djakarta		Java outside Djakarta		Outer islands		Total	
	Number	Total in $ Million	Number	Total in $ Million	Number	Total in $ Million	Number	Total in $ Million
1. Manufacturing	27	40.77	11	19.81	1	2.00	39	62.58
2. Mining	—	—	—	—	3	158.50	3	158.50
3. Fishery	—	—	—	—	7	11.50	7	11.50
4. Forestry	—	—	—	—	13	79.50	13	79.50
5. Communications	3	8.23	—	—	1	0.53	4	8.76
6. Pharmacy	4	4.15	—	—	—	—	4	4.15
7. Commerce	3	2.10	—	—	—	—	3	2.10
8. Public Works, Real Estate	7	8.14	—	—	—	—	7	8.14
9. Plantations	—	—	—	—	4	6.90	4	6.90
Total	44	63.39	11	19.81	29	258.93	84	342.13

(1) Includes capital of Indonesian partners in joint ventures.
Source: Foreign Investment Board.

Appendix VII

Percentage of Employed Population (10 years and over) At Work by Economic Sector and Region [1]

ECONOMIC SECTOR

Statistical Region	Agriculture, Forestry, Fishing	Mining and Quarrying	Manufac- turing	Construc- tion	Commerce	Transport and Commu- nications	Services	Others and Not Stated	Total
West Java	11.8	0.0	1.1	0.4	2.2	0.3	2.5	0.2	18.4
Central Java	13.7	0.0	1.7	0.3	2.5	0.2	2.0	0.2	20.6
Jogjakarta	1.7	0.0	0.4	0.1	0.4	0.0	0.4	0.0	2.9
East Java	17.8	0.1	1.2	0.2	2.7	0.3	2.7	0.2	25.2
TOTAL, Java-Madura	44.9	0.1	4.4	0.9	7.8	0.8	7.6	0.5	67.1
North Sumatra & Atjeh	4.9	0.0	0.3	0.1	0.6	0.1	0.9	0.1	7.0
Djambi, Riau & West Sumatra	3.2	—	0.1	0.1	0.4	0.1	0.4	0.1	4.4
South Sumatra & Lampung	4.1	0.0	0.3	0.1	0.4	0.1	0.5	0.0	5.5
Kalimantan	3.4	0.0	0.3	0.0	0.4	0.0	0.7	0.1	5.0
Bali	1.5	—	0.1	0.0	0.2	0.0	0.3	0.1	2.3
North & Central Sulawesi	1.6	—	0.1	0.0	0.1	0.0	0.2	0.0	1.9
South & Southeast Sulawesi	3.4	0.0	0.3	0.1	0.4	0.1	0.4	0.1	4.7
Nusatenggara	1.7	—	0.1	0.0	0.0	0.0	0.2	0.0	2.1
TOTAL, Outside Java	23.9	0.1	1.4	0.4	2.6	0.4	3.6	0.6	32.9
INDONESIA	68.8	0.2	5.8	1.3	10.4	1.2	11.2	1.1	100.0

(1) Excludes Djakarta, East Nusatenggara, Maluku, West Irian.
Number of sample households—Total: 21,305   Urban: 4,019   Rural: 17,286
Source: Central Bureau of Statistics, Djakarta; Angkatan Kerdja Penduduk per Daerah, Survey Sosial Ekonomi Nasional Tahap Kedua Nov. 1964-Feb. 1965.

Appendix VIII

Percentage of Employed Population (10 years and over) By Occupation and Region

OCCUPATION

Statistical Region	Professional, Technical, etc.	Administrative and Managerial	Clerical Workers	Sales Workers	Farmers, Fishermen, Loggers, etc.	Mining & Quarrying Workers	Transport and Communications	Craftsmen, Production Process Workers & Others	Services, Sport, Recreation Workers, Not Classified, and Not Stated	Total
West Java	1.6	0.9	2.1	12.3	64.7	0.1	2.3	12.7	3.3	100.0
Central Java	2.3	0.9	1.9	12.5	66.0	0.1	1.4	11.8	3.1	100.0
Jogjakarta	4.6	2.0	2.5	13.9	56.7	—	1.1	16.7	2.5	100.0
East Java	1.9	0.4	2.7	11.4	70.6	0.0	1.5	9.3	2.1	100.0
TOTAL, Java-Madura	2.1	0.8	2.3	12.1	67.0	0.1	1.7	11.3	2.7	100.0
North Sumatra & Atjeh	2.7	1.7	1.9	8.5	70.6	0.0	2.1	9.2	3.3	100.0
Djambi, Riau & West Sumatra	4.4	2.2	1.3	9.5	72.8	—	1.7	6.4	1.7	100.0
South Sumatra & Lampung	2.0	0.8	2.9	8.2	73.3	0.5	1.7	9.2	1.5	100.0
Kalimantan	2.3	1.5	2.3	8.4	69.6	0.3	1.0	8.5	6.2	100.0
Bali	2.5	0.4	1.8	8.4	67.4	—	1.0	16.4	2.2	100.0
North & Central Sulawesi	2.2	0.3	1.3	3.2	82.5	—	0.3	4.6	5.6	100.0
South & Southeast Sulawesi	1.8	1.3	2.1	9.5	72.4	0.1	1.2	10.4	1.2	100.0
West Nusatenggara	3.1	1.1	1.8	3.7	81.6	—	0.4	5.2	3.1	100.0
TOTAL, Outside Java	2.6	1.3	2.0	8.1	72.6	0.1	1.4	8.9	3.0	100.0
Total	2.3	0.9	2.2	10.8	68.8	0.1	1.6	10.5	2.8	100.0

(1) Excludes Djakarta, East Nusatenggara, Maluku, West Irian.
Number of Sample Households — Total: 21,305   Urban: 4,019   Rural: 17,286
Source: Central Bureau of Statistics, Djakarta: Angkatan Kerdja Penduduk per Daerah, Survey Sosial Ekonomi Nasional Tahap Kedua, Nov. 1964 — February 1965.

Appendix IX

Percentage of Population (10 Years and Over)
By Educational Standard and Age

ALL INDONESIA

Age in Years	Below Primary School	Primary School	General Secondary School	Special Secondary School	General High School	Special High School	Academy	University	Not Stated	Total
10 — 14	11.7	4.0	0.2	0.0	—	—	—	—	0.4	16.4
15 — 19	5.8	4.3	0.9	0.2	0.1	0.0	0.0	—	0.1	11.4
20 — 24	5.9	2.8	0.6	0.2	0.2	0.1	0.0	0.0	0.1	10.0
25 — 29	8.7	2.0	0.4	0.2	0.1	0.1	0.0	0.0	0.1	11.6
30 — 34	8.8	1.3	0.1	0.1	0.0	0.1	0.0	0.0	0.1	10.6
35 — 39	8.6	1.1	0.2	0.1	0.0	0.0	0.0	0.0	0.1	10.1
40 — 44	7.2	0.8	0.1	0.1	0.0	0.0	0.0	0.0	0.1	8.2
45 — 49	6.5	0.6	0.1	0.0	0.0	0.0	0.0	—	0.1	6.2
50 — 54	5.1	0.3	0.0	0.0	0.0	0.0	0.0	0.0	0.0	5.5
55 — 59	2.8	0.2	0.0	0.0	0.0	0.0	—	0.0	0.1	3.0
60 — 64	3.2	0.1	0.0	0.0	0.0	0.0	—	0.0	0.0	3.3
65 — 69	1.2	0.0	0.0	—	—	—	—	—	0.0	1.2
70 — 74	1.0	0.0	0.0	0.0	0.0	—	—	—	0.0	1.1
75 and over	1.0	0.0	0.0	—	—	—	—	—	0.0	1.0
Not stated	0.0	—	—	—	—	—	—	—	0.1	0.2
Total	76.5	17.6	2.6	0.9	0.6	0.4	0.1	0.0	1.3	100.0

Number of Sample Households — Total: 21,305   Urban: 4,019   Rural: 17,286
Source: Central Bureau of Statistics, Djakarta: Sifat2 Demografi Penduduk Indonesia, Survey Sosial Ekonomi Nasional Tahap Kedua, Nov. 1964 — February 1965

Appendix X

Percentage of Employed Population (10 Years and Over) By Educational Standard and Region [1]

Statistical Region	Below Primary School	Primary School	General Secondary School	Special Secondary School	EDUCATION General High School	Special High School	Academy	University	Not Stated	Total
West Java	77.9	17.5	1.9	0.8	0.6	0.2	0.1	0.1	0.9	100.0
Central Java	81.8	14.2	2.0	1.2	0.3	0.2	0.1	0.0	0.2	100.0
Jogjakarta	73.7	19.1	2.7	1.8	1.0	1.1	0.4	0.2	–	100.0
East Java	82.1	14.6	1.3	1.0	0.4	0.4	0.1	0.0	0.1	100.0
TOTAL, Java-Madura	80.5	15.5	1.7	1.0	0.5	0.3	0.1	0.1	0.4	100.0
North Sumatra & Atjeh	65.9	24.2	6.0	0.7	1.0	0.8	0.1	0.1	1.2	100.0
Djambi, Riau & West Sumatra	74.5	18.9	2.4	2.4	0.4	1.1	0.1	0.1	0.1	100.0
South Sumatra & Lampung	72.7	22.4	2.3	1.6	0.7	0.2	0.1	0.1	0.1	100.0
Kalimantan	81.9	13.7	2.0	1.0	0.3	0.6	0.1	0.1	0.5	100.0
Bali	76.4	19.6	1.1	1.6	0.5	0.7	0.1	–	–	100.0
North & Central Sulawesi	70.9	23.5	5.0	0.1	0.3	–	–	–	0.1	100.0
South & Southeast Sulawesi	87.2	8.8	1.7	0.8	0.9	0.6	–	0.1	0.1	100.0
West Nusatenggara	81.9	14.6	2.2	0.8	0.3	0.1	0.1	–	–	100.0
TOTAL, Outside Java	75.7	18.4	3.0	1.2	0.6	0.6	0.1	0.1	0.4	100.0
INDONESIA	78.9	16.4	2.2	1.1	0.5	0.4	0.1	0.1	0.4	100.0

(1) Excludes Djakarta, East Nusatenggara, Maluku, West Irian.
Number of sample households — Total: 21,305   Urban: 4,019   Rural: 17,286
Source: Central Bureau of Statistics, Djakarta: Angkatan Kerdja Penduduk per Daerah, Survey Sosial Ekonomi Nasional Tahap
    Kedua, Nov. 1964 — Feb. 1965.

Appendix XI

Percentage of Population By Age and Sex

Age in Years	Urban			Rural			All Indonesia — Total		
	Male	Female	Total	Male	Female	Total	Male	Female	Total
0	3.1	2.7	2.9	2.8	2.6	2.7	2.8	2.6	2.7
1	1.8	1.7	1.8	2.1	1.8	1.9	2.0	1.8	1.9
2	3.9	3.4	3.6	3.9	3.7	3.8	3.9	3.6	3.8
3	3.3	3.3	3.3	3.7	3.5	3.6	3.7	3.5	3.6
4	3.4	3.1	3.3	3.9	3.7	3.8	3.8	3.7	3.7
5 — 9	16.2	14.8	15.5	17.6	17.4	17.5	17.5	17.0	17.3
10 — 14	12.6	12.3	12.5	11.6	9.9	10.8	11.8	10.2	11.0
15 — 19	9.1	9.9	9.5	7.5	7.3	7.4	7.7	7.6	7.7
20 — 24	7.0	8.5	7.8	5.7	7.3	6.5	5.8	7.5	6.7
25 — 29	6.7	8.2	7.4	6.5	9.1	7.8	6.6	9.0	7.8
30 — 34	6.5	7.7	7.1	6.5	7.7	7.1	6.5	7.7	7.1
35 — 39	6.7	6.5	6.6	6.9	6.7	6.8	6.9	6.7	6.8
40 — 44	5.5	4.9	5.2	5.7	5.4	5.6	5.7	5.4	5.5
45 — 49	4.2	3.9	4.0	4.5	3.9	4.2	4.4	3.9	4.2
50 — 54	3.5	3.0	3.2	3.8	3.7	3.8	3.8	3.6	3.7
55 — 59	2.2	1.9	2.1	2.2	1.8	2.0	2.2	1.9	2.0
60 — 64	2.0	1.8	1.9	2.5	2.1	2.3	2.4	2.0	2.2
65 — 69	0.8	0.7	0.7	0.9	0.8	0.8	0.9	0.8	0.8
70 — 75	0.7	0.7	0.7	0.8	0.8	0.8	0.8	0.7	0.7
75 — and over	0.6	0.8	0.7	0.7	0.7	0.7	0.7	0.7	0.7
Not Stated	0.2	0.2	0.2	0.2	0.1	0.1	0.1	0.1	0.1
Total	100.0	100.0	100.0	100.0	100.0	100.0	100.0	100.0	100.0

Number of sample households — Total: 21,305   Urban: 4,019   Rural: 17,286
Source: Central Bureau of Statistics, Djakarta: Sifat2 Demografi Penduduk Indonesia, Survey Sosial Ekonomi Nasional
Tahap Kedua, Nov. 1964 — Feb. 1965.

Appendix XII

Percentage of Population by Monthly Per Capita Expenditure, Regions of Indonesia, and Urban-Rural[1]

Region	Monthly Per Capita Expenditure in Old Rupiahs									% of Total Urban Population	% of Total Rural Population	% of Total Population
	Up to 2,000	2-3,000	3-4,000	4-5,000	5-6,000	6-7,000	7-8,000	8-10,000	10,000 & over			
West Java	0.5	1.5	2.7	3.2	2.9	2.3	1.6	2.0	2.7			19.3
Central Java	3.3	4.6	4.2	2.8	2.0	1.1	0.6	0.7	0.7			19.9
Jogjakarta	0.3	0.6	0.6	0.4	0.2	0.1	0.1	0.1	0.1			2.5
East Java	4.9	5.5	4.5	3.1	1.9	1.2	0.7	0.6	0.8			23.2
Total: Java-Madura	9.1	12.2	12.0	9.4	6.9	4.7	3.1	3.4	4.3			64.9
Total: Java-Madura (Urban)	2.3	6.4	9.9	10.3	8.6	5.4	4.9	6.2	7.7	61.8		
Total: Java-Madura (Rural)	9.9	13.0	12.3	9.3	6.7	4.6	2.8	3.0	3.8		65.3	
North Sumatra & Atjeh	0.1	0.4	0.8	1.2	1.1	0.9	0.7	0.9	1.6			7.7
Djambi, Riau, & West Sumatra	0.1	0.4	1.0	0.9	0.8	0.6	0.4	0.5	0.7			5.3
South Sumatra & Lampung	0.1	0.4	0.6	0.6	0.7	0.6	0.5	0.8	1.1			5.3
Kalimantan	0.1	0.2	0.2	0.4	0.4	0.5	0.5	0.7	1.7			4.7
Bali	0.6	0.5	0.4	0.4	0.3	0.1	0.0	0.1	0.1			2.6
North & Central Sulawesi	0.0	0.2	0.1	0.1	0.2	0.2	0.1	0.2	0.8			1.9
South & Southeast Sulawesi	1.3	1.0	1.0	0.6	0.5	0.3	0.3	0.3	0.3			5.7
West Nusatenggara (Lesser Sundas)	0.2	0.4	0.3	0.3	0.2	0.1	0.1	0.2	0.3			2.0
Total: Outside Java	2.4	3.5	4.5	4.6	4.2	3.2	2.6	3.6	6.6			35.1
Total: Indonesia	11.4	15.6	16.5	14.0	11.1	7.9	5.7	7.0	10.8			100.0
Total: Indonesia (Urban)	3.5	9.5	14.2	14.1	12.6	9.6	8.2	11.1	17.2	100.0		
Total: Indonesia (Rural)	12.5	16.5	16.8	13.9	10.9	7.7	5.4	6.4	10.0		100.0	

Note: The levels of monthly per capita expenditure used in this table should not be taken as reflecting purchasing power in Indonesia today. They are given in old rupiahs (i.e., the currency before the 1,000:1 revaluation of the rupiah in December 1965). Nor would it be accurate to assume that expenditure levels are now 1/1,000th of the levels in the table; price adjustments and inflation since the end of 1965 have completely altered statistical spending levels. The percentages in the table nevertheless indicate the **relative** expenditure levels in geographical regions and in urban vs. rural areas.

(1) Excludes DCI Djakarta, East Nusatenggara, Maluku, West Irian.

Source: Compiled from Pengeluaran Untuk Konsumsi Penduduk, Survey Sosial Ekonomi Nasional Tahap Kedua, (Nov. 1964 — Feb. 1965), Biro Pusat Statistik, Djakarta.

Appendix XIII

Average Per Capita Monthly Expenditure by Items of Consumption, Region, and Urban-Rural (In Old Rupiahs)[1]

Item	Java-Madura Urban	Java-Madura Rural	Java-Madura Total	Outside Java Urban	Outside Java Rural	Outside Java Total	All Indonesia Urban	All Indonesia Rural	All Indonesia Total
Cereals & cereal products	2,071	1,928	1,944	2,304	2,515	2,488	2,160	2,131	2,134
Cassava & cassava products	90	121	118	153	260	247	114	169	163
Fish & seafood	306	282	285	837	601	631	509	392	406
Meat & eggs	330	108	132	395	271	287	355	164	186
Milk & milk products	51	5	10	57	18	23	54	10	15
Vegetables & fruits	645	398	425	716	550	571	672	451	476
Other food	719	474	501	1,155	899	931	885	621	652
Prepared food	359	193	211	882	284	360	559	225	264
Alcoholic beverages & tobacco	303	235	243	705	335	382	456	270	292
Housing, fuel, light & water	428	323	335	560	351	377	479	333	350
Miscellaneous goods & services	524	166	206	660	352	392	575	231	271
Clothing, footwear & headwear	277	199	207	461	342	357	347	248	260
Durable & semidurable goods	145	72	80	202	114	125	166	87	96
Consumer taxes & insurance premiums	12	2	3	25	4	6	17	2	4
Extra expenditure for festivals & ceremonies	116	134	132	129	144	142	121	137	135
Food Total	4,874	3,744	3,869	7,204	5,733	5,920	5,764	4,433	4,588
Non-Food Total	1,502	896	963	2,037	1,307	1,399	1,705	1,038	1,116
Total	6,376	4,640	4,832	9,241	7,040	7,319	7,469	5,471	5,704

Note: The absolute figures in this table are of no value whatsoever since they are expressed in old rupiahs (i.e., the currency before the revaluation of 1,000:1 in December 1965), and because of subsequent inflation. They can, however, be used as an indicative measure of spending patterns if the amounts spent on particular items are taken as a percentage of the total average expenditure or the total average expenditure in a particular region.

(1) Excludes DCI Djakarta, East Nusatenggara, Maluku, West Irian.

Source: Compiled from Penguluaran Untuk Konsumsi Penduduk, Survey Sosial Ekonomi Nasional Tahap Kedua (Nov. 1964 – Feb. 1965), Biro Pusat Statistik, Djakarta.

Appendix XIV

Direction of Indonesian Exports, 1967[1]

Main Trading Partners/Areas	Value ($ '000)
Singapore	64,777.9
Philippines	22,046.3
Malaysia	1,070.8
Thailand	6,521.4
Southeast Asia	88,055.8
West Asia	2,179.9
Hong Kong	12,887.5
Japan	155,624.4
Taiwan	54.9
China (Mainland)	675.8
North Asia	170,019.1
Africa	1,146.6
Australia	60,228.6
Australia/Oceania	72,022.8
USA	101,458.7
North America	101,624.1
Latin America	2,107.9
UK	25,916.8
Belgium/Luxembourg	8,890.9
France	7,401.4
Netherlands	79,855.2
West Germany	55,119.3
Western Europe	183,057.4
Poland	5,985.1
Russia	14,788.9
Rest of Europe	25,670.3
Total Exports	657,802.5

(1) Preliminary
Source: Central Bureau of Statistics

Appendix XV

Source of Indonesian Imports, 1967

Main Countries and Areas	Value ($ '000)
Malaysia	1,152
Singapore	17,210
Cambodia	2,591
Thailand	8,395
Burma	3,444
India	8,266
Pakistan	7,230
Hong Kong	59,832
Republic of Korea	1,550
North Korea	1,067
Japan	181,877
Taiwan	14,118
China (Mainland)	54,196
Africa	10,626
Middle East	190
Australia and Oceania	13,048
US	58,259
Latin America	564
Netherlands	97,559
UK	22,492
Belgium/Luxembourg	2,744
France	6,741
West Germany	507
Switzerland	3,556
Italy	16,075
Austria	1,097
Denmark	1,804
Sweden	1,256
East Germany	4,832
Hungary	3,667
Poland	8,139
USSR	4,722
Czechoslovakia	9,586
Yugoslavia	7,707
Finland	1,283

Total imports: $649 million

Appendix XVI

Indonesian Exports through May 1968 [1]

($ Millions)

Period	Total Export	Rubber (Estate)	Rubber (Smallholder)	Petroleum Products	Tin Ore	Copra	Coffee (Estate)	Coffee (Smallholder)	Tea	Tobacco	Palm Oil	Exports Excluding Oil
1952	934.3	200.6	223.3	191.3	86.1	53.1	5.5	12.5	23.5	23.2	26.6	743.0
1953	840.3	138.9	133.9	204.6	80.6	57.7	13.5	17.4	28.6	31.8	28.6	635.6
1954	866.5	104.8	166.4	227.1	59.5	51.4	17.7	21.8	39.8	34.6	26.7	639.4
1955	945.5	171.8	259.7	215.8	59.5	35.4	7.3	8.7	31.2	30.8	24.2	729.7
1956	926.2	154.5	206.2	255.5	62.0	39.2	7.6	22.4	29.8	29.4	27.1	670.9
1957	954.4	145.9	203.6	302.8	55.5	40.5	8.2	21.2	29.8	33.6	26.0	651.6
1958	790.7	108.8	153.2	315.2	35.4	18.2	4.2	14.3	24.8	30.2	23.7	475.5
1959	931.0	143.4	275.9	285.7	36.1	27.6	5.0	14.0	20.3	24.4	19.2	645.3
1960	840.8	134.0	243.2	220.8	50.6	29.1	2.6	11.1	27.7	33.3	20.0	620.0
1961	788.2	122.5	184.6	260.9	33.3	34.7	2.4	11.4	25.6	24.6	21.4	527.3
1962	663.7	101.6	196.9	215.8	34.9	14.8	2.9	9.6	20.6	16.2	17.8	447.9
1963	695.6	95.2	147.4	268.7	18.9	13.6	3.8	16.0	17.8	18.9	20.0	426.9
1964	724.2	98.5	135.2	267.4	31.6	23.5	7.1	19.5	17.0	21.8	26.9	456.8
1965	707.7	86.5	135.4	271.9	30.9	18.0	8.4	23.2	16.9	18.7	27.3	435.8
1966	678.7	90.8	132.1	203.6	30.7	15.1	7.2	25.3	17.0	24.0	33.3	475.1
1967	657.8	62.6	103.9	237.8	48.8	13.3	8.4	36.9	9.5	14.4	23.4	420.0
Jan./May '66	289.6	42.8	55.5	81.7	14.5	6.2	3.3	6.7	8.9	18.6	10.2	207.9
Jan./May '67	257.3	27.4	41.0	98.8	12.6	2.6	1.7	9.3	4.3	9.7	9.3	158.6
Jan./May '68	270.2	26.8	44.3	106.0	12.0	10.6	3.2	10.0	6.8	10.1	8.7	164.2

(1) Excludes West Irian. In 1965, 1966, and 1967, exports from West Irian totalled $10 million, $9 million, and $17 million respectively.
Source: Central Bureau of Statistics

Appendix XVII

Major Imports by Commodity Groups, January — July 1968

($ million)

Import Category	Item	Total Imports [1]	% [1]
Group A	Rice	86.89	42.8
	Fertilizer	33.86	16.7
	Wheat flour	26.91	13.3
	Cambrics	17.18	8.5
	Weaving yarn	14.59	7.2
	Cotton	11.68	5.8
	Newsprint	2.34	1.2
	Serum and vaccines	2.13	1.1
	Asphalt	1.70	0.8
	Jute	1.47	0.7
	Other	4.29	2.1
	TOTAL, Group A	203.06	100.0
Group B	Textiles	10.35	9.1
	Galvanized iron sheets	7.10	6.3
	Pharmaceuticals	5.45	4.8
	Radios, TV's, telephones	4.65	4.1
	Chassis and parts	3.14	2.8
	Cement	3.13	2.8
	Tobacco	2.96	2.6
	Silk weaving yarn	2.87	2.5
	Engine oil	2.78	2.4
	Celluloid, cellophane	2.48	2.2
	Other	68.64	60.5
	TOTAL, Group B	113.55	100.0
Group C	Artificial silk (rayon) woven textiles	33.58	60.3
	Cloves	7.89	14.2
	Gold, silver, platinum	6.53	11.7
	Painting material	1.89	3.4
	Cigarette paper	1.57	2.8
	Plate glass	0.69	1.2
	Paper, excl. newsprint	0.63	1.1
	Other paper	0.56	1.0
	Locks	0.50	0.9
	Cloth for textile screen printing	0.47	0.9
	Other	1.39	2.5
	TOTAL, Group C	55.73	100.0

Major Imports by Commodity Groups, January — July 1968

($ million)

Import Category	Item	Total Imports	%
Commodities outside Groups A, B, or C	Motorcycles, also incomplete	1.15	16.7
	Kerosene	0.54	7.8
	Silk woven ribbon	0.47	6.9
	Plate glass	0.35	5.2
	Muslin cloth	0.32	4.7
	Surgical instruments	0.30	4.4
	Other sugars	0.23	3.3
	Cloth and rubber shoes	0.22	3.3
	Bicycle spare parts	0.16	2.3
	Waterproof cloth	0.12	1.8
	Other	3.00	43.6
	TOTAL, outside Groups A, B, or C	6.88	100.0
TOTAL		$379.21	

(1) Does not include imports without letter of credit.
Source: Ministry of Trade

Appendix XVIII

Net National Product of Indonesia by Industrial Origin, 1960 and 1964

(Billions of Rupiahs)

Industry	1960	(%)	1964 Constant (1960) Prices	(%)	1964 Current Prices	(%)
Agriculture, forestry, fishing	205.2	52.4	217.5	51.5	3,616.3	56.2
Farm food crops	132.0		137.5		2,451.9	
Farm cash crops	26.9		32.1		388.1	
Estate crops	11.7		12.4		179.5	
Animal husbandry	18.1		19.3		190.8	
Forestry & hunting	9.0		6.8		123.1	
Fishing	7.5		9.4		282.9	
Mining & quarrying	12.0	3.1	13.9	3.3	22.4	0.4
Manufacturing	48.1	12.3	50.7	12.0	648.1	10.0
Large, medium	19.4		18.9		163.8	
Small	28.7		31.8		484.3	
Construction	7.1	1.8	7.7	1.8	135.3	2.1
Electricity, gas	0.9	0.2	1.4	0.3	4.0	0.1
Transport & communications	13.9	3.4	14.0	3.3	108.1	1.7
Wholesale & retail trade	59.4	15.2	73.4	17.3	1,121.5	17.4
Banking, other finance	3.3	0.8	3.4	0.8	45.3	0.7
Ownership of dwellings	7.4	1.9	8.3	2.0	126.5	2.0
Public administration & defense	16.1	4.1	12.6	3.0	196.3	3.0
Services	22.1	5.6	24.2	5.7	423.3	6.5
Net domestic product	394.8	100.8	427.1	101.0	6,447.1	100.1
Net investment income from abroad	−3.0	−0.8	−4.2	−1.0	−4.2	−0.1
Net national product	391.8	100.0	422.9	100.0	6,442.9	100.0

Source: Statistik Indonesia (Statistical Pocketbook of Indonesia) 1964-1967, Biro Pusat Statistik, Djakarta.